REVELATION

Jesus' Messages to Seven Pastors
and
John's Vision of the Last Days

JOHN DAVID CLARK, SR.

Revelation: Jesus' Messages to Seven Pastors
and John's Vision of the Last Days
© 1992 John David Clark, Sr.

ISBN-13: 978-1-934782-08-8

First printing, 1992
Second printing, 2023

----
cover design by Donna Nelson

For information, write to:

Books – Revelation
PO Box 99
Burlington, NC 27216–0099

Visit us at these websites:

www.PastorJohnsHouse.com
www.GoingtoJesus.com
www.Isaiah58.com

For video sermons, songs, testimonies, and Bible lessons:
www.youtube.com/TheSpiritistheWitness

and for good music all day long, go to:
www.SongsofRest.com

Author's Notes

- In English, the singular and plural forms of "you" are identical. However, in biblical Hebrew and Greek, there are obvious differences. Therefore, to more perfectly convey the biblical writers' messages in verses where the English word "you" appears, I have italicized the "y" of all plural forms, such as *y*ou, *y*our, *y*ours, and *y*ourselves.

- Translations of Old and New Testament scriptures are my own. Following standard practice, whenever a word is added to the translation for clarification, that word is italicized.

- Conflicting rules exist as to how punctuation should be used, none of them being adequate for every situation. My Readers will find that I subscribe to a freer punctuation style. Of special note, I do not include within quotation marks any punctuation that is not a part of what is quoted. To do otherwise, in my opinion, leaves too much room for misrepresentation of the original author's intent.

BOOKS OF THE BIBLE AND THEIR ABBREVIATIONS

Old Testament Books

Genesis	Gen.	Ecclesiastes	Eccl.
Exodus	Ex.	Song of Solomon	Song
Leviticus	Lev.	Isaiah	Isa.
Numbers	Num.	Jeremiah	Jer.
Deuteronomy	Dt.	Lamentations	Lam.
Joshua	Josh.	Ezekiel	Ezek.
Judges	Judg.	Daniel	Dan.
Ruth	Ruth	Hosea	Hos.
1Samuel	1Sam.	Joel	Joel
2Samuel	2Sam.	Amos	Amos
1Kings	1Kgs.	Obadiah	Obad.
2Kings	2Kgs.	Jonah	Jon.
1Chronicles	1Chron.	Micah	Mic.
2Chronicles	2Chron.	Nahum	Nah.
Ezra	Ezra	Habakkuk	Hab.
Nehemiah	Neh.	Zephaniah	Zeph.
Esther	Esth.	Haggai	Hag.
Job	Job	Zechariah	Zech.
Psalms	Ps.	Malachi	Mal.
Proverbs	Prov.		

New Testament Books

Matthew	Mt.	1Timothy	1Tim.
Mark	Mk.	2Timothy	2Tim.
Luke	Lk.	Titus	Tit.
John	Jn.	Philemon	Phlm.
Acts	Acts	Hebrews	Heb.
Romans	Rom.	James	Jas.
1Corinthians	1Cor.	1Peter	1Pet.
2Corinthians	2Cor.	2Peter	2Pet.
Galatians	Gal.	1John	1Jn.
Ephesians	Eph.	2John	2Jn.
Philippians	Phip.	3John	3Jn.
Colossians	Col.	Jude	Jude
1Thessalonians	1Thess.	Revelation	Rev.
2Thessalonians	2Thess.		

Table of Contents

"I was in the Spirit on the LORD's day."

The island of Patmos is mentioned only once in the Bible, but the remarkable event which took place there has made Patmos familiar to every student of Scripture. John, the disciple especially loved by Jesus, was on Patmos Island "because of the word of God and because of the witness of Jesus Christ," and one day, as John communed in prayer with God, he was taken into heaven and given the most astonishing vision ever of the end of the world.

These are the things John saw.

Original Introduction, 1992

For a long time now, Christian ministers have sounded the warning that the Lord Jesus could return "at any moment" and that every prophecy of the events which precede his coming has been fulfilled. I do not want to seem frivolous, but to hear these men speak, one would have to think that Jesus missed his cue! Obviously, if those who teach that doctrine had been sent from God, then Jesus would have returned long ago. The only reasonable explanation for the failure of their predictions of an "any-moment" return of Jesus is that there are still many events that must first come to pass. Ironically, one indication that the return of Jesus is not imminent is the many who claim that it is. Jesus said the very first sign of the beginning of the end is that many deceivers would come in his name, saying, "The time is at hand" (Lk. 21:8).

I certainly agree that we should always be prepared for the return of our Lord, and I also know that if the Father chose to do so, He could send His Son back to earth this very moment. But I believe that the Father knew from the beginning when He would send His Son back for His saints and that His Son's prophecies concerning the end of the world can be trusted.

The question, "Are you ready for Jesus to come?" may be a good question to ask, but the more appropriate question is, "Are you ready for Jesus *not* to come?" because that is the reality; it is not time for Jesus to return. So, the real issue is, are we ready to stay here and do the work that remains to be done? Are we prepared to endure what this world and the body of Christ will suffer before the coming of the Lord?

Much talk about Jesus coming at any moment makes God's people look foolish to the world. How long can ministers expect to keep the respect of people in this world while prophesying falsely of a soon return of Jesus? How many years can the "any-moment" return of Jesus be proclaimed before the world begins to consider the preaching of the gospel itself to be as empty a promise as that one has been? What the saints should be proclaiming is that we have entered into the "beginning of sorrows", which marks the beginning of the end; however, "the beginning of sorrows" began a long time ago, and we have still not gone beyond it. As things are, though, after hearing for such a long time that the end is at hand, people in general are not alarmed by that message and just shrug it off as the rambling of misguided voices declaring a discredited gospel.

Nevertheless, we are not discouraged. God has, from the beginning, planned these things so as to conceal the truth from the proud. The sheep will hear the voice of the Shepherd when he speaks, knowing that "all who have ever come before are thieves and robbers." The Spirit's voice appeals to the sincere child of God as no other voice can. To the heart set on the things of God, the voice of the Shepherd is as easily distinguished from that of a hireling as is day from night.

Jesus will not come tonight, or tomorrow, next week, or next year. His return is still years away, probably more than a decade, and possibly many years longer than that. The saints must suffer through "great tribulation" not once but *twice* before the coming of the Lord, as a careful reading of Revelation will show.

We begin our study of Revelation by studying John's vision of Jesus himself, Jesus' seven messages to the seven pastors in the ancient Roman province of Asia, and John's vision of heaven. After that, we will study the order of the end-time events that John saw. I do not hesitate to confess ignorance of some of the details concerning John's prophetic visions. What I am giving here is the general order of end-time events into which those details will fit, whatever they are. I am open to comments or questions which any Reader may have. Indeed, I ask for such correspondence.

May God use this study to better prepare you, my dear Reader, to stand in the Final Judgment, washed from every stain of sin by the blood of God's Son Jesus Christ, the Savior of the world. To him belongs all honor, and the praise of every tongue, to the glory of God the Father.

New Introduction, 2023

Over thirty years have passed since I wrote the first edition of this book. In the meantime, as I predicted, Jesus did not return. Nor is it yet time for his return. We are still many years away from the blessed appearance of our Lord Jesus, and so, the message of this edition is the same as that of the first, namely, since Jesus is not coming soon, we should focus on learning to walk in the Spirit in this present world so that we may bless others and please God.

The doctrine of an "any-moment" return of Jesus can discourage and confuse sincere believers, and escaping that confusion and discouragement is important, for in doing so, we may focus on our true mission: doing the will of God in this world.

My heartfelt gratitude is offered to the saints whom God has placed in my life. Their love of the truth – indeed, their demand for it – has often challenged me to pursue the knowledge of God so that I, too, may be prepared for Jesus not to come soon.

.

REVELATION

Jesus' Messages to Seven Pastors
and
John's Vision of the Last Days

JOHN DAVID CLARK, SR.

PART 1

Revelation 1:1 – 5:14

John's Vision of Jesus,
Jesus' Messages to Seven Pastors,
and John's Vision of Heaven

Chapter 1
John's Vision of Jesus
Revelation 1:1 – 20

Revelation 1

¶1a. A revelation from Jesus Christ,

Note: Some scholars translate John's opening words as "a revelation *of* Jesus Christ", rather than "a revelation *from* Jesus Christ". However, while this revelation must have taught John much about Jesus, it is the fact that Jesus is the source of this revelation which is John's emphasis.

1b. which God gave him

Note 1: Both the Old and the New Testaments make reference to the Father's giving of various blessings to the Son. This is evidence that the Father is indeed greater than the Son, just as Jesus said (Jn. 14:28). Here are some of the things that the Scriptures say the Father gave to His Son:

1.	Life itself	Ps. 21:4; Jn. 5:26
2.	Power to give life to others	Jn. 17:2
3.	Angels to watch over him	Ps. 91:11–12
4.	All authority in heaven and earth.	Mt. 28:18
5.	Complete authority to judge	Jn. 5:22
6.	A work to do	Jn. 17:4
7.	Disciples	Jn. 17:6, 12
8.	Words to say; a doctrine	Jn. 17:8; 7:16
9.	Power to heal and deliver	Acts 10:38
10.	Glory on earth and in heaven	Jn. 17:22, 5
11.	Eternal life for us	Acts 2:33; Heb. 9:12
12.	This revelation of the future	Rev. 1:1

Note 2: If the Father gave these things to the Son, then there was a time when the Son was without them.

1c. to show his slaves what must soon happen, and he made it known by sending his angel to his slave, John,

2. who testified of the word of God and of the witness of Jesus Christ, as much as he saw.

Note: This is the order of communication: God to Jesus; Jesus to his angel; the angel to John; and John to the seven pastors of the seven Assemblies of God in the Roman province of Asia.

3a. Blessed is the one who is reading and those who hear the words of this prophecy and who keep the things written in it,

Note: The blessing is not simply for those who read or hear the words of this prophecy but for those who *take heed* to the things they read or hear.

3b. for the time is near.

Note 1: John said "the time is near" because that is what Jesus told him at the end of his revelation (Rev. 22:10). But Jesus could not have been telling John that his Second Coming was near because with this revelation, it was revealed to John that Jesus' Second Coming was many years away. Jesus was talking about the nearness of the earliest events that would lead to the end, for the first seal that the Lamb opens has to do with a great apostasy which began to take place in John's time.

The book of Revelation is divided into two main parts. The second part, which contains the prophecies dealing with the end of the world, is the better known of the two. The first part, however, contains John's messages from Jesus for the seven pastors still ministering in the Roman province of Asia at that time. In those messages, Jesus reveals to those men what will soon happen in their Assemblies. So, in addition to the beginning of end-time events, the phrase, "the time is at hand", applied to things that were about to happen in the Asian Assemblies.

Note 2: When the New Testament began, all believers thought that Jesus would return very soon. For example, James wrote, "The coming of the Lord is at hand" (Jas. 5:8b). This is obviously a failed prophecy, but it is not the only prophecy to have failed or been delayed because of misconduct on the part of God's people. For example, Moses, by killing an Egyptian (Ex. 2:11–12), delayed one of God's promises to Abraham for thirty years (Gen. 15:13 with Ex. 12:40). A number of other prophecies have likewise not come to pass because of the disobedience of certain people (Num. 25:10–13 with 1Sam. 2:30; Ex. 6:6–8 with Num. 14:32–34). So, a failed prophecy is not necessarily a false prophecy; it could be a true prophecy whose fulfillment depended upon the obedience of believers which did not follow.

As an elderly apostle, Paul said that all the saints in the Roman province of Asia (where the seven Assemblies were located) had abandoned the true faith (2Tim. 1:15). Their apostasy swiftly infected the whole body of Christ on earth, and that affected the timing of future events, including the return of Jesus for his saints.[1] Paul, knowing this would happen, warned the saints that Jesus would not return until after a great apostasy had taken place (2Thess. 2:1–4), and Jesus warned his disciples to beware of false teachers who would say (even after the great apostasy), "The time is at hand" (Lk. 21:8). So, at the beginning of this New Covenant, Jesus' return may have been near, but if so, after the great apostasy of the body of Christ, it was postponed. And two thousand years later, we are still waiting.

Note 3: The converse of the above is also true. Paul and Peter both taught that believers can hasten the fulfillment of prophecy by obeying God (2Cor. 10:6; 2Pet. 3:12).

¶4a. John. To the seven Assemblies that are in Asia:

Note 1: The Greek word translated "Assemblies" here, and throughout my New Testament translation, is *ekklesia*. Almost all

---

[1] For more on this horrendous apostasy, see *The Iron Kingdom Series, Vol. 2: The Jerusalem Council*, available for online reading at GoingtoJesus.com.

Christian translators mistranslate *ekklesia* as "church", ignoring the indisputable fact that ancient Greeks never used *ekklesia* that way.[2]

Note 2: If the apostasy in Asia had already begun to take place when John wrote this, then these remnants of the original Assemblies were small congregations, especially those in the little towns of Thyatira, Philadelphia, and Laodicea.

4b. Grace to you and peace from the One who is, and who was, and who is to come, and from the seven spirits that are before His throne,
5a. and from Jesus Christ, the faithful witness, the firstborn from the dead, and ruler over the kings of the earth.

Note 1: "The One who is, and who was, and who is to come" is the Father, not the Son. Jesus is mentioned as a separate person in verse five. This is also seen in Revelation 4 and 5, where "the One who was, and who is, and who is to come" is sitting on the throne, and then, the slain Lamb, who is Jesus, appears before Him (Rev. 4:8; 5:6–7).

Note 2: Paul once made mention of "the whole family in heaven and on earth" (Eph. 3:15). Here, John passes along to the family of God on earth pleasant greetings from some of the family of God in heaven: the Father, the Son, and the seven spirits that stand before God's throne.

5b. To him who loves us, and washed us from our sins in his blood,
6. and has made of us a kingdom, priests to his God and Father. To him be glory and dominion forever and ever. Amen!

---

[2] The proper definition of "church" is a building used for religious purposes. The Greek word from which "church" comes is *kuriakon* ("belonging to a Lord"). William Tyndall (c. 1494–1536) refused to mistranslate *ekklesia* as "church", and for his efforts to produce a faithful English Bible translation, churchmen hunted him down and murdered him. King James, in order to secure the support of such churchmen, commanded his translators to mistranslate *ekklesia* as "church", forbidding the correct translation, "assembly", or as Tyndall preferred, "congregation".

7. **Behold, he is coming with the clouds, and every eye will see him, even those who pierced him, and all the tribes of the earth will mourn because of him. Yes, Amen!**

Note: Even in the apostles' time, some began teaching the bizarre doctrine that Jesus had already returned (2Tim. 2:16–18), but John was obviously still looking for Jesus to come back.

¶8. **"I am the Alpha and the Omega, says the L**ORD **God, the One who is, and who was, and who is to come, the Almighty."**

Note: Verse 8 is an unanticipated exclamation from the Father. Another such interjection, this time from the Son, can be seen in Revelation 16:15.

¶9. **I, John, *your* brother and partner in the tribulation, and kingdom, and perseverance in Christ Jesus, was on the island called Patmos because of the word of God and because of the testimony of Jesus Christ.**

Note 1: John was still in Judea long after Jesus ascended into heaven (Gal. 1:18; 2:1, 9), so he must have come to Patmos Island late in his life.

Note 2: We have no specific information about why or how John came to be on Patmos Island, other than his statement that he was there "because of the word of God and because of the witness of Jesus Christ." This tells us that John was on Patmos as a result of persecution (cf. Rev. 6:9); however, traditional explanation notwithstanding, John does not say he was *exiled* to Patmos; he may have only been hiding from persecution on the island.

Patmos is mentioned but three times[3] in extant ancient literature, and none of those writers refer to Patmos as a place of exile or as a penal colony. Description of Patmos as a place of exile or imprisonment comes from Christian historians writing at a later

---

[3] Once each by Thucydides, Pliny, and Strabo.

date. One of them claimed that John was condemned to labor in mines on the island, but there is no evidence that mines were on Patmos or that the Romans worked slaves there.

Note 3: John may even have fled to Patmos to escape persecution from apostate believers. We know that late in his life, John was unwelcome in some congregations (3Jn. 1:9–10) because of the widespread apostasy of the body of Christ at that time (1Jn. 2:18–19; 4:1; 2Tim. 1:15).

10a. I was in the Spirit on the LORD's day,

Note: It is not only unbiblical but also anachronistic to say that the LORD's day is Sunday. The only "LORD's day" that John knew was the day that God set aside as holy: the Jewish Sabbath day. John knew nothing about the emperor Constantine's elevation, in the fourth century, of the Day of the Sun as a weekly holy day.

10b. and I heard behind me a loud voice like a trumpet,
11. saying, "What you see, write in a book, and send it to the seven Assemblies: to Ephesus, and to Smyrna, and to Pergamon, and to Thyatira, and to Sardis, and to Philadelphia, and to Laodicea."

Note: The voice belonged to Jesus, as the following verses show, and what Jesus said tells us that there were but seven Assemblies remaining in the province of Asia that were recognized by God. The Lord did not say, "to seven *of* the Assemblies", but "to the seven Assemblies". Likewise, in verse 4, John addressed this book to "the seven Assemblies that are in Asia".

12. And I turned to see the voice that was speaking to me. And when I had turned, I saw seven golden lampstands,
13. and in the midst of the seven lampstands was one like a son of man, wearing a robe extending to his feet, and girded about the chest with a golden sash.
14. His head and his hair were white as wool, like snow, and his eyes were like a flame of fire,

15. and his feet were like fine brass glowing in a furnace, and his voice was like the sound of many waters.
16. And he held seven stars in his right hand, and out of his mouth came a sharp, double-edged sword, and his face was like the sun shining in its strength.
17a. And when I saw him, I fell at his feet like a dead man,

Note 1: John used "like" or "as" about ninety times in this book, and understandably so. Much of what he saw, beginning with this vision of the glorified Jesus, was beyond human experience, and John could describe what he was seeing only by saying it was "like" something known on earth.

Note 2: The experience of falling down – indeed, even passing out – as a result of a heavenly visitation is not uncommon in Scripture (e.g., Ezek. 1:28–2:2; Dan. 8:17–18, 27). When John and the others saw Jesus after his resurrection, Jesus was in the earthly body with which John was familiar, and so, none of them passed out as John did here, when Jesus appeared in his glorified spiritual body.

Note 3: John saw no nail prints in the hands of the glorified Jesus because glorified bodies have no scars. They are perfect in every way. If a believer dies with one arm, he will have two arms when he is raised from the dead and given a glorified body. All physical blemishes will be done away with when the physical body is replaced with the one God will give His people.

17b. but he placed his right hand on me, saying, "Do not be afraid. I am the first and the last,
18a. and the one who lives and was dead, and behold, I am alive forever and ever! Amen!

Note: Jesus had to tell John who he was because John did not recognize him. Jesus put on this glorified body after he ascended (cf. Jn. 17:5; Acts 3:13), and John had not seen him since then.

18b. And I have the keys of death and of hell[4].

Note: That Jesus holds the keys to both death and hell contradicts the Christian myth that attributes to the Devil[5] the power to cast sinners into hell and torment them after they die.

19. Now, write down the things you have seen, and the things which are, and the things which will come to pass after these things.

Note: Like Paul (Gal. 1:11–12), John did not receive what he wrote from a man, but from Jesus Christ. The fact that these messages came from Jesus serves as John's credentials for ministering these things to the saints, and in fact, in the kingdom of God, there are no other credentials except what comes from Jesus.

20. The mystery of the seven stars that you saw in my right hand and of the seven golden lampstands: the seven stars are the messengers of the seven Assemblies, and the seven lampstands are the seven Assemblies."

Note: Some years ago, I went out at dusk to pray before that night's prayer meeting. I walked along the railroad tracks that ran behind large warehouses near my home, and as I prayed, the holy Spirit came upon me and began to speak through me in an indignant tone. It was as if the millions of pieces of gravel along the tracks were the people of earth, and God was speaking to them through me. This is some of what the Spirit, with intense scorn, said: "What difference does it make, what *men* say about anything? [The Spirit spoke the word "men" with supreme contempt.] If *men* call a man a prophet, does *that* make him a prophet? If *men* call a man a pastor, does *that* make him a pastor? What difference does

---

[4] The Greek word is "Hades", but to avoid distraction, I have elected to use the more familiar word, "hell".

[5] Throughout this book, I use the familiar word "Devil" in order to avoid distraction. The word means "Accuser", which was Satan's function and title in heaven before he was cast out by Jesus. However, since he has been cast out of heaven, his accusations are no longer valid, and his title now might better be "Slanderer", as some have it.

it make, what *men* say about anything! Am *I* confused by *your* delusions?"

Even though God was angrily demanding an answer, not a single stone along the tracks could render one. They were, of course, completely insensible to my voice. And unless God touches our hearts, we humans are as dead to Him as those railroad stones were to me.

Then the holy Spirit began to laugh through me – powerfully laugh – but without the first hint of joy. It was a terrifying, threatening laughter which echoed off the long tin roofs of the warehouses along the tracks. I literally staggered under its power. God's fury burned through my eyes as His laughter roared from my throat. The laughter consumed me, and I could not speak, but my heart was begging God, "Please, God, don't ever let me hear you laugh at me like this!"

Then the Spirit began to speak the words that it spoke through David long, long ago (Prov. 1:24–26): "Because I called and *you* refused, because I stretched out my hand and no one regarded it, because *you* disdained all my counsel and did not want my reproof, I will also laugh at *your* calamity. I will mock when *your* terror comes."

It was nearly dark when my prayer ended, and I was left standing alone on the tracks. How utterly worthless are our thoughts and ways, and how desperately we need God's thoughts and the knowledge of His ways! God is not confused by our delusions; we can only confuse one another.

I tell this story to emphasize a critical point. God being the Creator means that whatever He says, is, but as for us, we make nothing true by speaking it. There is nothing human about God; He cannot die, and He cannot lie. Even if the entire world were to join hands and proclaim a thing to be true, God would not be moved by it, for nothing is true unless He says it (Prov. 11:21a; 16:5). The claims and pronouncements of men carry no weight whatsoever in heaven. Only the man God calls a pastor is a pastor. Only the man God calls a prophet is a prophet. Only the man God anoints is anointed. And God recognizes no assembly of worshippers as being an Assembly of His unless He created that Assembly by His Spirit.

When Jesus sent messages to the seven pastors of the seven Assemblies in Asia, he sent them to men who were pastors *in God's sight* over congregations that were Assemblies of believers *in God's sight*. He sent no messages to any other pastors in the province of Asia. Those apostate pastors and their assemblies in Asia may not even have considered these seven Assemblies to be legitimate, but then, God is not confused by our delusions.

The Seven Assemblies in Asia

My Credentials for Writing Chapter 2: Jesus' Messages to the Seven Pastors

In both the Old and New Testaments, the main word for "angel" actually means "messenger". Sometimes, the word refers to heavenly messengers, such as the angels Jacob saw in a vision (Gen. 28:12), or Gabriel, who was sent to Daniel (Dan. 8:16; 9:21), and then, centuries later, to Zacharias and Mary (Lk. 1:19, 26–27). But the word can also refer to earthly messengers, such as the servants that Jacob sent to meet his brother Esau (Gen. 32:3), or the two messengers John the Baptist sent to Jesus (Lk. 7:19, 24), or even John the Baptist himself (Mt. 11:10; Mal. 3:1a). Here in Revelation, Jesus was not telling John to send messages to angels; that would have made no sense. Men do not write to angels. Indeed, an angel brought these messages to John (Rev. 1:1). So, the messengers to whom John was writing were men, the pastors of the seven Assemblies that remained in Asia.

I didn't learn this on my own; Jesus revealed it to me. This is how it happened:

In 1990, some dear friends were visiting our home when the Spirit spoke to me and said, "Get alone and read the Bible." It felt odd to leave our company; at the same time, I was excited to find out why the Lord wanted me to go read the Bible. So, I went to my office and sat down to read. But which book? The thought came to me to read in Revelation, since I had not done so in a while. I had studied Revelation intensely while in seminary, at one point becoming so familiar with the Greek text that I preferred to read it in Greek rather than in English. But that had been fourteen years earlier, and so I opened my English language Bible instead. I started reading in Revelation 2, where – so I had always thought – Jesus was giving John messages for the seven Assemblies in Asia.

When I read the first words of Revelation 2, "To the angel of", the Spirit spoke to me and said, "These messages are to the pastors of the Assemblies, not to the Assemblies themselves." I was surprised. Was this true? Was Jesus telling John to send these messages to individual pastors instead of to the Assemblies? How could I know for sure that I had heard from the Lord? Then, I read further, "I know your works, and your labor, and your patience, and that you cannot tolerate those who are evil." Then it came to me how I could "test the spirit" and make certain that the voice I had just heard was Jesus.

I remembered that in English, the word "you" is spelled the same way whether it refers to an individual or a group, but in biblical Greek, there is a difference between the singular and plural forms of "you", as you can see here:

English	Greek
you (singular)	σύ (singular)
you (plural)	ὑμεῖς (plural)

I arose from my chair, walked across the room to my bookshelf, and opened my Greek New Testament. There it was. The "you" and "your" in these seven messages were singular! Jesus was not addressing the whole congregation; he was speaking to the pastors! And he had really spoken to me! I immediately forsook the opinion which I had for so long held, namely, that the seven messages from Jesus were messages to the seven Assemblies, and I proceeded to read Revelation 2 and 3 as John understood them, and as Jesus intended for them to be understood.

But there is more to my testimony that must be told. As I said, while in the seminary, I became quite familiar with the Greek text of Revelation. My final exam in one Greek course was to sit alone with my professor in his office and to translate whatever portions of Revelation he would choose. It was expected of me to know all the vocabulary, to be able to explain the morphology, and to answer any other question concerning the text that my professor may ask. The day of my exam, there was nothing that he asked me that I could not fully answer. He was so impressed that he even went to a different book, the gospel of Mark, and chose a random passage which I had not studied and asked me questions about those verses.

Now, I had to tell that part of the story in order to bring out the essential point, which is that although I knew the Greek text of Revelation very well, I remained ignorant of what the text meant until the Spirit of God spoke to me fourteen years later! The knowledge of Greek, in itself, had revealed nothing to me; it was the Spirit of God alone that taught me the truth. This is what Jesus meant when he said that the Spirit would guide us into all truth (Jn. 16:13). The knowledge of Greek is only the knowledge of Greek; it is not the knowledge of God. That knowledge comes only through the Spirit.

By leading me to get alone with Him, and then speaking to me that day in my office, Jesus gave me the credentials I need to explain these messages in Revelation to you. Peter said, "If any man minister, let it be with the strength that God supplies" (1Pet. 4:11), and it is with the strength God gave me those many years ago that I minister to you in the following pages the messages in the second and third chapters of John's book of Revelation.

Chapter 2
Jesus' Messages to the Seven Pastors
Revelation 2:1 – 3:22

First Message: To the Pastor at Ephesus

Ephesus was the capital of the province of Asia in John's time, and within its walls was a huge, world-renowned temple dedicated to Artemis,[6] goddess of the moon and of hunting. The original temple was made of the purest white marble and is considered to have been one of the Seven Wonders of the Ancient World. The temple was about 370 feet long, 180 feet wide, and contained over 100 columns up to 60 feet high. The nearby theater in Ephesus, into which some of Paul's companions were dragged in Acts 19, could hold over 24,000 people.

The Ephesian Assembly loved Paul, but at Paul's last meeting with their elders, he prophesied that some of them would turn from the faith, "speaking perverse things in order to draw away disciples after themselves" (Acts 20:30). Later, when this began to happen, Paul sent Timothy to Ephesus to salvage as many souls as he could from the apostasy that was taking place (1Tim. 1:3–4). If these messages came to John after that apostasy, as appears to be the case, then this is a message for the pastor of the faithful remnant of the Ephesian Assembly, the ones who did not follow the false teachers.

Paul summoned Timothy away from Ephesus, replacing him with Tychicus (2Tim. 4:9–12), but since Jesus does not call this pastor by name, we do not know if this message is for Tychicus.

---

[6] The King James translation of the Ephesians' chant in Acts 19:28 and 19:34 is, "Great is Diana of the Ephesians!" That was an intentional mistranslation by the king's translators; they substituted the Roman name "Diana" for the Greek "Artemis", which is in the original biblical text. Most modern translations correct that error and use "Artemis".

Revelation 2

¶1. "To the messenger of the Assembly in Ephesus, write:

¶He who holds the seven stars in his right hand, who walks in the midst of the seven golden lampstands, says these things:

2. I know your works, and your labor, and your patience, and that you cannot tolerate those who are evil. And you have put to the test those who make themselves out to be apostles, but are not, and you have found them liars,

Note: This pastor had the wisdom and boldness to expose those in Ephesus who falsely claimed to be apostles of Christ. Such men were found in other cities as well (e.g., 2Cor. 11:13–15; Gal. 1:6–7; 5:12). They were not immoral wretches, any more than the religious leaders who opposed Jesus were immoral wretches. They were, instead, zealous and devout ministers; otherwise, they would have deceived no one with their claim to be ministers sent by Christ.

3. and you have patience, and you endured for my name's sake and did not grow weary.
4. Nevertheless, I have against you that you have left your first love.

Note: This pastor was a good and wise man, and had been faithful in difficult times. But Jesus saw a flaw in him which would, if not corrected, disqualify him from continuing as God's messenger for the saints in Ephesus: he had left his "first love". But what is one's first love?

Typically, when a newly converted soul starts his journey with Jesus, he looks up to all others in the kingdom of God as better and wiser than himself. He senses his need of guidance and is willing to receive it. Then, as he grows in grace and knowledge, he begins to discern the body more perfectly, and with that discernment comes an awareness of faults in some saints whom he previously held in high esteem.

This developing ability in Christ to make righteous judgments of older saints' character can be confusing for new believers. I have seen many of them condemn themselves for what they were beginning to discern, telling themselves they shouldn't think such thoughts. Sometimes, such believers even try to repent for seeing what the Spirit is showing them, not realizing that they are just growing in grace and knowledge. They must be taught that as the mind of Christ develops within them, they will see what God sees, and what God sees in His children is not always pleasant. Solomon said, "In much wisdom is much grief, and he who increases knowledge increases sorrow" (Eccl. 1:18); so, it is impossible to escape the sorrow Christ feels for some believers when we grow spiritually, for as we grow in the Spirit, we attain to the knowledge that Christ has about them.

My father, "Preacher Clark", helped rescue me and others from leaving our first love for wayward brothers and sisters by putting together two of Jesus' sayings in a sweet, special way. First, he quoted this from Jesus: "As often as *you* did it to one of the least of these my brothers, *you* did it to me" (Mt. 25:40). Then, he told us that it was not up to us to determine who are "the least" among God's children, for Jesus himself revealed who they are: "Whoever breaks one of the least of these commandments and teaches men to do so shall be called least in the kingdom of heaven" (Mt. 5:19). So, wayward ministers are the least in the kingdom of God, and our attitude toward them reveals our degree of godliness. The pastor in Ephesus had left his first love by ceasing to love believers who were disobeying God and teaching others to do the same. Jesus was displeased with him because he still loved those fallen souls, "not wanting any to perish, but for all to come to repentance" (2Pet. 3:9).

Before coming to Christ, if I discovered a distasteful fault in someone, it would adversely affect my love for him. But as I grew in Christ, I discovered that seeing a brother's fault did not diminish my love for him at all. I could keep the backslider on a pedestal in my heart simply because he belonged to God. With that attitude, faults or failures in a fellow believer could not make me love him

less. In other words, I did not leave my first love for a fellow believer who fell away from righteousness.

The Ephesian pastor's discernment was excellent, but discernment without sufficient love of God can be more of a problem than
an asset. Over time, a pastor will see among God's people some of
the best and some of the worst that the kingdom of God has to offer, and he must be able to deal with each spirit according to the
will of God. While no pastor should allow false teachers to teach
in the Assembly under his care, those same false teachers must be
shown the love of God as long as there is hope for them. Jesus requires his servants to follow his example in everything, including
hating sin. Pastors must learn to hate sinners with the love of God.

5. **Remember, therefore, from where you have fallen, and
    repent, and do the first works. Otherwise, I will come
    upon you suddenly and remove your lampstand from
    its place, unless you repent.**

Note: Jesus' threat to remove the Assembly from this pastor's
care may seem too severe a punishment for such a devoted and ca-
pable servant of God, but at stake was hope for the souls for whom
God cared. God loves all His children, even the bad ones, and if
we become so bitter toward the wayward that we leave no door
open for them to repent, we are no longer useful to our heavenly
Father in restoring lost sheep to the fold. That is why Jesus commanded this good man to repent and why he threatened to take the
congregation away from him if he did not.

6. **Yet, you do have this, that you hate the deeds of the
    Nicolaitans, which I also hate.**

Note 1: Hating is a godly attribute if one hates what God hates,
the way God hates it.

Note 2: Theories abound, but no one knows who the
Nicolaitans were, or what their deeds were that Jesus hated.

7. **He who has an ear, hear what the Spirit is saying to the Assemblies! To him who overcomes will I give to eat of the tree of life that is in the paradise of my God.**

<u>Lesson from Jesus' message to the pastor in Ephesus:</u>

God's servants are required not merely to hate *what* God hates, but to hate *the way* God hates. Jesus sternly warned this very good pastor that his congregation would be taken from him unless he returned to his first love. He could return to his first love because, as Preacher Clark astutely observed, he had not *lost* his first love; he had *left* it. The pastor's love for brothers who had gone astray (the "wolves" whom Paul prophesied would arise in Ephesus) had to be regained; otherwise, if God ever forgave those false teachers, the pastor would be unable to minister to them. The man of God must know how to be right and merciful at the same time; he must not close his heart to those who are wrong.

Second Message: To the Pastor at Smyrna

By the time John wrote his letter, Smyrna was over two thousand years old, well-known, and highly regarded throughout the known world. Not much of ancient Smyrna can be excavated because the large city of Izmir, Turkey, sits on top of it. Smyrna was important as a port city, and it boasted the largest agora (the equivalent of a modern shopping mall) in the ancient world.

¶8. **"And to the messenger of the Assembly in Smyrna, write:**

¶The first and the last, who was dead and is alive, says these things:
9. **I know your works, and your suffering, and poverty (but you are rich), and the slander of those who claim to be Jews, and are not, but are a synagogue of Satan.**

Note 1: There is no proof for the existence of a Jewish community in Smyrna in John's time, and so, it is unlikely that Jesus was referring to Jews falsely claiming to be Jews. Rather, this pastor was being slandered by people who claimed to be the body of

Christ, the New Testament "Israel of God" of which Paul spoke (Gal. 6:16). In other words, unlike some of the apostate believers in Ephesus, these people did not belong to Christ at all; they just thought they did.

Paul taught that only those who receive God's Spirit are Jews in this covenant (Rom. 2:28–29; 8:9). The apostates with which the pastor in the city of Ephesus dealt had received the Spirit, apparently, and so, though falsely claiming to be apostles, they did belong to God; they were Jews in God's sight. However, here in Smyrna, people were falsely claiming to belong to God, that is, they were falsely claiming to have received the Spirit. And because of such teaching, confusion arose among the Assemblies as to who really had the Spirit and who did not, so much so, that the apostle John felt compelled to explain to believers how to tell who really has the holy Spirit (1Jn. 4:1–3). And since Patmos Island is not far from Ephesus, John may have written that letter to help them.

Note 2: In telling this pastor that those who falsely claimed to be God's people were "a synagogue of Satan", Jesus was saying that Satan was the originator and the director of their assemblies.

10. Do not fear the things you are about to suffer. Behold, the Devil is now about to cast some of *you* into prison so that *you* might be tested, and for ten days, *you* will have tribulation. Be faithful unto death, and I will give you the crown of life.

Note: This faithful pastor loved his congregation, and Jesus warned him that his faith was about to be tried by seeing some of his sheep cast into prison by Satan. (Note that the "yous" in the first and last sentences in verse 10 are singular, while the "*yous*" in the middle sentence are plural.) This pastor was about to suffer, but his suffering would be the imprisonment and affliction of others, not himself! So, Jesus charged him to remain steadfast in the faith when those he loved suffered.

11. He who has an ear, hear what the Spirit is saying to the Assemblies! He who overcomes will not be harmed by the Second Death.

Note: The "Second Death" is not hell; it is a far worse place called "the Lake of Fire", of which we will learn more later.[7]

Lesson from Jesus' message to the pastor in Smyrna:

The fact that Satan was personally involved in the persecution of these believers is a testimony to the effectiveness of this impoverished pastor's ministry, for it indicates that their faith in Christ was sufficient to deal with that degree of spiritual warfare. Few of God's children ever mature in spirit enough to become targets of Satan's wrath. Jesus found no fault with this good shepherd and encouraged him only to "be faithful unto death".

Third Message: To the Pastor at Pergamon

Pergamon was a special city for a number of reasons. In 133 BC, when King Attalus III died without an heir, he bequeathed Pergamon and its territory to Rome. Within the city was a world-renowned medical school and the second largest library in the ancient world. The largest library was in Alexandria, Egypt, and the Egyptians, fearing that the library at Pergamon would surpass theirs, curtailed shipments of papyrus to Pergamon in order to slow down Pergamon's production of manuscripts. But Pergamon would not let the scarcity of papyrus slow down its progress; scholars there developed the use of animal skins for writing in the place of papyrus. This new writing material became known as "parchment", and its use quickly spread to other nations.

The most noteworthy building that remains of ancient Pergamon is the altar of Zeus, chief of the Greek gods. It was dismantled in the late nineteenth century and transported to Berlin, Germany, where it now stands in the Berlin Museum. The photo on the following page is a picture of this altar:

---

[7] For more on this subject, read my online gospel tract, "The Second Death", at GoingtoJesus.com.

By Lestat (Jan Mehlich) - Own work, CC BY-SA 3.0. *Wikicommons*. https://common-
s.wikimedia.org/wiki/File:Berlin_-_Pergamonmuseum_-_Altar_01.jpg#/media/
File:Berlin_-_Pergamonmuseum_-_Altar_01.jpg

¶12. **"And to the messenger of the Assembly in Pergamon,
write:**

**¶He who has the sharp, double-edged sword says these
things:**
13. **I know your works, and where you are living – where
Satan's throne is – and yet you hold fast my name, and
did not deny my faith even in the days in which
Antipas, my faithful martyr, was slain among *you*,
where Satan dwells.**

Note 1: Jesus did not reveal why he referred to Pergamon as
"where Satan's throne is."

Note 2: Though living in an extremely difficult situation, the
pastor in Pergamon had been faithful, even in the face of death.
Given the task of being a pastor in the city where Satan's throne
was, he had upheld the standard of truth in the Assembly, except in
a few cases which Jesus proceeds to mention.

14. **Yet, I have a few things against you because you have
there some holding the doctrine of Balaam, who taught
Balak to lay a stumbling block before the sons of Israel,
to eat food offered to idols and to commit fornication.**
15. **And you also have there some who hold the doctrine of
the Nicolaitans.**

Note 1: Jesus faulted this pastor, not because of what the pastor himself was teaching, but because of what he was allowing others to teach to his congregation. It is important to note that Jesus held this one individual – the pastor – personally accountable for the conduct and spiritual well-being of the members of the Assembly in his charge. A pastor is accountable for what his congregation does because pastors have a God-given mandate to maintain God's order, purity, and joy in his congregation.

This concept of a pastor's accountability to God for his flock's behavior is not restricted to New Testament leaders. At Mount Sinai, God emphasized to Moses that he would be personally accountable for Israel's conduct. Notice that the only time "you" is plural is in verse 21:

Exodus 23
20. Behold, I am sending an angel before you [singular] to protect you along the way and to bring you to the place that I have prepared.
21a. Beware of him, and obey his voice. Do not provoke him, for he will not pardon *y*our [plural] transgression.

In verse 20, all the "yous" being singular, God was promising Moses that His angel would go before *Moses* to bring *Moses* to the Promised Land. Of course, this was good news for the Israelites because it meant that God's angel would go before them, too – as long as they followed Moses. Then, in verse 21, we have this: "Beware of him, and obey his voice. Do not provoke him, for he will not pardon *y*our transgression." The verbs "beware", "obey", and "provoke" are singular, meaning that God was commanding the man Moses to fear the angel and submit to him. But the reason for this warning was that the angel "will not pardon *y*our [plural!] transgression." *God would hold Moses accountable for Israel's actions!* In other words, Moses was being told that if he failed either to obey *or enforce* God's law, he would suffer for it.

Jesus, likewise, holds the pastors of these seven Assemblies personally accountable for the conduct of their congregations.

Note 2: One false doctrine that the pastor in Pergamon was allowing to be taught among his sheep was what Jesus called "the doctrine of Balaam" (verse 14). There were few sins in the Old Testament of such evil cunning that they were actually given titles. One was "the sin of Jeroboam" (2Kgs. 3:3; cf. 1Kgs. 12:26–33), to which God referred for centuries, even mentioning it after the nation of Israel was destroyed (2Kgs. 23:15). Likewise, the sin called "the doctrine of Balaam" did such damage to Israel that although it was committed in Numbers 25 (see also Num. 31:16), Jesus mentioned it here, in the last book of the Bible.

Balaam taught sinners how to persuade God's people to blend with them religiously, socially, and politically. He taught the Moabites how to use the good nature of God's people against them by advising the Moabites to approach Israel as friends, to worship the God of Israel and to invite Israel to join them in their worship, and to intermarry with them. Israel fell into the trap, and thinking they were opening their hearts to others in love, they were opening their hearts to the influence of wicked spirits. Thus Balaam, to borrow a phrase from the prophet Daniel, "destroyed many with peace" (Dan. 8:25). God's people were persuaded that to be "inclusive" was good, but the first of the Ten Commandments is that the God of Israel is exclusively God (Ex. 20:3).

Such an "inclusive" mindset is typical of a proud, sophisticated society. Worldly people can become proud of not knowing, or rather, not believing in "the truth", but they become fools when they go so far as to deny that there is a truth to know, and then reject those who do know the truth and testify to it. This pastor, living in the sophisticated city of Pergamon, had caved in to the pressure to be inclusive, and in doing so, he had left the door open for unclean spirits to come and go as they pleased in his Assembly.

Note 3: Jesus was also displeased that the pastor was tolerating those who taught "the doctrine of the Nicolaitans". As I have said, no one knows what this doctrine was because Jesus did not explain it, but his primary point was that this pastor was not protecting the body of Christ from evil influences, even though he had authority from God to do so. Maybe the pastor did not understand the authority he had, but Jesus understood it, and he insisted that this man use it.

Note 4: There is a small but telling difference between Jesus' message to this pastor concerning the Nicolaitans and his message to the pastor in Ephesus: the absence of the phrase, "which I also hate." Jesus was able to say to the pastor at Ephesus that he *also* hated the way of the Nicolaitans because that pastor hated it. Here at Pergamon, Jesus could not say that he also hated the doctrine of the Nicolaitans, for this pastor, unfortunately, did not hate it. In the sophisticated culture of Pergamon, it may have been news to this pastor that Jesus hated anything, including false doctrine, or that Jesus would not tolerate those who taught false doctrine, or that Jesus expected him to enforce a standard of holy exclusiveness in his Assembly. The pastor obviously did not understand that being inclusive with the spirits of this world is not wisdom; rather, it is "enmity against God" (Jas. 4:4).

16. So, repent! Otherwise, I will come to you soon, and I will wage war against them with the sword of my mouth.

Note: Because this pastor loved his congregation (though he did not know how to love them as Jesus did), Jesus was able to motivate him to do his duty for them by warning him, "If you don't fix the problem, I will make war against them!" With this threat, Jesus was using this pastor's love for the Assembly to motivate him to stop those in his congregation who were teaching false doctrine.

17. He who has an ear, hear what the Spirit is saying to the Assemblies! To him who overcomes will I give to eat of the hidden manna, and I will give him a white stone, and upon the stone a new name written which no one knows except the one who receives it.

Lesson from Jesus' message to the pastor in Pergamon:
This pastor did not understand that loving God's people includes enforcing a standard of holiness for them. The love of God

for His people demands that His unruly children be warned. It is good for believers when the world is tolerant, for by tolerating all faiths, they inadvertently tolerate the true one. But God demands purity of faith and conduct among the saints, and the body of Christ is to be perfectly *intolerant* of every false way (cf. Ps. 119:104, 128). Paul once told the Corinthians, quite forcefully, that even though it is none of our business to judge those outside the body of Christ, God certainly requires believers to exercise judgment among them-selves (1Cor. 5:9–13; 11:31). Tolerating heresy is no virtue for a pastor; it is dereliction of duty. The cultural pressure on this Assembly was the pressure *to appear good* rather than *to be good,* and this pastor had yielded to the pressure.

Fourth Message: To the Pastor at Thyatira

Thyatira was a relatively minor city, situated on a road connecting the two larger cities of Pergamon and Sardis. An important part of the economy of Thyatira was the production of purple dye. Lydia, a woman whom Paul met in Philippi, was "a dealer in purple cloth" from Thyatira (Acts 16:12–14).

¶18. **"And to the messenger of the Assembly in Thyatira, write:**

¶The Son of God, who has eyes like a flame of fire and whose feet are as fine brass, says these things:

19. **I know your works, and love, and faith, and service, and your patience. And your last works are greater than the first.**

20. **However, I have against you that you put up with your wife – Jezebel! – who calls herself a prophetess, but who teaches and misleads my servants to commit fornication and to eat things offered to idols.**

21. **And I gave her time to repent, but she will not repent of her whoredom.**

Note: God's great patience had been demonstrated in His patience with this wicked woman. However, she had rejected His mercy, and now, her opportunity for mercy had passed.

22. **Behold, I am casting her onto a sickbed, and those who commit adultery with her, into great affliction, unless they repent of her works.**
23a. **And I will kill her children with death.**

Note: Jesus was greatly displeased that this pastor had not restrained his wife when she puffed herself up to be a prophetess, or one might say, co-pastor. She was teaching the same doctrine of Balaam that was being taught in Pergamon, that is, teaching God's servants to be inclusive and "to eat food offered to idols and to commit fornication" (2:14). Jesus told this pastor that he was about to do three things: (1) strike his wife with a debilitating disease, (2) afflict her followers with the same disease, but give them a last chance to repent, and (3) kill her children.

Jesus did not tell this pastor to communicate this message to the ones involved; he just let him know what he was about to do.

23b. **And all the Assemblies will know I am the one who examines the minds and hearts,**

Note 1: What Jesus is about to do to the pastor's wife and her followers at Thyatira will be so terrifying that news of it will spread throughout the body of Christ in this part of the world.

Note 2: After these angry comments to this pastor, Jesus spoke no more to him. In the middle of verse 23, the "yous" become plural because Jesus began speaking to the Assembly as a whole, encouraging the faithful among them to hold on to what they still had until he came.

23c. **and I will give to each of *you* according to *your* deeds.**
24. **But to *you* I say, to those who are left in Thyatira, as many as do not hold that doctrine, who have not known 'the deep things of Satan', as they say, I put no other burden on *you*.**
25. **Only hold fast what *you* do have until I come.**

Note: It is possible for believers to keep themselves pure and acceptable to God even if their leaders do not. The pastor, his wife, and others in the Assembly in Thyatira had strayed far from righteousness, but some in this congregation had not followed their perverse example, and Jesus was pleased with them. No child of God is obligated to follow a pastor who is going the wrong way.

26. **And he who overcomes and keeps my works until the end, to him will I give authority over the nations,**
27. **and he will rule over them with an iron rod (like potters' vessels, they will be shattered), as I also received from my Father,**
28. **and I will give him the morning star.**
29. **He who has an ear, hear what the Spirit is saying to the Assemblies!**

<u>Lesson from Jesus' message to the pastor in Thyatira:</u>

This pastor had fallen victim to the same worldly pressure that the pastor in Pergamon had begun to fall into, but there was a difference. While the situation in Pergamon was grim, Jesus let that pastor know he could still correct it, and he commanded him to do so. Here in Thyatira, however, the pastor had allowed evil to continue for so long that it had grown beyond his strength to correct. He had several worthy virtues, including the zeal to labor more than ever, but he had tolerated evil for too long, and it had taken root in the Assembly.

Paul told the Corinthians, "If we would judge ourselves, we would not be judged" (1Cor. 11:31). This body had not judged itself, and so, Jesus had to come and bring judgment in order to make things right again.

Fifth Message: To the Pastor at Sardis

Five centuries before Christ, and two centuries before Alexander the Great made it a Greek city, Sardis was the capital of this region. At the time John wrote this message, however, Sardis was no longer a great city. Still, the prosperous Jewish community in Sardis boasted the largest synagogue outside of Palestine.

Revelation 3

¶1. "And to the messenger of the Assembly in Sardis, write:

¶He who has the seven spirits of God and the seven stars says these things:
I know your works, that you have a reputation that you are alive, but you are dead.

2. Be watchful, and strengthen the things that are left, which are about to die, for I have not found your works perfected before my God.

Note: When I was a young man, just beginning my ministry, the Lord spoke to me and said, "Do not expect or desire any big thing, but make your work perfect." It is a terrifying thought to me to be judged, as this pastor was, as having failed to do that. If Jesus commands it, we can do it. And woe to us if we do not.

3. Remember, therefore, how you received and heard, and hold fast, and repent! If you do not watch, I will come upon you like a thief, and you will not know what hour I will come upon you.

4. Yet, you have a few names in Sardis who have not defiled their garments, and they will walk with me in white, for they are worthy.

Note 1: We can paraphrase what Jesus said like this: "You have *only* a few names in Sardis who have not defiled their garments." This means, sadly, that most of the saints in Sardis had defiled their garments by following this pastor's lead and were no longer worthy to walk with Jesus.

Note 2: The apostle Paul warned the saints to "abstain from every form of evil" (1Thess. 5:22). That is sound advice. But it is equally sound advice to warn the saints to abstain from a mere form of good. This pastor had begun to live on his reputation rather than maintain a living connection with God, and Jesus had nothing good to say about him. There were a few good things

about him that kept him from being hopeless, but Jesus warned
him that even those things were about to die.

5. **He who overcomes, the same shall be clothed in white
    garments, and I will not blot his name out of the Book
    of Life, but will confess his name before my Father and
    before His angels.**
6. **He who has an ear, hear what the Spirit is saying to the
    Assemblies!**

Note: This pastor was one of two, the other being in Laodicea,
whose spiritual condition was so bad that he was in danger of having his name blotted out of the Book of Life. He had a reputation
among men for being spiritually alive, but he was dead to the
things of God. He had fallen from life in the Spirit into a life of
appearances, and Jesus bluntly warned him to repent and to remember how he started out.

Lesson from Jesus' message to the pastor in Sardis:
    A pastor may fool the people around him, but he can never fool
God, who knows the heart. Here in Sardis, as in Thyatira, a few
saints had kept themselves pure, though most had not, in spite of
this pastor's miserable spiritual condition. Those believers did not
follow their pastor. They kept their relationship with Christ alive
through the Spirit and did not allow their pastor's ways to "defile
their garments".

Sixth Message: To the Pastor at Philadelphia

Philadelphia was a city of moderate significance in the ancient
world. It came under Roman control when King Attalus III died
and bequeathed his kingdom, which included this city and
Pergamon, to Rome. Four years later, Rome consolidated its hold-
ings in this area to form the Roman province of Asia.

¶7. **"And to the messenger of the Assembly in Philadelphia,
    write:**

¶These things says the one who is holy, who is true, who has the key of David, who opens and no one closes, and closes and no one opens:

Note: The key of David is mentioned in Isaiah 22:15–25. Here in Revelation 3, Jesus confirms that Isaiah's words were a prophecy about him by quoting from it in reference to himself. Isaiah 22:22 says, "The key of the house of David will I [God] lay upon his [Jesus'] shoulder. He will open, and no one will shut; and he will shut, and no one will open."

The key of David is the key of the king's house, and with it came the authority to decide who would enter and who would not. Jesus told his disciples, "I am the door" (Jn. 10:9), and he warned them that only those who come to God through him will be saved (Jn. 14:6).

8. **I know your works. Behold, I have set before you an open door which no one can shut, for you have little power, and yet, you kept my word and did not deny my name.**
9a. **Behold, I am giving** *you* **some from the synagogue of Satan, those who claim to be Jews and are not, but are lying.**

Note: Claims of men have never carried any weight in heaven, as Jesus demonstrated while he was on earth (Jn. 2:23–25). At times, Jesus even rebuffed his own disciples when they claimed to believe in him (e.g., Jn. 16:31). Much less is he impressed now with men's claims of faith in him. Jesus considers them to be lying who claim to believe and to be in the body of Christ, that is, to be Jews in a New Testament sense, if they have not received the Spirit of God. (See the note under 2:9.)

9b. **Behold, I will make them come and bow down at your feet, and they will know that I love you.**
10. **Since you have patiently kept my word, I also will keep you from the time of trial that is about to come upon the whole world, to try those who dwell on the earth.**

11. I am coming quickly. Hold on to what you have, so that no one will take your crown.

12. He who overcomes, him will I make a pillar in the temple of my God, and he will never again depart from it, and I will write upon him the name of my God, and the name of the city of my God, the New Jerusalem that is coming down out of heaven from my God, and my new name.

13. He who has an ear, hear what the Spirit is saying to the Assemblies!

Lesson from the message to the pastor in Philadelphia:

This pastor was under the same kind of pressure to compromise the gospel which other pastors had given in to, but he had been faithful. He did not have much spiritual strength, but as a reward for his perseverance in the faith, Jesus promised both to keep him from the hard trial which was coming and to compel his adversaries to acknowledge that God loved him. Jesus loved this man and encouraged him to be faithful, lest someone steal the crown of life that awaited him.

Seventh Message: To the Pastor at Laodicea

Laodicea was closely associated with another small town nearby, Colossae. In Paul's letter to the Colossians, he mentions Laodicea five times, asking the Colossians to allow the Laodiceans to read their letter, and for them, in turn, to read the letter he had written to the Laodiceans. We do not have Paul's Laodicean letter.

¶14. "And to the messenger of the Assembly in Laodicea, write:

¶The Amen, the faithful and true witness, the beginning of the creation of God, says these things:

15. I know your works, that you are neither cold nor hot. I would that you were either cold or hot.

16. So, because you are lukewarm, and neither hot nor cold, I am about to vomit you out of my mouth.

Note: This pastor had too much love for God to give himself completely to the world, but he also had too much love for the world to give himself completely to God. Jesus wanted him to be one way or the other.

17. **Because you say, 'I am rich, and increased with goods, and have need of nothing,' and you do not know that you are wretched, and pathetic, and poor, and blind, and naked,**
18. **I advise you to purchase from me gold refined by fire so that you may be rich, and white garments so that you may clothe yourself and the shame of your nakedness not be exposed, and eyesalve to anoint your eyes so that you may see.**

Note: Previously, Jesus mentioned those who claimed to be something they were not; now, it is the pastor himself who was claiming to be something he is not. When someone is in such poor spiritual condition that he thinks he is doing well, he is in danger of being cast out of the kingdom of God. That is what Jesus meant when he warned this pastor that he was about to vomit him out of his mouth.

19. **As many as I hold dear, I rebuke and chasten. Be zealous, therefore, and repent!**
20. **Behold, I have been standing at the door, and I am knocking. If anyone hears my voice and opens the door, I will enter in to him and dine with him, and he with me.**

Note: This pastor was in the worst spiritual condition of any of the seven. His unwise assessment of himself was based upon earthly wealth, not upon the righteousness of God. However, because Jesus still loved him, he sternly rebuked him and warned him that he was in grave danger of losing his soul.

21. **He who overcomes, him will I grant to sit with me on my throne, as I also overcame and sat with my Father on His throne.**

22. He who has an ear, hear what the Spirit is saying to the Assemblies!"

Lesson from Jesus' message to the pastor in Laodicea:

Throughout these seven messages, but here especially, it is instructive to see how Jesus does not confuse love with indulgence. When a pastor loves a congregation too much to reprove sin, he is loving his flock with a fleshly love, not the love of God. In response to this pastor's pathetic spiritual condition, and as a good example for us all, Jesus both rebuked him and expressed his love for him.

Colossae

Though the city of Colossae was also in the province of Asia, just a few miles south of Laodicea, Jesus sent no message to the pastor there. Was this because the pastor and his congregation had completely fallen into apostasy, so that God no longer acknowledged them as His? It is impossible to say, but it does make one wonder why Jesus sent no message there, and it may explain why these messages were sent to "*the* seven Assemblies that are in Asia", instead of "seven *of the* Assemblies that are in Asia".

Summary of the Seven Messages

To rightly understand these seven messages, we must recognize that they were messages from Jesus to real pastors who were facing real life situations. These seven Assemblies do not represent seven time periods, or "church ages", as some teach; nor should they be in any other way spiritualized.

In these letters, Jesus held the pastors personally accountable not only for what they themselves were teaching and doing, but also for what they were allowing to be taught and done in their congregations. None of them were judged by Christ on the basis of their education, the size of their congregations, or their wealth. They were all judged solely on the basis of how faithfully they were transmitting the will and word of God to the Assemblies entrusted to them. In the kingdom of God, a man's worth is measured by his value to the spiritual well-being of those around him.

It is a pastor's particular privilege and duty to be a steadfast source of spiritual strength and direction for the saints of God. If he is not, he is a failure. But if he is, then he has fulfilled his commission to be a "shadow of a great rock in a weary land" and is a success.

Lastly, at the conclusion of each of these seven messages are promises which are attended by the same exhortation: "He who has an ear, hear what the Spirit is saying *to the Assemblies!*" In other words, Jesus offered each promise to all the Assemblies, not just to the pastor. And to every child of God everywhere, Jesus still offers these precious promises:

- To him who overcomes will I give to eat of the tree of life that is in the paradise of my God (2:7).

- He who overcomes will not be harmed by the Second Death (2:11).

- To him who overcomes will I give to eat of the hidden manna, and I will give him a white stone, and upon the stone a new name written which no one knows except the one who receives it (2:17).

- He who overcomes and keeps my works until the end, to him will I give authority over the nations, and he will rule over them with an iron rod (like potters' vessels, they will be shattered), as I also received from my Father, and I will give him the morning star (2:26–29).

- He who overcomes, the same shall be clothed in white garments, and I will not blot his name out of the Book of Life, but will confess his name before my Father and before His angels (3:5–6).

- He who overcomes, him will I make a pillar in the temple of my God, and he will never again depart from it, and I will write upon him the name of my God, and the name of the city of my God, the New Jerusalem that is coming down out of heaven from my God, and my new name (3:12:–13).

- He who overcomes, him will I grant to sit with me on my throne, as I also overcame and sat with my Father on His throne" (3:21–22).

As with all of God's promises, we obtain them by faith (Heb. 6:12), for it is faith in Christ Jesus which makes us "more than conquerors" and enables us to overcome the world and everything in it. John said in a letter to beloved saints, "This is the victory that overcomes the world – our faith" (1Jn. 5:4).

Chapter 3
John's Vision of Heaven
Revelation 4:1 – 5:14

Revelation 4

¶1. **After these things, I looked, and there was an open door in the sky! And the first voice that I heard speaking to me like a trumpet said, "Come up here, and I will show you things that must come to pass hereafter."**

Note: John's being caught up to heaven is not symbolic of the saints being caught up to meet the Lord, as some say. He is simply John, and this is John's testimony about Jesus taking him into heaven and revealing the future to him.

2. **Immediately, I was in the Spirit, and behold, a throne was set in heaven, and on the throne sat One**
3. **whose appearance was like a stone of jasper and sardius, and a rainbow encircled the throne, in appearance like an emerald.**

Note 1: John mentions the word "throne" twelve times in the eleven verses of Revelation 4. Everything John sees here, he describes by its relation to the throne: *on* the throne, *around* the throne, *out of* the throne, *before* the throne, or even the puzzling phrase, "*in the midst of* the throne".

Note 2: Throughout Revelation, the One sitting on the throne is the Father, never Jesus.

4. **And around the throne were twenty-four thrones, and on the thrones sat twenty-four elders clothed in white garments, and on their heads were crowns of gold.**

5. **And out of the throne came flashes of lightning, and voices, and peals of thunder. And seven lamps of fire were blazing before His throne, which are the seven spirits of God,**

Note: These seven flames are not just flames; they are living beings whose form is that of fire, created to stand before God and serve Him. In Revelation 1:4, you may recall, John told the Assemblies that along with the Father and the Son, these seven spirits sent them greetings.

6. **and before the throne was something like a sea of glass, like crystal. And in the midst of the throne and around the throne were four things that were alive, full of eyes in front and behind.**
7. **The first living thing resembled a lion, and the second living thing resembled a calf, and the third living thing had a face like a man, and the fourth living thing resembled an eagle in flight.**
8. **And each one of these four living things had six wings round about, and they were full of eyes within, and they took no rest day or night, saying, "Holy! Holy! Holy! LORD God Almighty, who was, and who is, and who is to come!"**

Note: John had never seen such creatures as these four heavenly beings and had no name for them. His description of these creatures brings to mind the cherubim of Ezekiel's visions (Ezek. 1:3–10; 10:14–15), but these are not the same creatures. Here, each of them has but a single face: one, the face of a lion, another, the face of a calf, then of a man, and lastly, of an eagle in flight. Those are the same four faces Ezekiel saw on the cherubim, but in Ezekiel's case, each cherub had all four faces on its one head!

9. **And whenever the living creatures give glory and honor and thanks to Him who was sitting on the throne, to Him who lives forever and ever,**

10. the twenty-four elders fall down before Him who sits on the throne, and they worship Him who lives forever and ever, and they throw their crowns before the throne, saying,

11. "You are worthy, our Lord and God – O Holy One! – to receive glory and honor and power, for you created all things, and by your will did they come into being and were created."

Note: These twenty-four elders are overcome with God's glory and fall down like this several times during John's revelation (Rev. 5:8, 14; 11:16; 19:4), which means that between those times, the elders are by some means returned to their thrones, with their crowns back on their heads.

Revelation 5

The Scroll

¶1. Then, in the right hand of Him who sits on the throne, I saw a scroll, with writing on the inside and on the outside, sealed with Seven Seals.

Note: It is remarkable that in the midst of these astonishing scenes, with amazing new creatures praising God, and with lightning bolts flashing and thunders roaring, John's attention was captured by a scroll in the hand of God.

2. And I saw a strong angel proclaiming with a loud voice, "Who is worthy to open the scroll and to loose its seals?"

Note: There are degrees of power and varieties of gifts among heavenly beings, just as within the body of Christ, for in saying that this is a "strong" angel, it is obvious that other angels have less power than this one. Later in Revelation, John will also see an angel with a special gift of power over fire (Rev. 14:18), which implies that some angels do not have that gift. Further, the Bible speaks of "archangels" (Jude 1:9 with Rev. 12:7), that is, angels with authority over other angels. All of this tells us that there is government, a holy order, in heaven.

3. And no one in heaven above, nor on earth, nor beneath the earth was able to open the scroll, nor even to look at it.

4. And I began to weep bitterly because no one was found worthy to open the scroll, nor even to look at it.

Note: It is surprising that John did not know that Jesus was worthy to open the scroll, which suggests that John is learning in this revelation just how great the Lord is. If that is the case, then the extent of the Son's glory was about to be revealed to him as never before.

5. Then one of the elders said to me, "Stop crying. Behold, the Lion of the tribe of Judah, the Root of David, has overcome to open the scroll and its Seven Seals."

Note: One of the titles for Jesus is "son of David", but the elder referred to Jesus as "the Root of David", thus emphasizing the fact that David came from the Son of God, not vice versa. The Son of God entered into the lineage of David when he came to earth and took on the form of Mary's son, Jesus. Prior to that, he was in heaven with the Father, and being God's agent in the creation of all things, the Son was the root not only of David but also of every other creature.

6. And then I saw, standing in the midst of the throne and of the four living things, and in the midst of the elders, something like a slaughtered lamb, with seven horns and seven eyes, which are the seven spirits of God sent out into all the world.

Note 1: John does not say this lamb is Jesus, and it is not certain that John yet knows that it is.

Note 2: Apparently, a person in a glorified body can appear in whatever form he chooses. In Revelation 1:7, Jesus told John that the world will see him in the wounded, fleshly body that he had while on earth (cf. Zech. 13:6). Then, in Revelation 1:13–16, John saw Jesus in a body as radiant as the sun. Here, Jesus appears as a slaughtered lamb with seven horns and seven eyes instead of the usual two. Later, in Revelation 19, Jesus appears on a horse, as a mighty warrior.

7. And it came, and it took the scroll from the right hand of Him who sat on the throne.

Note 1: John began his book of Revelation by describing it as a revelation which God gave to Jesus, but while on earth, Jesus told his disciples, "Of that day or hour, no one except the Father knows, not even the angels who are in heaven, nor even the Son" (Mk. 13:32; Mt. 24:36). This apparently means that John is witnessing the moment when the Father gives that revelation to Jesus, for this scroll contains very detailed revelations concerning the order of end-time events. If this is the moment the Father fully revealed the future to His Son, it is touching to think that Jesus brought his beloved disciple John up to heaven to witness the event.

Note 2: The future that was revealed when the Lamb opened the scroll would be different if the Lamb had not paid the price for our sins. For all of us, the future would have been eternally dismal if the Lamb had failed to redeem us. But a blessed future was purchased for us with the blood of the Lamb of God, and it is freely given to all who believe in him.

8. And when it took the scroll, the four living things and the twenty-four elders fell down before the Lamb, each one having a harp and golden bowls full of incense (which are the prayers of the saints).

Note: This worship of the Lamb of God is a new thing. All that John had known, and all that had ever been known, was that every creature should worship only the One sitting on the throne, that is, God. Even Jesus said the same while on earth (Mt. 4:10; Lk. 4:8).

9. **And they sang a new song, saying, "You are worthy to take the scroll and to open its seals because you were slaughtered. And with your blood, you purchased us for God out of every tribe and tongue and people and nation."**

10. **"And you made them kings and priests to our God, and they shall reign on the earth!"**

Note: The ones singing in verse 9 are not the same ones singing in verse 10. The elders, having been redeemed from earth, would have sung verse 9, praising God for purchasing them from among men with the blood of the Lamb. Verse 10, however, would have been sung by the four living creatures, for they sing of Jesus making "them" (the twenty-four elders) kings and priests to God.

11. **And I looked, and I heard as it were the sound of many angels around the throne and the living creatures and the elders, and the number of them was myriads of myriads, and thousands of thousands,**

12. **saying with a loud voice, "Worthy is the Lamb that was slain to receive power, and riches, and wisdom, and strength, and honor, and glory, and praise!"**

Note: For the angels in heaven to worship Jesus as well as God was unprecedented, and it is remarkable that the angels sensed that it was the will of God for them to do so. But even this revelation to John of the Son's glory, astonishing as it was, must have paled in his eyes in comparison to the glory revealed in what happened next.

13. **And then I heard every created thing that is in heaven, and on earth, and beneath the earth, and upon the sea, and everything that is in them, all saying, "To Him who sits on the throne and to the Lamb, be blessing, and honor, and glory, and might forever and ever! Amen!"**

Note: All creation is glorifying God all the time, whether or not any creature is aware of it or intends to do it. David hinted at this when he said, "The heavens declare the glory of God" (Ps. 19:1).

God even uses the wrath of evil men to bring Him glory (Ps. 76:10). What is new here is that John sees all creation glorifying the Son *along with the Father.* Before the Son of God was revealed and glorified, all creation had praised God alone, unaware that the Son even existed. Jesus told his disciples that it was the Father's will "that all should honor the Son just as they honor the Father" (Jn. 5:23), but this is the first time the Bible records all creation doing it.

14. And the four living things kept saying, "Amen!" And the elders fell down and worshipped.

Note: To this point in Revelation, no prophecy of end-time events has been given to John. But when the Lamb takes the scroll from the hand of the Father and opens its Seven Seals, the order of end-time events begins to unfold for him, for heavenly beings looking on, and for us.

Conclusion

It bears repeating that only because Jesus suffered and died for us does the future contained in the scroll exist. The Reader will remember Paul's famous statement that if anyone is in Christ, everything is made new. Paul was saying that in Christ, we are given a new life right now, in this world, and that we are given *a new past*,[8] for in Christ, Abraham becomes our father, and our family tree contains all the righteous from Abel to this day. But more than that, in Christ, *we are given a new future,* the future that was revealed when the Lamb opened the Seven Seals which bound the scroll that the Father held in His omnipotent hand.

---

[8] I am indebted to Sandy Sasser for this insight.

PART 2

Revelation 6:1 – 22:21

The Order of End-Time Events

My Credentials for Writing Part 2: The Order of End-Time Events

In early 1992, Lee Ann Burkhart, a member of my weekly Bible study group, suggested that we read the book of Revelation. I had little interest in prophecy and was reluctant to read Revelation, but with Lee Ann's gentle voice, the Spirit was leading me to do so. At that time, if someone had lined up all the people on earth based on who was most likely to write a book on prophecy, I would have been at the end of the line. All the commentaries I had read concerning Revelation seemed contrived and strained, and Christian prophecy teachers seemed as confused as they were confident. It was obvious to me that God had not revealed the order of end-time events to any of them, though I did believe He would reveal it when the appropriate time came.

I assented to Lee Ann's request to read Revelation on one condition, namely, that we simply read through the book to become familiar with what was in it, and nothing else. We would not spend any time trying to figure it out. It was not that I was completely disinterested in Revelation; I had carefully read Revelation a number of times, in both Greek and English. Once, I had even made a chart of the events in Revelation to acquaint myself with what John saw; at the same time, I knew that the God who revealed it to John would have to reveal it to me if I was ever to understand it.

When we finished our reading of Revelation, which took several weeks, two remarkable things happened. The first was that, as we closed our Bibles the night we completed the book, another member of the group said, "Let's read it again." The second remarkable thing was that I agreed to do it. I had never gone over the same material twice in a row, but this time, I felt the Lord leading us to do it, and so, the next week when we met, we began again to read Revelation.

When we reached Revelation 7 in our re-reading of the book, one of the men in our Bible study, Billy Highfill, asked me a question, and God used Billy's question to unlock our understanding of the order of end-time events. (I will say more about this later.) And that done, what we found was that the events of the last days will happen, in the main, in the order that John wrote them down.

Chapter 4
The Seven Seals
Revelation 6:1–8:6

Revelation 6

The First Seal: A White Horse

¶1. And I saw that the Lamb opened the first of the Seven Seals, and I heard one of the four living things say, like the sound of thunder, "Come!"

2. And I looked, and there was a white horse! And the one sitting on it held a bow, and a crown was given to him, and he went out conquering, and to conquer.

Note 1: One evening, just a few days before he was crucified, Jesus sat down on the Mount of Olives, and four of his closest disciples came and asked him about the signs of the end of the world and of his Second Coming (Mt. 24:3; Mk. 13:3–4). Peter, James, John, and Andrew then listened as the Lord of heaven and earth quietly described the order of end-time events. Jesus described there the same events John describes here, and in the same order. The first sign Jesus gave them was that "many will come, using my name, and they will deceive many" (Mt. 24:4–5; cf. 2Pet. 2:1–2). That first prophecy of Jesus, that a false gospel would be proclaimed in his name and would conquer men's souls, is also the first end-time event revealed to John in Revelation.

Note 2: The white horse does not represent military warfare. That kind of warfare takes place next, during the time of the red horse. The white horse here represents spiritual warfare in which the souls of men are conquered; it is an imitation of the white horse which Jesus will ride when he returns to earth (Rev. 19:11). Paul was warning believers of this ungodly religious spirit when he said that Satan was now presenting himself to them as "a messenger of light" and that the men they had begun to follow were Satan's ministers, falsely claiming to speak for Christ (2Cor. 11:13–15). He told his beloved Galatians, "There are certain men determined to alter the gospel of Christ," and he scolded them for having turned so quickly to "another gospel" (Gal. 1:6–7). He warned the Philippians of "evil workers" who promoted a way of worship contrary to the Spirit of God (Phip. 3:2–3). And we have already mentioned that Paul sent Timothy, and then Tychicus, to Ephesus to salvage what they could of the body of Christ there (1Tim. 1:3; 2Tim. 4:12).

But Paul's warnings did not prevail. The spirit on the white horse won the hearts of the saints, and before Paul died, he witnessed a sweeping apostasy within the body of Christ. Paul was a success in the eyes of God, but Paul was rejected by most of God's people, including his own converts, while he was still living. But it did not stop there, for it was revealed to John that the spirit on the white horse would not only go forth conquering but that it would continue to conquer. And so, in time, the apostasy that claimed to be the gospel has dominated Western Society for almost two thousand years.

Note 3: The time required for individual end-time events varies. We are not told how much time passes for each of the seals, or for the events which transpire after them. The earliest events of the Seven Seals took centuries to completely unfold, while others which come later do not require much time at all.

The Second Seal: A Red Horse

¶3. **And when he opened the second seal, I heard the second living creature say, "Come!"**

4. **And there came out another horse, fiery-red! And it was given to him who rode on it to take peace from the earth so that men would slaughter one another, and a great sword was given to him.**

Note 1: The great apostasy seduced and polluted the body of Christ with worldliness. And as a result of the rise of that false gospel, the righteous influence on mankind of the true gospel waned, and that reduction of the saints' effect as "the salt of the earth" resulted in greater strife among nations. This is in line with the order of the end-time events that Jesus gave to his four disciples on the Mount of Olives, for the second major development, he said, would be "wars and rumors of wars" (Mt. 24:6).

Note 2: Peace is increasingly being taken away. In the first edition of this book, I wrote, "*I believe that at this moment, in 1992, we are well into the effect of this troublesome spirit on the earth. How much more widespread the conflicts will grow only God can tell, but I believe that conditions can become much worse. On the Mount of Olives, Jesus added to his description of this time of strife by saying, 'Nation shall rise against nation, and kingdom against kingdom' (Mt. 24:7a). Who knows what violence is still to come?*" Since that first edition was published, matters have indeed grown much worse. There are a decreasing number of places on earth where people feel safe, and conditions will no doubt become even worse than they are.

Now, in 2023, mankind is still suffering through this time of terror, the time of the red horse.

The Third Seal: A Black Horse

¶5. And when he opened the third seal, I heard the third living creature say, "Come!" And I saw a black horse, and the one who sat on it held a balance in his hand.

6. Then I heard a voice in the midst of the four living things say, "A quart[9] of grain for a denarius, and three quarts of barley for a denarius, and do not harm the oil and the wine!"

Note 1: Jesus did not mention this event on the Mount of Olives.

---

[9] Literally, a *choenix*, which is a little less than a quart.

Note 2: In John's time, a quart was a day's ration for an ordinary working man, and a denarius was an ordinary working man's daily wage (cf. Mt. 20:2). So, it appears that this mysterious third seal, still being kept secret by God, has to do with the world's commerce and food supply.

Note 3: Since, in the Bible, oil and wine are often associated with God's people, the enigmatic commandment, "Do not harm the oil and the wine," may indicate that the saints' needs will be supplied during this extraordinary black horse time.

Note 4: After the time of the mysterious black horse, it will be easy for believers to see where they are in the order of end-time events, for the events following the black horse will be impossible to miss.

The Fourth Seal: A Pale Green Horse

¶7. And when he opened the fourth seal, I heard the fourth living creature say, "Come!"
8a. And I looked, and there was a pale green horse!

Note: The Greek word suggests this was a sickly, greenish-grey or greenish-yellow color.

8b. And the name of him who sat upon it was Death, and Hell[10] was following him, and authority was given to him over a fourth of the earth, to slay with the sword, and with famine, and with deadly disease, and by the beasts of the earth.

Note 1: At current population levels, over two billion people will die during this horrific event. Jesus said this about it: "There will be famines, and pestilences, and earthquakes in various places" (Mt. 24:7b). With the present increase in perplexing, incurable diseases, natural disasters, and growing strife among na-

---

[10] Death is the name of the spirit that rides the horse, and Hell [Hades] is the name of the spirit that was following him. They are spiritual beings with God-given power associated with death and hell.

tions, the death of over two billion people in a relatively short time is no longer unimaginable.

Note 2: When the first four seals were opened, these are the events which took place:

- A false gospel is proclaimed that conquers men's souls.
- Wars and threats of war increase.
- Unspecified events will transpire which apparently affect the world's commerce and food supply.
- One fourth of mankind is killed.

These first four seals are distinguished from the last three by the four horses that were sent out when the seals were opened. On the Mount of Olives, Jesus set apart these same four events by calling them "the beginning of sorrows" (Mt. 24:8), adding "the end is not yet" (Mt. 24:6). Then Jesus proceeded, as John did, to tell of worse things to come.

The Fifth Seal: Martyrs

¶9. **And when he opened the fifth seal, I saw beneath the altar the souls of those who had been slain because of the word of God and because of the witness of the Lamb which they possessed.**

Note 1: The "witness of the Lamb" is the holy Spirit. It is God's witness that Jesus is His Son and our Lord (1Jn. 5:6b, 9).

Note 2: The souls under the altar had been killed for the same reason that John said he was on Patmos, that is, "because of the word of God and because of the witness of Jesus Christ" (Rev. 1:9).

10. **And they cried out with a loud voice, saying, "How long, O Master, holy and true, will you not judge and avenge our blood upon those who dwell on earth?"**

Note: These saints had lived righteous lives on earth and were now in the presence of God. They spoke to God, and He, to them.

However, they were discontent with their present condition, for they wanted something they did not yet have, namely, justice. They were still laboring in prayer for something from God; they were not enjoying perfect peace and rest. According to popular Christian mythology, saints enter into eternal rest when they die, but that is not the case. God will not give His saints perfect peace and rest until after the Millennial Reign (Rev. 7:17; 21:4) when He destroys this heaven and this earth (Rev. 21:1).

11. And a white robe was given to each of them, and it was said to them that they should wait for a while, until their fellow servants and their brothers should finish their course, who were about to be killed as they also had been.

Note 1: Of this fifth seal, Jesus said, "They will turn *you* over to persecution, and they will kill *you*; *you* will be hated by all nations because of my name. And during that time, many will be offended, and betray one another, and hate one another" (Mt. 24: 9–10; Lk. 21:12–17).

Note 2: The fifth-seal event is called "great tribulation" by the heavenly elder who spoke with John (Rev. 7:14). This tells us that the body of Christ will still be on earth at this time; otherwise, the saints would not be here to suffer tribulation at all.

Note 3: There are even more martyrs to come after this. This tribulation will precede by a number of years another time of tribulation for believers which will take place during the reign of the Beast. This means that the body of Christ will not only go through the "great tribulation" of this fifth seal, but it will also suffer through a second, and greater, tribulation during the reign of the Beast, during the time of the seventh seal.

Note 4: As with all the seals, the events of the fifth seal naturally follow the events of the fourth and will lead into the disasters of the sixth seal. Because some influence of Jesus' gospel will remain in the world, the disasters of the fourth seal will motivate men to fear God and repent. Then, the persecution during the fifth seal of those who turn to Christ will motivate God to bring about the disasters of the sixth seal.

The Sixth Seal: Extraordinary Natural Disasters

¶12. **And I saw when he opened the sixth seal, and there was a great earthquake, and the sun became black as sackcloth made of hair, and the whole moon became like blood,**

Note: This blackness will be a temporary condition. Later in Revelation, the sun is functioning normally again (e.g., Rev. 9:2).

13. **and the stars of heaven fell to earth the way a fig tree, shaken by a strong wind, drops her summer figs.**
14. **And the sky was split apart like a scroll being rolled up, and every mountain and island were shaken out of their places.**

Note: All this was God's righteous response to the slaughter of so many of His saints during the fifth seal time. Isaiah foretold of this event when he said, "And all the host of heaven shall come apart, and the heavens shall be rolled up like a scroll, and all their host shall fall down, the way leaves fall from a vine or like figs falling from a tree" (Isa. 34:4).

15. **And the kings of the earth, and the great men, and the military leaders, and the rich, and the powerful, and every slave and free man hid themselves in caves and among the rocks of the mountains,**
16. **and they said to the mountains and to the rocks, "Fall on us, and hide us from the face of Him who sits on the throne and from the wrath of the Lamb!**
17. **For the great day of his wrath has come, and who is able to stand?"**

Note 1: The prophet Isaiah spoke of this day: "Go into the rock, or hide yourself in the ground, in terror at the LORD's presence and from the splendor of His majesty. The haughty looks of the great man will be humbled, and the pride of common men will be abased, and the LORD alone will be exalted on that day. For the day of the LORD of Hosts is upon everyone who is proud and haughty, and upon everyone who lifts himself up, and he will be abased. And the haughtiness of man will be brought down, and the loftiness of men will be brought low. And the LORD alone will be exalted on that day. And they will go into crevices in the rocks and holes in the ground, in terror at the LORD's presence and away from the splendor of His majesty when He rises to shake the earth" (Isa. 2:10–12, 17, 19).

Note 2: The preaching of the true gospel during the time of the fifth seal made men aware of God's hand in these awesome events. That sinners feared "the wrath of the Lamb" tells us that they knew about Jesus and that they had heard of the coming day of God's wrath. However, the tormenting fear which sinful men feel is the kind of fear that springs from an evil heart, and with time, it fades away. These terrified sinners will resume their ungodly lifestyles as soon as the temporary disturbances in the natural order subside, and they will again go about their sinful lives, "eating and drinking, marrying and giving in marriage" until Jesus comes, just as Jesus predicted (Mt. 24:37–39; Lk. 17:24–30).

Note 3: The sixth seal continues through Revelation 7.

Revelation 7

The One Hundred Forty-Four Thousand Are Sealed

¶1. **And after this, I saw four angels standing at the four corners of the earth, holding the four winds of the earth so that no wind would blow on the land, nor on the sea, nor on any tree.**

2. **Then I saw another angel ascending from the east, having the seal of the living God, and he cried out with a loud voice to the four angels to whom it was given to harm the land and the sea,**

3. saying, "Do not harm the land, nor the sea, nor the trees until we seal the slaves of our God on their foreheads!"

4. And I heard the number of those who were sealed, one hundred forty-four thousand, sealed out of every tribe of the sons of Israel:

5. from the tribe of Judah, twelve thousand sealed; from the tribe of Reuben, twelve thousand; from the tribe of Gad, twelve thousand;

6. from the tribe of Asher, twelve thousand; from the tribe of Naphtali, twelve thousand; from the tribe of Manasseh, twelve thousand;

7. from the tribe of Simeon, twelve thousand; from the tribe of Levi, twelve thousand; from the tribe of Issachar, twelve thousand;

8. from the tribe of Zebulun, twelve thousand; from the tribe of Joseph, twelve thousand; from the tribe of Benjamin, twelve thousand sealed.

Note 1: These one hundred forty-four thousand are sealed here, during the time of the sixth seal. The resurrection does not happen until the seventh trumpet, and so, these cannot be Old Testament Jews, resurrected from the dead. We are told nothing else here about this mysterious group. It may be that they are the same one hundred forty-four thousand described in Revelation 14, but that is not told us.

Note 2: Jews of our time cannot know from which ancient tribe they are descended, but it may be that progress in genetics research will make that knowledge available to men in the future. At any rate, God knows which tribe every Jew on earth today came from, and in providing this list for us, He may also be signaling that mankind will attain to that knowledge by the time of the sixth seal.

Note 3: The tribe of Dan is missing from this list, while the tribe of Levi is included. In the Old Testament, Dan was always numbered among the tribes, while Levi was not, being the priestly tribe. No reason for this change is given, though John must have noticed it.

¶9. **After these things, I looked, and there was a vast multitude that no one was able to number, out of all nations and tribes and peoples and languages, standing before the throne and before the Lamb, clothed in white robes, and palm branches in their hands,**

10. **and they cried out with a loud voice, saying, "Salvation belongs to our God, who sits on the throne, and to the Lamb!"**

11. **And all the angels had been standing around the throne, and around the elders and the four living things, and they fell on their faces before the throne and worshipped God,**

12. **saying, "Amen! Blessing, and glory, and wisdom, and thanksgiving, and honor, and power, and strength belong to our God forever and ever! Amen!"**

¶13. **Then answered one of the elders, saying to me, "These who are arrayed in white robes, who are they? And where did they come from?"**

14. **And I said to him, "My lord, you know." And then he told me, "These are they who are coming out of the great tribulation, and they washed their robes and made them white in the blood of the Lamb.**

Note 1: As I said earlier, although the elder told John that this is "the great tribulation", it will not be the worst tribulation that God's people will face before Jesus returns. Another time of great tribulation will come some years after this, at the hands of the world ruler whom God calls "the Beast".

Note 2: Earlier, I mentioned the evening in 1992 when Jesus used a question from an astute student of the scriptures, Billy Highfill, to open my understanding to the order of end-time events. Billy's question had to do with the scene described in the verses above. It was this: "Are these martyred saints the same saints who are killed by the Beast?" In reply, I started to say yes, they were the same, but the Spirit stopped me, and I felt a light begin to shine within me. It suddenly was quite clear that these martyrs were not, and could not, be the same martyrs the Beast would slay, for when these saints are martyred, the Beast has not yet come. That seems so simple and obvious now, but until Jesus opens one's eyes, the simplest truth remains a mystery. In any case, that simple question was the key God used to help me, and I am very thankful for it. And once God gave us that answer, the rest of the end-time events of Revelation fell easily into place for us.

Note 3: The blood of Jesus was red; it was human blood. The "blood" of the pre-existent Son of God is the invisible holy Spirit. The blood of Mary's son Jesus was just like ours; no one could have washed a garment in that blood and made it white. The blood of God's Son from heaven is spiritual, and both Jesus and Paul said we must drink it (Jn. 6:54; 1Cor. 12:13). That blood has power; it raised Jesus from the dead (Heb. 13:20); it justifies and sanctifies sinners (Rom. 5:9; Heb. 10:29); it cleanses men's souls and makes their spiritual garments white; and it is still flowing.

When the natural blood of Jesus fell on the soldiers who crucified him, they washed it off, as they should have, but when the blood of God's Son fell on the disciples on the day of Pentecost, *it* washed *them*. The human blood of Christ Jesus had to be shed at Calvary in order for his soul-cleansing blood, the Spirit, to be shed on Pentecost morning (cf. Acts 2:33).[11]

15. Therefore, they are before the throne of God, and they serve Him day and night in His temple, and He who sits on the throne will dwell among them.
16. They will not hunger any longer, nor thirst any longer, nor will the sun ever beat down on them, nor any heat,
17. for the Lamb who is in the midst of the throne will be their Shepherd, and he will guide them to fountains of

---

[11] For more on this subject, see my online gospel tract, "The Blood of Christ", at GoingtoJesus.com.

living waters, and God will wipe away every tear from
their eyes."

Note: This promise of eternal rest from pain and discomfort
will be realized on the new earth, not this one. God will personally
dwell among His people and wipe away all their tears only after
the Millennial Reign and the Final Judgment, when this heaven
and earth are destroyed and God provides His children with a new
heaven and earth (Rev. 21:1–4).

Revelation 8

The Seventh Seal Reveals Seven Trumpets

¶1. And when he opened the seventh seal, there was silence in heaven for about half an hour.

Note: With the opening of the seventh seal, all of heaven senses
a terrifying fury from God and withdraws into complete silence.
Even the four living creatures fall silent – the same creatures John
said never cease crying out, "Holy! Holy! Holy!"

2. And then I saw the seven angels who stand before God,
and Seven Trumpets were given to them.

Note: Knowing that there will be seven trumpets has value because it was revealed to Paul that Jesus will return "at the last
trumpet", that is, the seventh one (1Cor. 15:51–52; cf. 1Thess.
4:16). With that knowledge, believers may better prepare themselves for the Lord's return and not be surprised by it, as the world
will be (1Thess. 5:2–4).

¶3. And then another angel came and stood at the altar,
having a golden censer, and much incense was given to
him to offer with the prayers of all the saints upon the
golden altar that is before the throne,

4. and the smoke of the incense went up before God with
the prayers of the saints from the hand of the angel.

5. And the angel took the censer and filled it with fire from
the altar, and he cast it to the earth, and there were

peals of thunder, and voices, and lightning flashes, and an earthquake.

¶6. And the seven angels who had the Seven Trumpets pre-pared themselves to sound the trumpets.

Note: The saints will suffer with the world through the earlier plagues of the Seven Trumpets, just as the Israelites in Egypt suffered through the earlier plagues with the Egyptians. But, again like the Israelites in Egypt, the saints who have "the seal of God", will be spared the latter calamities of the Seven Trumpets (cf. Rev. 9:4; Eph. 1:13).

Chapter 5
The Seven Trumpets
Revelation 8:7 – 14:20

Revelation 8

1st Trumpet: Hail and Fire Mingled with Blood
Scorch a Third of the Earth

¶7. And the first one sounded, and there was hail and fire mingled with blood, and it was cast to the earth, and a third of the earth was burned up, and a third of the trees was burned up, and all green grass was burned up.

Note 1: There is no explanation of where the blood came from. It may be that this blood is the blood of God's martyred saints, for if God stores up the tears of His people (Ps. 56:8), might He not also store up the blood of His martyrs?

Note 2: We are not told that men on earth hear the Seven Trumpets, just that the angels sound them.

2nd Trumpet: A Burning Mountain Ruins One Third of the Sea

¶8. Then the second angel sounded, and something like a big, burning mountain was cast into the sea, and a third of the sea became blood,
9. and a third of the creatures that live in the sea died, and a third of ships was destroyed.

Note: This burning mountain is not said to have come from heaven. On earth, the event in nature which could hurl mountain-sized, flaming boulders is called a "super-volcano". These volcanoes are gigantic (the Yellowstone caldera, for example, measures 35 by 45 miles), and they have immense explosive power.

3rd Trumpet: Wormwood Poisons a Third of Earth's Fresh Water

¶10. **And the third angel sounded, and a large star, blazing like a torch, fell from heaven, and it fell on a third of the rivers and on the springs of water.**

11. **And the name of the star is called "Wormwood", and a third of the waters became wormwood, and many men died from the waters because they were made bitter.**

Note 1: This object, unlike what is said of the previous one, did fall down from heaven. Since wormwood is from an earthly plant, the absinthe plant, it is unknown how an object from outer space can contain wormwood. Our ignorance does not preclude that possibility; however, this may be a reference to an angel who bears the name "Wormwood". All we know is that John says the waters were poisoned by this falling "star".

Note 2: Poisoning one third of earth's fresh water is conceivable. Fully twenty percent of earth's fresh water flows in one river, the Amazon, which drains almost the entire continent of South America and carries so much fresh water to the ocean that at the Amazon's mouth, the ocean is fresh water two hundred miles out. Moreover, about eighteen percent of the planet's fresh water is in Canada. From that, we can see how a huge object striking earth at the right place might ruin a large percentage of the earth's fresh water.

Note 3: The United States is not mentioned in Revelation. If the super-volcano in Yellowstone erupts, or if the star called Wormwood strikes the Western Hemisphere, that would explain why the United States, for all its present power and prestige, plays no discernible role in John's vision. If just those two calamities befall the Western Hemisphere, the nations in North and South America will lose their significance. Population levels will be reduced dramatically, and living conditions will be very poor.

4th Trumpet: Earth-Days Are Shortened by One Third

¶12. And the fourth angel sounded, and a third of the sun was struck, and a third of the moon, and a third of the stars so that a third of them was darkened, and the day did not shine for a third of it, and likewise the night.

Note: When Jesus was describing the order of end-time events, he said, "Except those days be shortened, no flesh will be saved. But for the sake of the elect, those days will be shortened" (Mt. 24:22). It is only with the revelation of this fourth trumpet event that we can understand that Jesus may not have been speaking of a reduction of the *number* of earth's days but of a reduction of the number of *hours* in a day. It may be that Wormwood's collision with earth increased earth's rotational speed from twenty-four hours to sixteen.

¶13. Then I looked, and I heard a lone eagle say with a loud voice as he flew in the midst of heaven, "Woe! Woe! Woe to those who live on the earth because of the remaining sounds of the trumpet of the three angels who are about to sound!"

Note: The first four seals were set apart from the last three by the appearance of four horses. Likewise, the first four trumpets are set apart from the last three by the cry of this eagle.

Revelation 9

5th Trumpet: Monstrous Creatures Torment Men
for Five Months

¶1. And the fifth angel sounded, and I saw a star from heaven that had fallen to earth, and the key to the shaft of the Abyss was given to him.

Note 1: This fallen star is a living creature, a fallen angel. Angels are again referred to as stars in Revelation 12:4.

Note 2: John did not see this star fall from heaven as he saw the star fall when the third trumpet sounded (8:10). This star is an angel who had already fallen.

Note 3: Most of the angels John sees carrying out God's plan for the end-times *come down* from heaven to perform their duties (e.g., Rev. 10:1; 18:1); they had not *fallen down*, as this angel had done. Nevertheless, fallen angels will play a significant part in end-time events, such as the four angels who are bound in the Euphrates River (vv. 14–15, below), and the three demons who gather the nations of earth against Israel (Rev. 16:13–14).

Note 4: John does not even attempt to explain what the Abyss is. The Abyss (also known as "the Bottomless Pit" or just "the Pit") is not hell. Hell is where sinners go after they die, and it is used as a holding place for them until the Day of Judgment when both sinners and the hell they occupy will be cast into a far worse place: the horrific Lake of Fire (Rev. 20:14–15). The Abyss is also a holding place, but it holds deadly and wicked creatures who have lived on earth, who instead of dying or being destroyed, have been cast into the Abyss to be used again on earth at a later date.

Satan will be cast into the Abyss when Jesus returns to reign on earth, and he will be held there until he is retrieved at the end of the Millennial Reign (Rev. 20:1–3, 7–8). So it is also with the coming world ruler called the Beast. When he appears, he will have already reigned once on earth (Rev. 17:11). He did not die but was consigned to the Abyss until God brings him up to reign again on earth for a few years immediately prior to Jesus' return (Rev. 11:7).

Because creatures who come from the Abyss have previously lived on earth, I sometimes refer to the Abyss as "God's recycling bin".

2. And he opened the shaft of the Abyss, and smoke came up out of the shaft like the smoke of a burning furnace, and the sun and the air were darkened with the smoke from the shaft.

3. And then, out of the smoke came locusts to the earth, and power was given to them like the power that scorpions of the earth have.

Note: The smoke came from the Abyss; John did not say the locusts did. Either the smoke was the locusts or the locusts formed within the smoke after it came out of the Abyss.

4. And it was said to them that they were not to harm the grass of the earth, nor anything green, nor any tree, but only the men who do not have the seal of God on their foreheads.

Note: When Paul spoke of "the seal of God", he was referring to the baptism of the holy Spirit (Eph. 1:12–13). There is, however, another seal which believers must receive in order to escape these fearsome creatures, and there is precedent for receiving a second seal from God. Israel was sealed to God at Mount Sinai when they entered into covenant with God. Then, centuries later, when God reached the end of His patience with His people, He commanded angels to go through the streets of Jerusalem and slaughter everyone in the city. However, before He sent them on their grisly task, He sent another angel ahead of them into the city to put a mark on those who would be spared (Ezek. 9). Every man in Jerusalem marked by the angel that day had already received the Old Testament seal of God: circumcision. But they had to be sealed again with an invisible mark in order for the destroying angels to pass them by. Such stories were written as warnings for us (Rom. 15:4; 1Cor. 10:11), that there will be a second sealing of believers to determine which of them will be saved.

5. And it was given to them not to kill but to torture them five months, and their torment was like the torment of a scorpion when it stings a man.

6. And in those days, men will seek death and will by no means find it, and they will long to die, but death will flee from them.

Note 1: Unlike any other seal or trumpet, the time involved in this painful plague is revealed: five months.

Note 2: It will do no one any good to say to the locusts, "I'm saved, and you can't make me doubt it." They will not be listening for anything man says; they will be looking for the seal of God. The religious claims of men will mean as much to those monstrous creatures as they meant to Jesus when he walked on earth, or as much as they mean to him now, which is absolutely nothing. Man's claims concerning his standing with God have never carried any weight in heaven. It is what God does that saves, not what man claims. And it will only be what God does in those days which will protect anyone from the stinging locusts. They will not be confused by man's delusions.

7. **And the appearance of the locusts was like horses prepared for battle, and on their heads were things like golden crowns, and their faces were like men's faces,**
8. **and they had hair like the hair of women, and their teeth were like lions' teeth.**
9. **And they had chests like breastplates of iron, and the sound of their wings was like the sound of many chariots with horses charging into battle.**
10. **And they have tails like scorpions, with stingers. And with their tails, they have power to hurt men five months.**

Note 1: John used "like" eight times in these four verses because he had never seen such creatures and had no name for them.

Note 2: Wise souls believe whatever God says, even if it seems impossible. In Revelation 1, for example, John told us that "every eye" will see Jesus when he returns. But before the mid-twentieth century, it was impossible for every person everywhere on earth to watch an event as it took place. No doubt, many skeptics in centuries past supposed that John was either speaking figuratively or just making the whole thing up. In our time, however, even atheists know that every eye on earth can watch an event as it is taking place, wherever on earth it happens. John's prophecy no longer seems make-believe because man has developed technology that makes what John prophesied possible.

In the same way, unbelieving souls today doubt that the scorpions John saw in his vision can ever really exist. They suppose that John was either speaking figuratively or just making the whole thing up. However, with advances in biogenetics, man is on the verge of producing unheard-of creatures, and in decades to come, when they do so, that generation will accept the possibility of the stinging locusts as easily as our generation takes for granted watching events from around the world as they happen.

Since earliest times, man has fantasized about mingling species. The ancients imagined and even worshipped strange mixtures of men and animals, such as snake-haired Medusa, centaurs, jackal-headed Anubis, and others. Men are now developing ways to produce such unnatural creatures, and in time, what they produce will bear witness to the truth of John's vision. The locusts will come.

11. They have as king over them the angel of the Abyss; his name in Hebrew is "Abaddon", but his name in Greek is "Apollyon".

Note: In both Hebrew and Greek, this angel's name means "the Destroyer". He is described in Revelation 9:1 as a "star from heaven that had fallen". In the Old Testament, he is the angel who passed over Egypt to kill all the firstborn of the Egyptians (Ex. 12:23), and he is mentioned elsewhere (Job 26:6; 28:22; Ps. 17:4; Prov. 15:11).

12. The first woe has passed. Behold, two woes are still to come after these things!

6th Trumpet: One Third of Mankind Killed,
and God's Two Witnesses

¶13a. And the sixth angel sounded,

Note: The sixth trumpet will continue until Revelation 11:15.

¶13b. and I heard a single voice from the four horns of the golden altar before God

14. telling the sixth angel who had the trumpet, "Loose the four angels who are bound in the great river Euphrates!"

15. And so, the four angels were loosed who were prepared for the hour, and for the day, and month, and year to kill a third of mankind.

Note 1: One fourth of mankind died during the fourth seal time. In the sixth trumpet time, an additional one third of mankind dies.

Note 2: This is the first mention in the Bible of the four angels bound in the Euphrates River, and John is not told anything about them, including when or why they were bound there. All we know is that they will be there, awaiting their appointed time of release. Whether they are there already or have yet to be cast into the Euphrates, we do not know.

16. The number of the soldiers on horseback was ten thousands times ten thousands. I heard their number.

Note: Such an army could not have been mustered in John's time. John adds, "I heard their number," as if he realized that people would have difficulty believing him. In John's time, an army of such size (at least 100,000,000)[12] was impossible to muster, even if every man, woman, and child in the entire known world were made a soldier. But in our time, such an army from either India or China can already be produced.

17a. And this is how I saw the horses in the vision, and those who sat on them:

Note: These creatures really were horses. Having grown up in an agrarian society, John knew locusts, and John knew horses. Though the locusts of the fifth trumpet were strange creatures, John still said that they *were* locusts, not something *like* locusts.

---

[12] Possibly, two hundred million, or more.

Likewise, he said in this verse that these strange creatures were horses, not something like horses.

17b. they had fiery red, and hyacinth-colored, and sulfurous-yellow breastplates, and the heads of the horses were like heads of lions, and out of their mouths issued fire, and smoke, and sulfur.

Note: I cannot remember how, but when I was a boy, I came into possession of a small vial of sulfur. Being curious, I poured out a small mound of the yellow powder onto a back porch step where I was sitting, and I decided I would set it on fire, just to see what would happen. It did not dawn on me then that it might have blown up and sent me flying into the next county, or the next world. But boys being what they are, I struck my match, leaned over and touched the match to the powder. There being no wind that day, the stream of smoke that arose from the sulfur went directly into my nostrils, and I suddenly found myself struggling for breath, for the fumes had begun to close up my breathing passages. I jerked my head away and soon recovered from the harrowing experience. Years later, when I read the parts of Revelation having to do with sulfur (also called "brimstone"), my back-porch experience helped me to appreciate what John was describing. The sulfur will choke many men to death.

18. By these three plagues, a third of mankind was killed: from the fire, and the smoke, and the sulfur that issued from their mouths.

19. Moreover, the power of the horses is in their mouths and in their tails, for their tails are like serpents, having heads, and with them, they do damage.

20. And the rest of mankind, those who were not killed by these plagues, did not repent of the works of their hands, that they should cease to worship demons and idols of gold, and of silver, and of bronze, and of stone, and of wood which can neither see, nor hear, nor walk.

21. Neither did they repent of their murders, nor of their sorceries, nor of their immorality, nor of their thievery.

Note: Paul said that as time passes, evil men "will grow worse and worse" (2Tim. 3:13). The reactions of men to God's judgments in Revelation demonstrate the truth of Paul's prophecy. When disasters struck the earth during the sixth seal, men cried out in fear of God and His Son, and, one assumes, they tempered their wicked lifestyles at least temporarily. However, here, during the plague of the sixth trumpet, men's hearts have been hardened to the point that they do not cry out in fear. And the downward spiral will continue, for later, at the time of the Seven Vials, men will go beyond merely not repenting; their hearts will be so completely hardened by that time that their reaction to the judgments of God will be to "blaspheme the God of heaven" (Rev. 16:11, 21).

Revelation 10

The Seven Thunders

¶1. **And I saw a strong angel descending from heaven, clothed with a cloud, and a rainbow upon his head, and his face was like the sun, and his feet, like pillars of fire,**

2. **and he held in his hand a little scroll, opened. And he set his right foot on the sea, and his left, on the land,**

3. **and he cried out with a loud voice, like a lion roaring. And when he cried out, Seven Thunders uttered their voices.**

4. **And when the Seven Thunders spoke, I was about to write, but I heard a voice from heaven, saying, "Seal the things which the Seven Thunders spoke, and do not write them."**

Note 1: If God hid from us what the Seven Thunders said, then we do not need that information. However, God obviously wanted us to know that before the seventh trumpet sounds, Seven Thunders will speak.

Note 2: Some time must pass to allow the Seven Thunders to speak. How much time, we are not told. But in revealing this information, God is making sure the saints living in these days will not be in expectation of the last trumpet immediately sounding.

The Time of the Gentiles[13] Nears Its End

5. **And the angel whom I saw standing on the sea and on the land raised his right hand toward heaven**
6. **and swore by Him who lives forever and ever, who created heaven and the things in it, and the earth and the things in it, and the sea and the things in it, that there shall be no more time,**
7a. **except in the days of the sound of the seventh angel, when he begins to sound his trumpet,**

Note 1: When the angel said, "There shall be no more time," he added, "except in the days of the sound of the seventh angel." The angel was not declaring the end of all time. If that were the case, there could be no thousand-year reign of Christ on earth.

The time that will end is the time of the Gentiles. The time of the Gentiles began a few years after Pentecost, when God first sent the gospel to Gentiles by the hand of Peter (Acts 10). Until that happened, if a Gentile wanted to serve the true God, he had to go to Israel and join himself to the Jews, but from that day until the time of the seventh trumpet, the door has stood open for Gentiles to enter into the kingdom of God as Gentiles, and God has for these two millennia poured out His Spirit on any soul, anywhere on earth, Jew or Gentile, who will believe the gospel of His Son and repent of his sins.

In Acts, as the door of the Gentiles opened, Israel's blindness to the gospel deepened, but the opposite will happen when the time of the Gentiles comes to its end, as Paul said: "Brothers, I would not have *y*ou ignorant of this mystery, that blindness has come upon Israel, in part, until the fullness of the Gentiles comes in" (Rom. 11:25). After the door to the Gentiles closes, God will send His Son again to the Jews, and after that, during the Millennial reign,

---

[13] Jesus' phrase was "the *times* of the Gentiles" (Lk. 21:24). If there is any significance to the plural form of "time", I do not know what it is.

the Gentiles who desire to serve God will again have to humble themselves to go to Israel to obtain mercy.

Note 2: While speaking with his disciples on the Mount of Olives about the last days – and years before anyone imagined there would be a "time of the Gentiles" – Jesus predicted the end of the time of the Gentiles, after they trample Jerusalem: "There will be great distress in the land, and wrath on this people. They will fall by the edge of the sword, and they will be led captive into all nations. And Jerusalem will be trampled underfoot by the Gentiles until the times of the Gentiles be fulfilled" (Lk. 21:23b–24).   In Revelation, other than revealing that Jerusalem will be trampled down for three-and-a-half years (Rev. 11:2), John does not give us any details about this trampling down of Jerusalem. That may be because this event is something spoken of by the Seven Thunders, and John was forbidden to record what the Seven Thunders said.

7b. and the mystery of God shall be accomplished, as He told His slaves, the prophets.

Note: Just as there is a basic seal of God (the baptism of the Spirit) and other seals may follow, so there is a basic mystery of the gospel and other mysteries may follow.   The mystery to which this angel referred is the one Paul spoke of in his letter to the Ephesians, the mystery of God's grace being extended to the Gentiles: "By revelation, the mystery was made known to me, which in other generations was not made known to the sons of men as it is now revealed to his holy apostles and prophets by the Spirit: the Gentiles are to be fellow heirs, and of the same body, and partakers with *the Jews* of His promise in Christ, through the gospel" (Eph. 3:3a, 5–6).

John Eats the Scroll

8. And the voice that I had heard from heaven spoke to me again, saying, "Go! Take the little scroll that is open in the hand of the angel who is standing on the sea and on the land."

9. And so, I went to the angel and told him to give me the little scroll. And he said to me, "Take it, and eat it up. It will make your stomach bitter, but in your mouth, it will be sweet as honey."

10. So, I took the little scroll out of the hand of the angel and devoured it, and it was in my mouth like honey, sweet, but when I had eaten it, my stomach was made bitter.

Note: John's experience here is not unique. The young priest and prophet Ezekiel was given a similar commandment to eat the prophecies that he would later deliver, and they, too, were sweet as honey in his mouth (Ezek. 2:8–3:3).

11. And they said to me, "You must again prophesy concerning many peoples, and nations, and tongues, and kings."

Note 1: We do not know who "they" are who spoke here to John. Both an angel and "a voice" previously spoke to John in this part of his revelation, so those two may be the "they" that spoke to him here. There are other speakers in Revelation as well that John does not identify.

Note 2: We are still in the sixth trumpet time. The seventh trumpet is sounded in Revelation 11:15.

Revelation 11

Note: After God begins to close the door for the Gentiles in Revelation 10, He begins to open the door for the Jews in Revelation 11. God promised He would send Elijah the prophet to Israel in order to begin the process: "Behold, I will send Elijah the prophet to *you* before the great and fearful day of the LORD comes" (Mal. 4:5). God did not let Israel know that He would send another prophet with Elijah; He kept that a secret until He revealed it here, to John.

God's Two Witnesses

¶1. And there was given to me a reed similar to a staff, saying, "Rise up and measure the temple of God, and the altar, and those who worship in it.

Note 1: Nothing else is said about this. I assume John did this, but if he did, we are not told what he found out. Nor is any reason given for taking these measurements.

Note 2: Since John was not commanded to return to earth to measure the temple in Jerusalem, it appears that the temple John was to measure was God's temple in heaven. Jesus offered himself to God for man's sins in that temple, and the outer court of heaven's temple is earth, where Jesus was killed before entering God's temple in heaven to offer himself.

2. But leave out the outer court of the temple, and do not measure it, for it is given to the Gentiles, and they will trample the holy city forty-two months.

Note 1: Forty-two months (1,260 days, or three-and-a-half years) is a repeated time period in Revelation. Besides Gentiles trampling the holy city for three-and-a-half years, God's Two Witnesses will prophesy in Jerusalem three-and-a-half years (verse 3, below), the Beast will reign over the earth for three-and-a-half years (Dan. 7:25; Rev. 13:5), and persecuted Israel will be given a place of safety for three-and-a-half years (Rev. 12:6).

Note 2: Other than it lasting forty-two months, John adds nothing to what Jesus said about the trampling of Jerusalem. (See *Note 2* under 10:7a, above.)

3. And I will give *power* to my Two Witnesses, and they will prophesy one thousand two hundred and sixty days, dressed in sackcloth."

4. These are the two olive trees and the two lampstands standing before the Lord of the earth.

Note: These two olive trees are men. Zechariah, like John, saw two olive trees standing before the Lord in heaven (Zech. 4:3, 11), but the connection between those two olive trees and God's Two Witnesses is not made clear.[14]

5. And if anyone attempts to harm them, fire comes out of their mouth and consumes their enemies, and if anyone attempts to harm them, this is how he must be killed.
6. These have authority to shut heaven so that no rain falls during the days of their prophecy, and they have authority over the waters, to turn them into blood, and to strike the earth with any plague, as often as they wish.

Note 1: We are not given the names of God's Two Witnesses. Many feel that, besides Elijah, the second witness is Enoch, since neither Elijah nor Enoch ever died (Gen. 5:23–24; 2Kgs. 2:11–12). But there is no indication in Scripture that dying disqualifies a man from being one of these witnesses. What difference would it make to God whether a man was alive or dead? Death cannot prevent God from using a man if He chooses to do so; death did not prevent God from using Jesus after he died. Moreover, Jesus said that his Father "is not God of the dead, but of the living, for to Him, everyone is alive" (Lk. 20:38). So, it is more likely that the second witness is Moses, not Enoch, for the following reasons:

- The Two Witnesses perform miracles which are connected with Moses and Elijah. Moses turned water into blood (Ex. 4:9; 7:19) and struck the earth with plagues (Ex. 9:13–14), and Elijah stopped the rain for three-and-a-half years (Jas. 5:17) and killed men by calling fire down from heaven on them (2Kgs. 1:10–12).

- Moses and Elijah were sent by God to the Jews, as these two men are.

- When God promised to send Elijah again, He also mentioned Moses (Mal. 4:4–6).

---

[14] The two gold-plated cherubim that stood before God in the Most Holy Place of Solomon's temple were also made of olive tree wood (1Kgs. 6:19–28).

- Moses and Elijah were alive on earth when Jesus was here, and they spoke to him about his approaching death (Mt. 17:1–3; Mk. 9:2–4; Lk. 9:28–31). Moses died and was buried (Dt. 34:5–6), but God raised Moses from the dead to prevent Satan from using his dead body (Jude 1:9), which explains why nobody was ever able to find Moses' grave.

- Moses and Elijah represent "the law and the prophets".

- The holy Spirit is God's witness that He has glorified His Son (1Jn. 5:6b, 9); therefore, receiving the Spirit is the only way a person can truly know and be a witness that Jesus has been glorified as Messiah and Lord (cf. Acts 2:36; 1Cor. 12:3). Moses and Elijah are exceptions to this rule, however. The Spirit had not yet been given when they witnessed Jesus in a glorious form (Mt. 17:1–3; cf. Lk. 9:29–31), but seeing him in that state qualified them to be witnesses for him.

Note 2: The importance of these two servants of God lies in their mission more than in who they are. The mission of God's Two Witnesses will be to prepare Israel for Jesus' Second Coming. We know this is true because that was also John the Baptist's mission. This is what the angel told John's father about John before he was born: "Many of the sons of Israel will he turn to the LORD their God. It is he who will go before him *in the spirit and power of Elijah* [emphasis mine], to turn the hearts of the fathers to the children, and the disobedient to the understanding of the righteous, to make ready a people prepared for the LORD" (Lk. 1:16–17; cf. Mal. 4:5–6).

Knowing that Elijah would come back to prepare Israel for the Messiah, Jesus' disciples were puzzled because they believed Jesus was the Messiah, but they had not seen Elijah. "And his disciples questioned him, saying, 'Why do the scribes say that Elijah has to come first?' Jesus answered and said to them, 'Elijah certainly is coming first, and he will restore all things. But I tell *you* that Elijah already came, and they didn't recognize him, but did with him whatever they pleased, and likewise will the Son of man also suffer at their hands.' Then the disciples understood that he spoke to them about John the Baptist" (Mt. 17:10–13).

It is as surprising as it is frustrating that nothing that the Two Witnesses say to Israel is revealed. We are only told that they will prophesy three-and-a-half years. It is difficult to believe that God would send them to preach the law and the prophets again, but in the absence of any information, we cannot say that He will not. We know they will be sent to prophesy among a people who rejected the Messiah the first time he came to them, for we are told that when the Messiah came into the world, "his own people did not receive him" (Jn. 1:11). But Jesus said Elijah would succeed and "restore all things", just as the angel who spoke to John the Baptist's father said that John would succeed and would "turn many of the sons of Israel to the LORD their God."

Note 3: Still, questions remain. Will the Jews recognize who the Two Witnesses are? Will the Two Witnesses ever prophesy beyond the borders of Israel? Will the Two Witnesses preach the gospel of Christ to the Jews? Or the law and the prophets, or both? And if they do proclaim Christ to them, what will they say? Will they preach Paul's gospel to them, or Peter's?[15] We do not know.

7. And when they have finished their testimony, the Beast that ascends from the Abyss will make war against them and overcome them, and he will kill them.

8. And their dead bodies will be in the street of the great city that is spiritually called "Sodom" and "Egypt", where also their Lord was crucified.

Note 1: The killing of these two prophets takes place later, during the time of the seventh trumpet, though John tells of it here.

Note 2: Within three years of their deaths, armies of the nations led by the Beast will viciously attack Israel, and only a bloodied, desperate remnant chosen by God will survive the attack. The lingering influence of the message that the Two Witnesses delivered to Israel will prove critical to the survival of that remnant.

---

[15] Peter's gospel for the Jews included works of the law, while Paul's gospel for the Gentiles did not.

Note 3: If the Beast kills the Two Witnesses at the beginning of his reign, then his slaying of the Two Witnesses could also be the beginning of the three-and-a-half years when Jerusalem will be "trampled underfoot by the Gentiles" (Lk. 21:24). By God's design, however, we have insufficient information to say with confidence that such is the case, and those two conquests may prove not to be the same event.

Note 4: The Beast will reign over the whole earth. This must include the land of Israel and Jerusalem in light of the fact that the Beast kills God's Two Witnesses in that city.

Note 5: The Beast may be of Jewish descent. This surprising possibility is suggested by several verses in the prophets. First, although the Beast will lead a multi-national force to destroy the nation of Israel, Isaiah speaks of a supremely wicked man closely associated with Lucifer who will destroy his own land and kill his own people (Isa. 14:20), the people whom God calls "the polluted people" (Ezek. 21:14, 29). Second, in consonance with John's Revelation that this man will suffer a fatal wound, Ezekiel speaks of a "mortally wounded,[16] wicked prince of Israel, whose day will come during the iniquity of the end time" (Ezek. 21:25) and who will be appointed "against the necks of the polluted, wicked people [Israel], those whose day will come at the time of iniquity of the end" (Ezek. 21:29). Further, if verse 30 of that same chapter in Ezekiel refers to God's judgment upon the Beast, which seems to be the case,[17] then the Beast was born in Israel, for God said, "In the place where you were created, in the land of your origin, will I judge you" (Ezek. 21:30), and as John saw, Jesus will destroy the Beast in the land of Israel (Rev. 19:20).

There is also a verse from Isaiah that speaks of an enraged man looking up into heaven and cursing his king and his God (Isa.

---

[16] There is a play on the Hebrew words here. The word translated "mortally wounded" could be translated "polluted", which would further associate the Beast with the Jews, "the polluted people" (Ezek. 21:14, 29).

[17] The reference (Ezek. 21:28b–32) is to the sword (the Beast) that God is using to destroy the nation of Ammon. An evil person can be the sword of the LORD (Ps. 17:13), as well as His hand (Ps. 17:14).

8:21), which the Beast will do as he prepares to do battle with Jesus (Rev. 13:6; 19:19). But he will see nothing but disaster and death, "and then, he will be cast into darkness" (Isa. 8:22), as John later sees happening (Rev. 19:19–20).

9. And some of the peoples, tribes, tongues, and nations will see their dead bodies three-and-a-half days, and they will not allow their dead bodies to be laid in a tomb.

Note 1: This is another example of a prophecy that was beyond human understanding until recent times. People everywhere on earth will be able to view the dead bodies of God's Two Witnesses, and as has been said, only within the last century has the technology existed that would allow people around the world to view a single event as it is taking place.

Note 2: The fact that these bodies are left unburied in the street does not necessarily mean that all of Israel despised them; it may be instead that the Beast will forbid anyone in Israel to bury them.

10. And those who dwell on the earth will rejoice over them, and celebrate, and send gifts to one another because these two prophets tormented those who dwell on the earth.

Note: John does not say that the people of Israel, specifically, are tormented by these prophets. They may have been, but it may also be the case, as I said, that the Beast rules this land as well as the rest of earth and will not allow Israel to bury God's Two Witnesses.

11. Then, after the three-and-a-half days, a breath of life from God entered into them, and they stood on their feet, and great fear fell on those who were looking at them.

12. And I heard a loud voice from heaven saying to them, "Come up here!" And they went up into heaven in a cloud, and their enemies watched them.

Note 1: Again, although the whole world hates the Two Witnesses, we are not told if their enemies include all the Jews.

Note 2: The world's gloating over the death of the Two Witnesses, and their glorifying of the Beast's power, will turn to the glory of God. What the Beast does to God's Two Witnesses will be part of God's plan, even though the Beast will think it is his idea. And after God allows men of earth to celebrate three-and-a-half days, He will show the Jews and the world His power by raising His Two Witnesses from the dead and carrying them up to heaven.

13. And on that same day, there was a great earthquake, and a tenth of the city fell, and seven thousand people were killed in the earthquake, and the rest were terrified and gave glory to the God of heaven.

Note 1: The door for the Jews into the kingdom of God is opening, and spiritually, they are moving in the opposite direction of the Gentiles. The preaching of God's Two Witnesses will have touched the hearts of many in Israel, and when the earthquake strikes Jerusalem, the Jews will be moved to "give glory to the God of heaven." Contrary to the Jews' reaction to their suffering, the Gentiles refused to repent and call on God when they suffered in Revelation 9, for their hearts were being hardened against the fear of God. While the Jews' crying out to the God of heaven suggests that their collective heart is beginning to turn back to the true God, we do not know what they understand about Him being the Father of Jesus, their Messiah, because we are told nothing about what the Two Witnesses will preach.

Note 2: In the Old Testament, both Jews and Gentiles used the term "God of heaven" in reference to Israel's God, beginning as early as Abraham (Gen. 24:3, 7) and continuing throughout Israel's history (e.g., Ps. 136:26), even to the latest Old Testament characters, including Daniel (Dan. 2:18–19), Nehemiah (Neh. 1:5), Jewish returnees from Babylonian captivity (Ezra 5:11–12), and the foreign kings Nebuchadnezzar (Dan. 4:34–35), Artaxerxes (Ezra 7:12, 21, 23), and Cyrus (2Chron. 36:23; Ezra 1:2).

¶14. **The second woe has passed. The third woe, behold, is coming quickly!**

7th Trumpet: "The Last Trumpet"

¶15. **And the seventh angel sounded, and there were loud voices in heaven, saying, "The kingdom of the world has become the kingdom of our LORD and of His Christ, and He shall reign forever and ever."**

Note: The angel did not say "the kingdoms" but "the kingdom of the world" because the world is the domain of one ruler, Satan. It is one kingdom under him, with his angels ruling over individual nations.

Satan told Jesus during the Temptation that all the kingdoms of the world had been given to him and that he could give it to whomever he would (Lk. 4:5–6). But Jesus wouldn't take it from the hand of Satan; he chose to wait for the time appointed by the Father, and when the seventh trumpet sounded, that time had come.

16. **And the twenty-four elders who were sitting on their thrones before God fell on their faces and worshipped God,**

17. **saying, "We give you thanks, LORD God Almighty, who is and who was, because you have taken your great power and have begun to reign.**

18. **And the nations were enraged, and your wrath has come, and the time for the dead to be judged, and to give the reward to your slaves, the prophets, and to the saints, and to those, small and great, who fear your name, and to destroy those who destroy the earth."**

¶19. **Then God's temple in heaven opened, and within His temple, the ark of His covenant was seen, and there were flashes of lightning, and voices, and peals of thunder, and an earthquake, and large hail.**

Note: Several major events take place during this seventh trumpet time, which continues until Revelation 16.

Revelation 12

Signs in Heaven

¶1a. And a great sign appeared in heaven:

Note 1: Jesus said that "great signs" would appear in heaven immediately prior to his return (Mt. 24:30; Lk. 21:11b, 25–28). In effect, God will use the sky as a screen on which to proclaim to the world the story of His Son, not with words, but with something that transcends language: the sun, moon, and stars. David wrote, "The heavens declare the glory of God" (Ps. 19:1a), but they have never declared the glory of God to the degree that they will at this time. Speaking of the sun, moon, and stars, David added, "There is neither speech nor language where their voice is not heard" (Ps. 19:3), and God will proclaim His Son's story with the "sign language" of the stars, so that all will be able to understand. In the sky, the world will see all the major events of Jesus' life displayed: his birth, Satan's attempt to kill him, his ascension into heaven, his cleansing of heaven, and Satan's subsequent attempt to destroy Israel and those who believe in Jesus.

Note 2: This "great sign" in the sky will provide the Gentiles with a last chance to believe the gospel and repent before the door closes upon them.

Note 3: By this time in Revelation, much will have changed in the heavens as well as on earth. Among those changes, a multitude of "stars" will have fallen to earth (Rev. 6:13), thus giving the night sky a different look from what it has now. Also, when the sixth seal was opened, John saw the sky "split apart like a scroll being rolled up" (Rev. 6:14), and that must have massively affected the appearance of the sky.

1b. a woman clothed with the sun, and the moon beneath her feet, and on her head a crown of twelve stars,

2. and she was with child and cried out with birth pangs, being in the agony of giving birth.

Note: This woman with a crown that had twelve stars represents Israel and her twelve tribes.

3. And another sign was seen in heaven, and there was a great, fiery-red Dragon with seven heads and ten horns, and seven crowns on his heads.

Note 1: The ancients understood "dragon" to refer to a wild, deadly, and monstrous beast. It was often used to refer to some sort of serpentine beast, but it was not restricted to that. For example, Cerberus, the three-headed watchdog of Hades, was sometimes referred to as a dragon.[18] John did not believe those ancient heathen myths, nor was he influenced by them, but he used "dragon" to communicate the extraordinarily dangerous and powerful nature of this creature.

Note 2: Nor was John describing Satan's physical appearance because even though Satan had been created with a perfectly beautiful body (Ezek. 28:12), he abandoned that body when he possessed the body of Judas. Now, he has no body at all, but is a spirit wandering the earth looking for someone whom he considers worthy to possess. Peter mentioned this when he said that Satan is wandering through the earth "seeking whom he may devour" (1Pet. 5:8).

4a. And his tail drew away a third of the stars of heaven, and he brought them to the earth.

Note: At this point in God's visual history of His Son, Jesus is not even born yet. Therefore, this scene is not depicting Satan and his angels being cast out of heaven. That comes later (verse 9), after Jesus lives on earth and ascends to the Father (verse 5), which agrees with what Jesus said a few days before his crucifixion, to

---

[18] It may be that Cerebus qualified to be called a "dragon" because he was sometimes described as having a mane that was made of serpents, and sometimes was given a serpent-like tail.

wit, the time was at hand for Satan to be cast out (Jn. 12:31; cf. Jn. 16:11).

This heavenly scene represents Satan while he still had access to heaven, using his God-given authority as "god of this world" (2Cor. 4:4), to bring over a third of the angels to earth, to rule over the world with him.[19] That, in itself, is not an evil deed. On the contrary, it was Satan's place to do that, as he said to Jesus during the Temptation.

4b. And the Dragon stood before the woman who was about to give birth so that when she gave birth, he could devour her child.

Note: As I mentioned, Peter said that Satan is wandering the earth "seeking whom he may devour." To devour, in his case, means to possess and control. So it is here with Jesus. Satan had no intention in the beginning to kill the baby Jesus. He knew Jesus was the Messiah, and he wanted Jesus to live because he expected to be Jesus' superior and to control him. That is why he offered Jesus his position as god of this world; he expected to be promoted to reign with God over all things (Isa. 14:13–14), as soon as Jesus accepted the position, which Jesus refused.[20]

5. And she bore a male child who is to rule all nations with an iron rod, and her child was caught up to God and to His throne.

6. And the woman fled into the wilderness, where she has a place prepared by God, so that they may nourish her there for one thousand two hundred and sixty days.

Note: We are not told what or where "the wilderness" is or what is meant by "one thousand two hundred and sixty days." The place in the wilderness to which Israel flees for safety may be her

---

[19] This "great sign" in the sky may be revealing to John that before being cast out of heaven, Satan possessed great authority over a multitude of angels. While Jesus was on earth, he mentioned "the Devil and his angels" (Mt. 25:41), but John did not understand what Jesus meant at that time.

[20] For more on this, see chapter 7 in my online book, *God Had a Son before Mary Did*, at GoingtoJesus.com.

own land,[21] but John does not tell us that. Israel's being nourished by God shows His continued care for them, even though they rejected and abused His Son. Indeed, in His great mercy, God has preserved the Jews as a people for two thousand years, even though He has punished them severely for their sin.

¶7. And there was war in heaven, Michael and his angels warring against the Dragon, and the Dragon waging war, and his angels,

8. but he did not prevail; neither was there place found for him in heaven any longer.

9. And the great Dragon was cast out, the ancient serpent who is called the Devil, and Satan, who deceives the whole world. He was thrown down to the earth, and his angels were thrown down with him.

Note: Casting Satan out of heaven was part of Jesus' reconciliation of heaven to God and his sanctification of heaven for his priestly ministry (Col. 1:20; Heb. 9:23).

10. And I heard a great voice in heaven saying, "Now have come the salvation and the power and the kingdom of our God, and the authority of His Christ, because the Prosecutor of our brothers[22] has been cast out, who prosecuted them day and night before our God.

Note: Satan and his angels being cast out of heaven means that every creature in heaven now is for us, and instead of a prosecutor watching for us to fail, we have "an Advocate with the Father, Jesus Christ the righteous" (1Jn. 2:1), who "is always alive to make intercession" for us (Heb. 7:25).

11. And they overcame him through the blood of the Lamb and through the word of their testimony, and they did not love their life, even to the death.

---

[21] See Appendix, "The Wilderness".

[22] In heaven, Satan held the office of Prosecutor while the law of Moses was in effect, as is seen in Zechariah 3:1–5.

Note: God has given us two unconquerable things by which we overcome Satan: (1) The blood of the Lamb, which is the holy Spirit, and (2) our testimony. No power can withstand the testimony of the simplest child of God, for a testimony is a confession of the work of God, which cannot be withstood (Eccl. 3:14).

12. **For this, rejoice, O heavens and those who dwell in them! Woe to the earth and the sea! For the Devil has come down among *you*, having great anger, knowing that he has little time."**

¶13. **And when the Dragon saw that he was cast down to the earth, he persecuted the woman who had given birth to the boy.**

14. **And they gave the woman two wings of a great eagle so that she could fly into the wilderness, to her place, where they will nourish her for a time and times and half a time, away from the face of the serpent.**

Note: We do not know who the "they" are who gave the woman the "two wings of a great eagle"; now do we know what those two wings represent.[23]

15. **Then the serpent spewed water like a river out of his mouth after the woman, to sweep her away with the flood.**

Note: Satan's persecution of the Jews began after he was cast out of heaven. There is no suggestion in the Bible that before his expulsion from heaven, Satan wanted to destroy the Jews, though they were at times hated by evil men. On the contrary, Satan would not have wanted Israel destroyed before the Messiah came, since he hoped to hand over his position as god of this world to the Messiah, which he tried to do during the Temptation (Mt. 4:9).

---

[23] God also told Israel at Mount Sinai, "I bore *you* on eagles' wings and brought *you* to me" (Ex. 19:4). So, God is the One who provides wings for Israel's escape. John does not tell us what the wings here in Revelation represent.

16. But the earth helped the woman, and the earth opened its mouth and swallowed up the river that the Dragon spewed out of his mouth.

Note: The "earth" here refers to believers, as it does in other prophecies (e.g., Ps. 2:10; Isa. 49:8–10; 66:8). The "sea", on the other hand, refers to the nations of the world (Isa. 60:5; Rev. 17:15). The earth opening her mouth to save Israel from Satan's flood represents believers influencing the nations not to harm Israel. Over the centuries, godly believers have thus helped Israel survive in a world that despises Jews.

17. And the Dragon was furious because of the woman, and went to make war against the remnant of her offspring, those who keep the commandments of God and have the witness of Jesus.

Note: Satan not only hates those through whom Jesus came, the Jews, but he also hates those who come from Jesus, the body of Christ. Indeed, Satan's principal object of hate now is the New Testament "Israel of God" (Gal. 6:16), which John defines as those who obey God and have the holy Spirit, which was poured out from heaven as a testimony to Jesus (1Jn. 5:6b; Rev. 19:10). Thus, John's definition of God's New Testament Israel agrees with what Paul told the saints in Rome: "If anyone does not have the Spirit of Christ, he does not belong to him" (Rom. 8:9b)

Revelation 13

The Beast

¶1a. And I stood upon the sand of the sea. And I saw, coming up out of the sea, a Beast

Note 1: We do not know by what name the world will know the Beast, but people will not see him as evil, and they will certainly not address him as "the Beast". That is God's name for him.

Whenever we read the Bible, we must remember that the Bible is written from God's viewpoint, not man's. Otherwise, we will be confused by the delusions that plague this wicked world and interpret the Scriptures the way the world sees them.

Note 2: The Beast is not the anti-Christ. The word "anti-Christ" appears nowhere in the book of Revelation, and for good reason. The book of Revelation is primarily a book about the future, and in John's time, the anti-Christ had already come, and many had already become like him (1Jn. 2:18; 2Thess. 2:7).

Note 3: The sea out of which the Beast comes represents "peoples, and multitudes, and nations, and languages" (Rev. 17:1–3, 15). This means only that the Beast is human; he is not an animal, though called, "the Beast".

Note 4: John previously said that the Beast came from the Abyss (Rev. 11:7), but there is no conflict here. The Beast came from both places. Both the prophet Daniel in ancient Babylon and the apostle John on Patmos Island referred to this man as a king (Dan. 7:17–25; Rev. 17:10–11), but the revelation to John was that this man is a king who "was, and is not [in John's time], and will ascend out of the Abyss" (Rev. 17:8). That is to say, after he reigned on earth at an unknown time in history, he was taken to the Abyss to be brought back to earth in the end-times to reign again.

Note 5: Since the Beast killed God's Two Witnesses during the sixth trumpet time (Rev. 11:7), we know that he first appears during the time of the sixth trumpet, not here, during the seventh, where John speaks more fully about him.

1b. with ten horns and seven heads, and upon his horns were ten crowns,

Note: The Beast, like the Dragon, has seven heads and ten horns (Rev. 12:3). The difference between the Beast and Satan is that the Beast's crowns are on his ten horns, while Satan's crowns are on his seven heads. Satan's seven heads are seven kings who have been especially useful to him, of which the Beast is one (Rev. 17:9–11), while the Beast's ten horns are ten kings who serve him (Rev. 17:12).

1c. and on his heads were names of blasphemy.

Note: We are not told what the names of blasphemy are, nor are we told why they are on the Beast's seven heads. We do know, however, that the seven heads of the Beast represent seven hills (Rev. 17:9), the seven hills of Rome, "the great city that reigns over the kings of the earth" (Rev. 17:18).

2a. And the Beast that I saw was like a leopard, and his feet were like a bear's, and his mouth was like the mouth of a lion,

Note: Daniel also saw the Beast, as well as the three great kingdoms that came before him. In John's vision, the Beast's being like a leopard with the feet of a bear and a lion's mouth indicates a relationship between the Beast and the three great world powers which precede him, for in Daniel 7, those three kingdoms are described as (1) a lion, (2) a bear, and (3) a leopard (Dan. 7:1–7, 17). This tells us that the Beast will incorporate in his kingdom elements of those three kingdoms.

2b. and the Dragon gave him his power, and his throne, and great authority.

Note 1: Where will the Beast's throne be? Jesus said (Rev. 2:12–13) that Satan's throne was in Pergamon, which is in modern, northwestern Turkey. But if Jesus was referring to the magnificent altar of Zeus, the chief of demons, that was in Pergamon, that altar was dismantled and transported to Germany in the late 19th century. It is now on display in the Pergamon Museum in Berlin. Therefore, it may be that the Beast will reign from that area.

Note 2: The Beast will act as god of this world after Satan gives him his power, and authority, and his throne.

3. And one of his heads seemed to be mortally wounded, but his mortal wound was healed. Then the whole earth marveled at the Beast,

Note: There are at least five reasons that the world will be in awe of the Beast:

- He alone will be able to kill God's Two Witnesses.
- He will receive a mortal wound, yet will miraculously recover from it.
- He will be exceptionally intelligent (Dan. 8:23) and will possess a supernatural ability to speak astounding things (Dan. 7:8, 25; Rev. 13:5a).
- He will seemingly have returned from the dead (Rev. 17:8–11).[24]
- He will persecute the body of Christ and Israel, both of whom the world hates.

4. **and they worshipped the Dragon who had given authority to the Beast, and they worshipped the Beast, saying, "Who is like the Beast, and who is able to make war against him?"**

Note: The world will not know who it is worshipping. Jesus once said to the Samaritans, "*You* don't know what *you're* worshipping" (Jn. 4:22), though the Samaritans thought they were worshipping the God of Abraham, Isaac, and Jacob. Likewise, the world will adore the Beast as their hero, but in worshipping him, they will be worshipping Satan, for the Beast will be Satan's visible representative, the exact reflection of his character.

5. **And there was given to him a mouth speaking great things and blasphemy, and authority was given to him to wage war forty-two months.**
6. **And he opened his mouth in blasphemy against God, to blaspheme His name and His dwelling, *that is,* those who dwell in heaven.**
7. **And it was given to him to make war against the saints and to overcome them, and authority was given to him over every tribe and people and language and nation.**

---

[24] This assumes that the world will be aware that the Beast previously lived and reigned on earth.

Note 1: John confirms Daniel's ancient prophecy that the Beast will overcome God's saints (Dan. 7:25), but John adds an important phrase by saying "it was given" to the Beast to do so. Satan is the one who gave the Beast his power, but more importantly, God is the One who ordained Satan to be god of this world, with authority to give dominion over the earth to whomever he will (Lk. 4:6). This is God's plan at work, not Satan's. Satan's plan had been to give his power and authority to Jesus (Mt. 4:8–9; Lk. 4:5–6).

Note 2: Neither John nor Daniel explained what it means for the Beast "to make war against the saints and to overcome them," but John uses a similar phrase in Revelation 11:7, where the Beast "makes war" against God's Two Witnesses and kills them. So, it seems that when the Beast makes war against believers, he will also kill them. However, he will not eradicate believers from the earth, for some will remain alive until Jesus appears in the sky and catches them up to be with him, which doesn't take place until Revelation 14.

8. **And they will worship him, all the inhabitants of the earth whose name is not written from the foundation of the world in the Book of Life of the Lamb who was slain.**

Note 1: Names that are in the Book of Life have been there from the creation of the world. There is no indication in Scripture that any names have been added to the Book of Life since the beginning. If someone's name was written in the Book of Life before the world began, he will be called to the grace of Christ, and if not, he will not be called. As Paul said, "He chose us before the foundation of the world, . . . having predestined us to adoption as His sons through Jesus Christ" (Eph. 1:4–5).

Note 2: Everyone whose name is not in the Book of Life will be deceived and will worship the Dragon and the Beast.

Note 3: Tragically, some of God's people will also love and follow the Beast. John did not say that every person who is in the Book of Life will refuse to worship the Beast. Unfaithful saints will fall under Satan's spell and serve him. God Himself will curse them to do that "because they did not receive the love of the truth, that they might be saved. And for that reason, God will send them a strong delusion so that they will believe the lie, so that they all might be damned who did not believe the truth, but took pleasure in unrighteousness" (2Thess. 2:10b–12).

9.   If anyone has an ear, let him hear!

10a. If anyone holds on to captivity, *into captivity* **he must go.**

Note: Some of God's children will refuse the liberty Christ purchased for them and will be taken captive, that is, led astray, by Satan.

10b. If anyone slays with a sword, he must be slain with a sword.

Note: For God's children to take up carnal weapons is to refuse the protection of the Spirit's weapons, which alone can save from sin and death. This standard for New Testament saints was established by Jesus when he told feisty Peter: "Put your sword back in its place! All who take up a sword will die by a sword!" (Mt. 26:52). And Paul, likewise, admonished the saints that if they would please their heavenly Father, they must not become "entangled in the affairs of this life" (2Tim. 2:4).

10c. Here is the patience and faith of the saints.

Note: It is by patience and faith that believers inherit the promises of God (Heb. 6:12). On the Mount of Olives, after saying that believers will be hated by all nations for his name's sake (Mt. 24:9), Jesus warned the four disciples who were with him that evening that only those who remain faithful will be spared God's wrath: "Because of a great increase of lawlessness, the love of many will grow cold, but he who endures to the end, the same shall be saved" (Mt. 24:12–13).

A Second Beast: the False Prophet

¶11. And I saw another beast coming up out of the earth, and he had two horns like a lamb, but he spoke like a dragon.

Note: Unlike the first Beast, who came from the sea, this second beast (later called "the False Prophet" – Rev. 16:13; 19:20; 20:10), will come from the earth, that is, from the body of Christ.[25] In other words, he is an apostate man of God, and other than his lamb-like horns, he is no longer like Jesus, the Lamb of God. His voice will be like that of a dragon, that is, his words will lead to death, just as Satan's words do.

While this man was serving God, he probably was an effective evangelist, winning souls to Christ, but now, he will use his influence to lead souls astray. He will certainly be an impressive figure, old enough to have suffered through some of the tribulations of the Seven Seals and/or Seven Trumpets, and will be able to tell thrilling stories about how God took care of him through those times. But something will have made him bitter, the way wise Ahithophel became bitter and turned against King David (2Sam. 15:12). Ahithophel's counsel to David was so perfect that it was "as if one had inquired in the oracle of God" (2Sam. 16:23). But he became bitter against David because of David's seduction of his granddaughter, Bathsheba, and David's murder of her righteous husband (2Sam. 11). Then, he became bitter against God because God forgave David's sin and did not have David executed as the law demanded (2Sam. 12).

We are not told what happened to the False Prophet of John's vision to cause him to turn from righteousness. But just as Israel did not see Ahithophel as evil when he turned against David, so the world (and many believers) will not see this man as evil when he turns against the Son of God.

12a. And he exercises all the authority of the first Beast in his presence.

---

[25] See *Note* under Revelation 11:16.

Note: The False Prophet will be completely under the control of the Beast. This fallen minister of Christ operated under the Spirit of God before his heart was darkened, but afterward, he will surrender himself to the power of Satan. However, he can exercise that deceitful power only when he is in the presence of the first Beast.

12b. And he set out to compel the earth and those who inhabit it to worship the first Beast whose deadly wound was healed.

Note: It is this wayward man of God, not the Beast himself, who initiates worship of the Beast. That way, the Beast can maintain an appearance of humility while the False Prophet declares the Beast's glory and demands that he is worthy of worship.

13. And he performs great signs, so that he even makes fire to come out of heaven to the earth before men.

14a. And he deceives those who dwell on the earth[26] by means of the signs that were granted him to do in the presence of the Beast,

Note: The body of Christ will be tried by this False Prophet more than by any false prophet in history. Jesus warned his disciples that if it were possible, even the wisest and most established of God's people would be deceived (Mk. 13:22). Paul also warned the saints that those who did not truly love the truth and stay faithful until the end will be taken captive by the delusive speech of this second beast, "whose coming is by the work of Satan, with every miracle, and deceptive signs and wonders" (2Thess. 2:9).

14b. telling the inhabitants of the earth to make an image of the Beast who had the wound from a sword and lived.

15. And it was granted him to give breath to the image of the Beast so that the image of the Beast should both

---

[26] Many manuscripts have, "deceives those who belong to me who dwell on the earth".

speak and cause to be put to death as many as will not worship the image of the Beast.

Note: Here again, the Beast can maintain an appearance of humility, since it is the image, not himself, that commands that people be executed if they do not worship the Beast.

16. **And he causes everyone, the small and the great, and the rich and the poor, both free men and slaves, that they give them a mark on their right hand or on their forehead,**
17. **so that no one is able to buy or sell except he who has the mark, the name of the Beast, or the number of his name.**

Note 1: This will result in a second time of great tribulation for believers before Jesus returns.

Note 2: Two things are not made clear by the Greek text of these verses:

1) It is impossible to say, based on the Greek text, whether it is the False Prophet or the image itself that makes everyone take a mark. The text in verse 16 could be translated either way: "it causes" or "he causes".

2) It is also impossible to say, based on the Greek text, whether two or three kinds of marks are mentioned in verse 17. I have translated it here as if there are three options: the mark, the name, and the number. However, the verse could be punctuated so as to have only two options: "he who has the mark: the name of the Beast or the number of his name."

18. **Here is wisdom. Let him who has understanding calculate the number of the Beast, for it is the number of a man, and his number is six hundred sixty-six.**

Note 1: By "the number of his name", John is referring to the way some ancient languages used letters of their alphabet for numbers. For example, Roman numerals were letters of the Roman alphabet (V=5, X=10, C=100, etc.). So, if one adds the numerical value of the letters of the Beast's name, whatever that name is, six hundred sixty-six will be the result.

Note 2: The Beast will be a man, not a governmental system. Sometimes, the term "beast" is used in prophecy as a term for a governmental system rather than for a single man (as in Daniel 7:1–7), but in this case, too many personal details are given about the Beast to allow for that.

Revelation 14

Jesus' Appearance on Mount Zion

¶1. And I looked, and there was the Lamb, standing on Mount Zion! And with him was a number, one hundred forty-four thousand, having his name and his Father's name written on their foreheads.

Note 1: This is the second mention of a group of one hundred forty-four thousand righteous souls. These may be the same one hundred forty-four thousand spoken of in Revelation 7, but John does not say so. This group was "purchased from the earth" (see verse 3, below), while the group in Revelation 7 came from the tribes of Israel. However, being from the tribes of Israel does not exclude them from having been purchased from the earth, for Israel, too, is an earthly nation.

Note 2: This is not the same appearance of Jesus that takes place in verse 14 when he appears to take his saints from the earth. John gives us no explanation for this appearance of Jesus on Mount Zion. Nor can this appearance be the Second Coming of Jesus, for that takes place in Revelation 19, and on that day, the Lord will descend from heaven and stand on the Mount of Olives, not on Mount Zion, as he does here. The Mount of Olives is on the east side of the Brook Kidron, which is east of Jerusalem. Mount Zion is on the west side of that brook, within the city of Jerusalem itself.

Note 3: The purpose of this visit of Jesus may be to set a mark on the Jews chosen to survive the coming attack of the Beast, and there would be precedent for that. Just before God sent Nebuchadnezzar's army to destroy Jerusalem, He sent an angel through the city to put a mark on those who would be spared (Ezek. 9).

2. **And I heard a sound from heaven like the sound of many waters and like the sound of loud thunder, and the sound that I heard was like harpists harping on their harps.**
3. **And they were singing a new song before the throne, and before the four living things and the elders, but no one was able to learn the song except the one hundred forty-four thousand who were purchased from the earth.**
4. **These are they who were not defiled with women, for they are virgins. These are the ones who follow the Lamb wherever he goes. These were purchased by Jesus from among men, firstfruits to God and to the Lamb,**
5. **and no lie was found in their mouth; they are without blemish.**

Note: Jesus said there are some who make themselves eunuchs for the sake of the kingdom of God (Mt. 19:11–12). This one hundred forty-four thousand belong to that category, and in Isaiah 56:3–5, God promised such souls a place in His kingdom better than that of sons and daughters. The special place given to these devoted saints is that they are privileged to attend the Son of God everywhere he goes. Not all of God's children are allowed to do that.

¶6. **And I saw an angel flying in the midst of heaven with everlasting good news to proclaim to the inhabitants of the earth, even to every nation and tribe and language and people,**
7. **saying in a loud voice, "Fear God, and give Him glory, for the hour of His judgment has come! And worship**

Him who made the heaven and the earth, and the sea and springs of waters!"

Note 1: With this, God offers the world a last chance to believe.

Note 2: Even at this late date, with the Lord Jesus about to appear on a cloud to catch his saints away, some people on earth will not have taken the mark of the Beast, for this angel calls upon men everywhere to fear God and worship Him, which he would not have done if everyone on earth was already hopelessly damned by receiving the mark (see verses 9–11, below).

¶8. **And another angel, a second one, followed, saying, "She has fallen! Babylon the Great has fallen, who caused all nations to drink of the wine of her whorish passion."**

Note: Babylon the Great, whom God also calls "the Great Whore" (Rev. 17:1), is a *fallen* thing out of which God calls His children before Jesus appears in the sky to catch away those who obey God and come out. The *destruction* of Babylon the Great takes place later, during the time of the seventh vial (Rev. 17:16).

¶9. **And then another angel, a third one, followed them, saying with a loud voice, "If anyone worships the Beast and his image and receives a mark upon his forehead or upon his hand,**
10. **he also will drink of the wine of the wrath of God, who has poured it undiluted into the cup of His wrath, and he will be tortured by fire and sulfur in the presence of the holy angels and before the Lamb,**
11. **and the smoke of their torment will ascend forever and ever, and they have no relief day or night who worship the Beast and his image, or whoever receives the mark of his name."**

Note 1: The only two choices for everyone on earth at this time will be to worship the Beast or be slain. No information is given us as to the type of death they will suffer who refuse to worship the Beast, but it probably will not be a swift and merciful execution.

So, it is more likely that the two choices for God's people will be torture and death in this world for not worshipping the Beast or eternal torture after death for worshipping him.

Note 2: The damned will be tortured "in the presence of the holy angels and before the Lamb." Isaiah prophesied about this element of eternal torment in the last chapter of his book. He said that those who are saved in the end will come up from time to time to New Jerusalem to worship God and that when they leave the holy city, they will view the damned in torment: "And it shall come to pass that from one new moon to the next, and from one Sabbath to the next, all flesh will come to worship before me, says the LORD. And they will go out and look at the dead bodies of men who rebelled against me, for their worm will not die,[27] and their fire will not be quenched, and they will be an abhorrence to all flesh" (Isa. 66:23–24).

Brother Stuart Hiser was given a vision of this frightful scene shortly after coming to Christ, and before Stuart even knew it was in the Bible! Here is his testimony, in his own words:

In the early 1990s, I dreamed that I was walking in the New Jerusalem. I was walking through the city, looking at all the dwelling places there. The streets were of transparent gold throughout the city, and the buildings all were bright white. All the colors were very bright and vibrant.

As I was walking, I came to a gate going out of the city, and then walked through the gate that led me to the outside of the city. There was green grass on both sides of the road, very pretty. As I was walking, I looked to my left, and out in the middle of the grass was a great big, transparent gold bubble. I could not see what was in the bubble. Then, all of a sudden, I had a feeling come over me of great fear and torment. It was terrifying. It consumed my whole body, and I knew – without even seeing them – that there were souls in great torment inside that bubble. Then the Spirit spoke to me and said, "You don't want to come here. Nobody wants to be here." It was terrifying. It was a year or more after this that I heard Pastor John explaining the difference between hell and the Lake of Fire, pointing out the scrip-

---

[27] This phrase means that the damned will always be tormented with regret.

tures in Isaiah 66, and I understood then what the Lord had shown me.

The feelings while I was walking through the city were overwhelming. I felt great joy, and peace filled my whole being, but it was not just that I felt that way; it was more like I was made of joy and peace. Everything in me was saturated with nothing but all the good and the glory of God that was around me there.

I will never forget that feeling when I looked at the bubble on the outside of the gate of the New Jerusalem in that dream. The feelings from being in the city with God's glory and then the feelings of torment from being outside the city looking at the bubble were so far apart! I know that I don't want to end up inside of that bubble with all those tormented souls. I don't have words to fully describe how that really felt. It is beyond this world, both the joy and the torment.

Note 3: The seventh trumpet was sounded in Revelation 11:15. Everything we have read since then has happened during the days of "the last trumpet", when Paul prophesied that Jesus will return to catch away his chosen people (1Cor. 15:52). Jesus did not come the moment that the trumpet sounded; the trumpet sound only signified the beginning of the time of the seventh trumpet.

12. Here is the patience of the saints, those who keep the commandments of God and the faith of Jesus.

¶13. And I heard a voice from heaven, saying, "Write, 'From now on, blessed are the dead who die in the Lord. Yes, says the Spirit, that they may rest from their labors, for their works follow them.'"

Note: This exhortation was for the saints of John's time and for all who have lived since then.

¶14. And I looked, and there was a white cloud! And sitting on the cloud was one like the Son of man, having on his head a golden crown, and in his hand a sharp sickle.

Note: This is Jesus. When he was on earth, he said that he would return "upon the clouds of heaven" (Mt. 24:30; 26:64; etc.), and he said it to John at the beginning of this book (Rev. 1:7; cf. 1Thess. 4:15–17).

15. And another angel came out of the temple, crying with a loud voice to the one sitting on the cloud, "Put in your sickle and reap, for the time to reap has come, for the harvest of the earth is ripe."

16. And the one who was sitting on the cloud thrust his sickle over the earth, and the earth was reaped.

Note 1: Again, this is Jesus' appearing, not his Second Coming.

Note 2: Many more saints will be raised from the dead to meet Jesus in the air than will be caught up to him from among the living. Jesus indicated how difficult it will be for believers to hold on to their faith through the time of the Beast when he said, "When the Son of man comes, will he find any faith on earth?" (Lk. 18:8).

Note 3: There are two resurrections. The first resurrection takes place here in Revelation 14, when Jesus appears in the clouds. It is often referred to as "the Rapture". The second resurrection will take place at the end of the Millennial Reign. The first resurrection is the "resurrection of life", and it is for those who have done good. The second resurrection is "the resurrection of damnation", and it is for those who have done evil (Jn. 5:28b–29).

Note 4: Jesus' raising of the faithful dead and his catching them up with living saints is an event of incomparable glory, but as with several other major events, John refers to it succinctly, saying only that "the earth was reaped." Paul gives us a fuller description of this holy moment, emphasizing that the saints who are caught up in the first resurrection will be given new, immortal bodies like the one Jesus has now (Phip. 3:20–21). And we learn from Paul's letter to the Corinthians that the Rapture will happen very quickly: "We will all be changed in an instant, at the twinkling of an eye, at the last trumpet" (1Cor. 15:51b–52a).

Note 5: After Jesus catches up the faithful, the only people left on earth will be those who have not believed in Jesus and the be-

lievers who took the mark of the Beast.   These all will suffer together through the Seven Last Plagues.

Note 6: Jesus has a new body, but not a new spirit. His new
body outshines the sun, but in spirit, he is still "meek and lowly"
(Mt. 11:29).   He is the King of angels and Lord of heaven and
earth, yet he humbly waited for this angel to tell him it was time to
reap the harvest of the earth.   The angel who commanded Jesus to
reap the harvest of the earth knew he was speaking to his King, but
he himself was humble enough to deliver this command from the
Father to the Son.

¶17. **And another angel came out of the temple that is in**
      heaven, he, too, having a sharp sickle.
18. **And another angel came out from the altar, having au-**
    thority over fire, and he shouted with a loud shout to
    the one who held the sharp sickle, saying, "Put in your
    sharp sickle, and gather the clusters of the vine of the
    earth, for her grapes are ripe!"
19. **And the angel thrust his sickle into the earth, and gath-**
    ered the vine of the earth, and cast it into the great
    winepress of the wrath of God.
20. **And the winepress was trampled outside the city, and**
    blood came out of the winepress as high as the bridles
    of horses for a distance of one thousand six-hundred
    stadia.[28]

Note: This prophecy of the Battle of Armageddon[29] does not
take place until Revelation 19, when Jesus returns to reign on
earth.

---

[28] That is, about two hundred miles.

[29] The name Armageddon means, "The hill of Megiddo".

Chapter 6
The Seven Vials
Revelation 15:1 – 19:10

Revelation 15

The Saints Stand before the Father

¶1. **And I saw another sign in heaven, great and marvelous: seven angels having the Seven Last Plagues, for in them is the wrath of God completed.**

Note 1: We are still in the time of the seventh trumpet, which began in Revelation 11:15.

Note 2: In chapter 12, God's first great sign in the sky proclaimed the story of Jesus to the world and offered them hope. This sign, however, will speak to a world of damned souls, declaring what God is about to do to them for rejecting the gospel of His Son.

Note 3: Before going on to describe the Seven Last Plagues that are about to strike the earth, John is ushered into the presence of God, where Jesus has taken the saints whom he just raptured.

¶2. **And I saw something like a sea of transparent glass mingled with fire, and those who overcame the Beast and his image and the number of his name standing on the glassy sea, holding harps from God.**
3. **And they sang the song of Moses, the slave of God, and the song of the Lamb, saying, "Great and marvelous are your works, LORD God Almighty! Righteous and true are your ways, O King of nations!**

4. **Who will not fear you, O LORD, and glorify your name? For *you* alone are holy! All nations will come and bow before you, for your righteous ways have been revealed.''**

Note: When the Father has welcomed His children home, He will tell them to go into heavenly chambers prepared for them and wait until the Seven Vials of wrath are poured out on the earth. This directive is not revealed in Revelation, but through Isaiah, who foretold of this loving admonition of God to the raptured saints: "Come, my people, enter into your chambers, and shut your doors behind you. Hide, so to speak, for a little while until the indignation is overpast. For behold! The LORD is coming out of His place to punish the inhabitants of the earth for *their* iniquity" (Isa. 26:20–21a).

¶5. **Then, after these things, I looked, and the temple of the tabernacle of witness in heaven was opened,**
6. **and out of the temple came the seven angels who had charge of the Seven Plagues, clothed with clean, bright linen, and girded around their chests with gold sashes.**
7. **And one of the four living creatures gave to the seven angels seven golden vials filled with the wrath of God who lives forever and ever.**
8. **And the temple was filled with smoke from the glory of God and from His power, and no one was able to enter into the temple until the Seven Plagues of the seven angels were accomplished.**

Note: There are only two other places in Scripture when God filled a place with such glory that no one was able to enter. The first was when Moses erected the tabernacle of God at Mount Sinai (Ex. 40). There, God's glory so filled the tabernacle that not even Moses could go in. The other instance was when Solomon dedicated the temple of God in Jerusalem; the glory of God so filled the temple that not even the high priest could enter (1Kgs. 8:10–11; 2Chron. 5:13–14). Here, when the glory of God fills His temple in heaven, all of heaven falls into silent anticipation as seven chosen angels begin pouring out vials containing the Seven Last Plagues.

Revelation 16

The Seven Last Plagues

¶1. Then I heard a loud voice from the temple saying to the seven angels, "Go, and pour out the Seven Vials of the wrath of God onto the earth!"

¶2. And the first went and poured out his vial onto the earth, and it became a foul and painful sore on the people who have the mark of the Beast and who worship his image.

Note: Many of the Jews may not have taken the mark of the Beast. Everyone who received the mark of the Beast was cursed to "drink of the wine of the wrath of God" and "be tortured by fire and sulfur . . . forever and ever" (Rev. 14:10–11a). It appears, then, that a number of the Jews will have refused to take the mark of the Beast, for when Jesus comes back to earth, they are granted grace to repent and believe the gospel. A refusal on the part of the Jews to take the mark of the Beast may also help explain why the Beast will hate them so much. Furthermore, since this painful plague is poured out upon those who received the Beast's mark, then if the Jews did not receive it, they will not be suffering with the rest of the world, and the world will no doubt be provoked by their lack of suffering, as many Europeans were provoked by the Jews' relative lack of suffering during the Black Death in the mid-14th century.

¶3. And the second angel poured out his vial onto the sea, and it became blood as from a dead man, and every living soul that was in the sea died.

Note: The parts of earth affected by the Seven Last Plagues are in nearly identical order with the parts of earth affected by the Seven Trumpets, but in these plagues, the devastation is complete. The plagues of the Seven Trumpets were tempered by mercy because there was still hope for mankind, and those plagues were intended to prod men to repent. These plagues, on the other hand, are poured out purely as punishment. It is to such an absence of mercy that the angel was referring when he said that whoever received the mark of the Beast would drink the "undiluted" wrath of God (Rev. 14:9–10).

¶4. **And the third poured out his vial into the rivers and the fountains of waters, and they became blood.**

5. **Then I heard the angel of the waters saying, "You are just, O Holy One, who is and who was, in making these judgments,**

6. **for they have poured out the blood of saints and prophets, and you have given them blood to drink. They are worthy."**

7. **And I heard the altar saying, "Yes, LORD God Almighty! Your judgments are true and just."**

¶8. **And then the fourth poured out his vial on the sun, and it was given to him to scorch men with fire.**

9. **And men were scorched with a fierce heat, and men blasphemed the name of the God who has authority over these plagues, and they did not repent to give Him glory.**

Note: At this point, with the exception of some of the Jews, no fear of God remains on earth; and so, God will withhold from mankind the grace that convicts of sin and leads to repentance.

¶10. **And the fifth poured out his vial on the throne of the Beast, and his kingdom was darkened, and they began to gnaw their tongues because of the pain,**

11. **and they blasphemed the God of heaven because of their pains and their sores, and they did not repent of their works.**

Note: With this plague, God gives living men a foretaste of their approaching eternal torment. Although the sun increases its intensity, the kingdom of the Beast is darkened, and men suffer excruciating pain – a foretaste for them of the Lake of Fire, where the damned will suffer horribly in absolute, suffocatingly thick darkness (Mt. 8:12; Prov. 20:20; 2Pet. 2:17).

¶12. And the sixth poured out his vial on the great river Euphrates, and its water was dried up to prepare the way for the kings from the east.

13. And I saw three unclean spirits like frogs come out of the mouth of the Dragon, and out of the mouth of the Beast, and out of the mouth of the False Prophet,

14. for they are miracle-working demon spirits, who go out to the kings of all the inhabited earth to gather them for the battle of the great day of God Almighty.

Note: God will be as much in charge of these unclean spirits from Satan, the Beast, and the False Prophet as He was of Pharaoh in Moses' day. God told Pharaoh, "I raised you up, to make you see my power" (Ex. 9:16), and God will also raise up the Beast to demonstrate His power. The Beast, motivated by virulent hatred of the physical descendants of Abraham (his spiritual descendants will be safely out of reach), will summon the armies of the world against the little nation of Israel. But his evil plan will only accomplish the purpose of God, who determined long ago to gather these armies for the Battle of Armageddon.

God chose the Assyrians to destroy the ten northern tribes of Israel, long before the Assyrian king had any plans to do so (Isa. 10:5–7). When the Assyrians marched on Israel, they had no idea that they were carrying out the plan God had put into the heart of their king. Likewise, when the Beast and his armies attack Israel, they will not know that they are fulfilling the hidden purposes of God. Thousands of years ago, through the prophet Ezekiel, God addressed the Beast, saying, "I will deceive you, and lead you on, and I will bring you up from the remote north, and I will cause you to come against the mountains of Israel" (Ezek. 39:2).

15. ("Behold, I am coming like a thief! Blessed is he who watches and keeps his garments, so that he does not go naked, and men see his shame.")

Note: Jesus interrupts John's prophecy to warn us all to keep ourselves pure so that we may be in heaven with him during these Seven Last Plagues.

16. And they gathered them to the place which is called in Hebrew, "Armageddon".

Note: The three demons of verse 14 are the "they" who gathered the armies of the Beast.

¶17. Then the seventh poured out his vial on the air, and a great voice came from the temple of heaven, from the throne, saying, "It is done."

18. And there were flashes of lightning, and peals of thunder, and voices, and there was a great earthquake such as has not occurred since men were on the earth, so mighty an earthquake and so strong.

19. And the great city was split into three parts, and the cities of the nations collapsed. And Babylon the Great was brought to remembrance before God, to give her the cup of the wine of His furious wrath.

Note: It bears repeating that, at this point, Babylon has already fallen (Rev. 14:8), but it has not yet been destroyed. It is impossible that fallen Babylon would come to God's mind here if she was not still around.

20. And every island fled away, and mountains were not found.

21. And large hail, weighing about a talent,[30] came down out of heaven upon men, and men blasphemed God because of the plague of the hail, for the plague of it was very great.

Note: The Battle of Armageddon, the last event to take place during the time of the seventh vial, will not take place until Revelation 19:11–21. No time passes during Revelation 17 and 18,

---

[30] Depending on the culture and time period, a talent could weigh as little as 57 pounds or as much as 130 pounds.

for an angel comes to John to show him the institution that God calls "the Great Whore" and "Babylon the Great".

Revelation 17

Spiritual Whoredom

¶1a. Then one of the seven angels who had the Seven Vials came,

Note: The fact that John recognized the angel tells us that angels are individually recognizable, like humans. Later, we also learn from John that angels are the size of humans.

1b. and he spoke to me, saying, "Come. I will show you the judgment of the Great Whore

Note 1: When the angel speaks to John about "the Great Whore", he is not referring to people guilty of fleshly immorality, but spiritual immorality. God speaks of spiritual whoredom in both testaments, and without understanding the concept of spiritual whoredom, one cannot understand Revelation 17 and 18, or indeed, much of the Bible itself.

God's covenant with Israel was, spiritually speaking, a covenant of marriage, with like responsibilities, expectations, and promises. The marriage took place at Mount Sinai, where God began the process by eloquently proposing to Israel: "If *you* will carefully listen to my voice and keep my covenant, *you* will be a treasured possession to me above all peoples, for all the earth is mine. And *you* will be to me a kingdom of priests and a holy nation" (Ex. 19:5–6a).

Israel accepted God's proposal (Ex. 19:8), and the date was set for the marriage (Ex. 19:10–11). On that wonderful day, God came down on Mount Sinai, and from the top of the mountain, He spoke the Ten Commandments, which I characterize as the wedding vows of the covenant. The third commandment of the ten made it clear to Israel that she would be required to be faithful to her Husband, whose holy name she was about to take upon herself: "You shall not bear the name of the LORD your God in vain, for the

LORD will not hold him guiltless who bears His name in vain" (Ex. 20:7).

God was fully committed to the marriage, but Israel was weak in her commitment. The gods of foreign nations attracted her, and she began to follow their ways and to worship them. This, in God's sight, was spiritual whoredom and made Israel a spiritual whore (Isa. 57:3; Ezek. 16:28). "The virgin Israel", said her broken-hearted Husband, "has done a very horrible thing" (Jer. 18:13). Through the prophets, God described in heart-rending detail the "very horrible thing" that Israel had done, reminding His faithless wife of how He had loved her, and of how unthankful and unfaithful she had been. Among the most touching of these descriptions is found in Ezekiel: "On the day you were born, your cord was not cut, nor were you washed with water to clean you up, nor were you rubbed at all with salt, nor were you even swaddled. No eye took pity on you to do any of these things for you out of compassion for you, but you were tossed out into an open field because you were abhorred on the day you were born. And when I passed by you and saw you squirming in your blood, I said to you, 'Live!' Yes, I said to you in your blood, 'Live!'" (Ezek. 16:4–6).

Israel did come to life, and God richly blessed and increased her. "I made you flourish like a plant of the field, and you grew and became great, and you came into full adornment. Your breasts were formed, and your hair was long, and yet, you were naked and bare. I passed by you again and looked at you, and behold, it was your time of love. And I spread my garment over you and covered your nakedness, and I swore to you and entered into covenant with you, says the Lord GOD, and you became mine. And your fame went out among the Gentiles because of your beauty, for it was perfect through my splendor which I had bestowed upon you. But you trusted in your beauty, and you played the whore because of your fame, and you poured out your fornication on anyone passing by; his it was" (Ezek. 16:7–8, 14–15).

"Surely, as a wife treacherously leaves her husband, so have you dealt treacherously with me, O house of Israel," God lamented through Jeremiah (Jer. 3:20). And through Isaiah, "Yea, you exposed *yourself to others* besides me and went up, widened your bed, and made your covenant with them. You loved their bed . . . and you brought *men* down to Sheol" (Isa. 57:8b, 9b). And in Ezekiel, God continued, "And you took some of your garments and made for yourself colorful high places, and you committed whoredom on them – which things have not been, nor shall be. And you took your beautiful objects made from my gold and from my silver which I had given you, and you made for yourself male images, and you committed whoredom with them. And you took your colorfully woven garments and clothed them, and you offered my oil and my incense before them, and my bread which I gave you – fine flour, and oil, and honey with which I fed you – and offered it before them for a placating aroma. . . . Moreover, you took your sons and your daughters, whom you had borne to me, and these you sacrificed to them, to be eaten! Was your fornication a small thing, that you slaughtered my children and gave them up, making them to pass over *the fire* for them? And in all your abominations and whoredoms, you did not remember the days of your youth when you were naked and bare, squirming in your blood. How weak is your heart, seeing you do all these things, the work of a brazen whore, building your arched place at the head of every street, and making your high place in every open square. . . . You adulterous woman, who takes strangers instead of her Husband!" (Ezek. 16:16–22, 30–32). "Your Maker is your Husband," God pleaded (Isa. 54:5a). "Whom do you dread or fear, that you dissembled and did not remember me?" (Isa. 57:11a).

For centuries, God pleaded with Israel, heartbroken at her betrayal of Him. "Oh, how the faithful city is turned to whoredom! She was filled with justice; righteousness lodged in her, but now, murderers. Your silver has become dross; your choice wine is diluted with water. Your princes are apostates and companions of thieves, all of them loving bribery and pursuing gifts" (Isa. 1:21–23a). "Your adulteries, your lewd whoredoms, are on the hills in the countryside. I see your abominations! Woe to you, Jerusalem! You will not be clean! When will it ever be?" (Jer. 13:27). "I cleansed you from your uncleanness and lewdness, and you would not be clean from your uncleanness; therefore, you will not be cleansed anymore until I have satisfied my wrath against you"

(Ezek. 24:13). "Because you have forgotten me, and cast me behind your back, you also must bear your lewdness and your whoredoms" (Ezek. 23:35). Then God concluded by saying, "I will strip her naked and expose her as in the day of her birth. And I will make her like the wilderness, and lay her waste like a desert, and I will kill her with thirst" (Hos. 2:3).

Note 2: God pleaded with Israel to come back to Him, even offering her mercy that went beyond the law. According to Moses' law, He reminded them, "If a man puts away his wife, and she goes from him and becomes another man's, will he return to her again? Would not that land be greatly polluted? But you have played the whore with many lovers; yet, come back to me! says the LORD" (Jer. 3:1). "Return, O backslidden Israel, says the LORD! My face will no longer frown on you, for I am merciful, says the LORD. I will not stay *angry* forever. Only acknowledge your sin, that you have rebelled against the LORD your God, and have dispersed your ways to strangers under every green tree, and have not obeyed my voice, says the LORD. Come back, O wayward children, says the LORD, for I am married to *you!*" (Jer. 3:12b–14a).

In spite of the Lord repeatedly telling Israel that He was the one speaking through Jeremiah, Israel stubbornly refused to believe the prophet, and in time, God's mind was alienated from His fallen wife (Ezek. 23:18). She so polluted herself and Jerusalem with heathen gods – her "lovers" (Ezek. 16:33; Hos. 2:7) – that God felt estranged from her and the holy city (Jer. 19:4). In other words, Jerusalem was fallen, but was not yet destroyed.

At the last, the unthinkable happened. God came to hate Israel (Jer. 12:8). He turned her out of His house and gave her up to her lovers, seeing that she preferred them. "What right", He asked, "does my beloved have in my house?" (Jer. 11:15a). And His anger matched His grief: "The LORD has sworn by the pride of Jacob,

'*I will damn myself* [31] if I ever forget any of their deeds!'" (Amos 8:7). "Jerusalem's sin is appalling!" cried Jeremiah. "She has become an unclean thing" (Lam. 1:8a).   When the end came and Jerusalem destroyed, she was left a pile of smoldering ruins, and Jeremiah was mortified: "The kings of the earth and all the inhabitants of the world would not have believed that foe or enemy could enter into the gates of Jerusalem" (Lam. 4:12).

Note 3: The end of the Old Testament did not bring an end to spiritual whoredom.   The apostle Paul repeatedly warned the body of Christ that they could fall into the same error that ruined Israel, saying, "All these things happened to them as examples, and they are written for our admonition" (1Cor. 10:11a).   But in Paul's second letter to the Corinthians, seeing the saints' hearts succumbing to the world's seduction, he wrote, "I am jealous over *you* with a godly jealousy, for I betrothed *you* to one husband, to present a chaste virgin to Christ. But I fear, lest, as the serpent led Eve astray by his craftiness, so *your* thoughts likewise be led astray from the simplicity that is in Christ" (2Cor. 11:2–3).

In spite of the best efforts of Paul and the other apostles, the body of Christ fell into spiritual whoredom.   When the Bride of Christ first entered into covenant with God, she was richly blessed, just as Israel was richly blessed when she started; however, also like Israel, she was unfaithful.   Turning from the pure gospel of God, the "chaste virgin" whom Paul had betrothed to God's Son began committing spiritual fornication with the spirits, the "gods", of this world.   Under the law, God's chosen people, Israel, fell into pride at being God's own and became the Great Whore of the Old Testament.   Under this covenant of grace, God's chosen people, the body of Christ, fell into pride at being God's own and became the

---

[31] The Hebrew construction here is an ancient way of making an oath of the greatest importance.   It was the ultimate oath that could be expected of anyone because the one making the oath was swearing on his own life that he would do what he had sworn to do.   It was so dreadful a curse that the curse itself was left unspoken.   When men took this oath, the unspoken curse was something like, "I will agree to be damned if I [fail to do as I say]."   But when God took this oath, since there is no one greater than He who could damn Him, the unspoken part of the oath would be something like, "I will damn myself if I [fail to do as I say]."

Great Whore of the New. Isaiah's condemnation of Israel's pride in her unique position with God came to apply equally to the unfaithful body of Christ: "Your wisdom and your knowledge turned you *from me*," God told the backslidden nation, "and you said in your heart, 'I *am*, and there is none besides me'" (Isa. 47:10b).

1c. [the Great Whore] who sits on many waters,

Note: The Great Whore did not come up from the waters, as the Beast did (Rev. 13:1). She only sat on them, as a queen. The waters on which the Whore sits "are peoples, and multitudes, and nations, and languages" (Rev. 17:15), which tells us that the institution which God calls the "Great Whore" is multi-national in scope.

Since the Whore is the fallen body of Christ, and in prophecy, the body of Christ is often referred to as "the earth" (see the note under Rev. 12:16), we can say that the Whore came from the earth, just as the False Prophet did.

The Beast came up from the sea, but he did not stay there; he went to the earth (God's people) and conquered it, as Daniel and John both prophesied he would do (Dan. 7:21; Rev. 13:7). The Whore, on the other hand, came from the earth but did not stay there; she went to the sea (people of the world), and by prostituting her spiritual influence, she was exalted by the kings of the world to sit with them "on many waters". Both she and the Beast left their place and went where they did not belong.

2. with whom the kings of the earth have committed fornication, and by the wine of her whoredom are the inhabitants of the earth made drunk."

Note: The Whore's involvement with the kings of the earth is a reference to backslidden believers' entanglement in the political affairs of men. Historically, the world's political systems always included religious elements. However, the body of Christ was created apart from all earthly institutions; it was never meant to be a part of this world. But after the body of Christ rejected Paul's gospel and drifted away from life and worship in the Spirit, she became entangled in men's political affairs. Then, the world embraced her and began drinking deeply of the potent wine of her infidelity to Christ.

3. So, he carried me away in spirit into a wilderness, and I saw a woman sitting on a scarlet-colored Beast that was full of blasphemous names and that had seven heads and ten horns.

Note 1: The angel said he would show John a woman whom he described as sitting "on many waters," but then he took John into a wilderness where John saw the woman sitting on the Beast instead. However, both are true of the Whore. Sitting on the Beast is symbolic of the fallen body of Christ being supported and carried along by worldly governments, and influencing the direction of those governments. Sitting upon many waters also represents the great influence she has over the peoples of the world.

Note 2: If the Great Whore were merely a worldly institution, her dependence upon worldly political power would not make her a whore in God's sight. God has never condemned sinners for going astray and joining forces with a worldly power; sinners are already astray, and they are the worldly power. The Whore was condemned because she belonged to God, and God had commanded her to walk in the Spirit and not to rely upon "the arm of flesh" (cf. 2Chron. 32:8). But when she blended with Rome, she traded her purity for earthly status and wealth, and her spiritual adultery with the kings of earth made her a whorish institution to God.

4. And the woman was arrayed in purple, and scarlet, and adorned with gold, and precious stone, and pearls, having in her hand a golden cup that was full of abominations and the filthiness of her fornication,

5a. and on her forehead was written a name: "Mystery: Babylon the Great,[32]

---

[32] Jeremiah helps identify the Great Whore as "Babylon the Great" when he describes Babylon (as the angel did to John) as a woman who dwells upon many waters and is "abundant in treasures" (Jer. 51:13a).

Note: Babylon the Great is a mystery only because what she really is, is hidden from men. She is not a mystery to God; He sees this institution exactly for what it is. Babylon is a mystery to men who see this evil institution as a force for good in the world, and it is her embrace of both saints and sinners as members that confuses them. Jesus once said, "That which is highly esteemed among men is an abomination in the sight of God" (Lk. 16:15), and nothing is so highly esteemed among men as their lofty religious creeds and somber ceremonies. However, nothing is more detestable to God than such things, for He gave His Son to bring us life instead of ceremonies, and for men to continue to serve Him with their carefully crafted creeds and rituals instead of walking in the Spirit that Christ died for is among the greatest of evils. Especially is this true for those to whom God has given His Spirit, for they are not merely walking in their fleshly ways, like men of the world, but they have forsaken the right way in order to do it.

5b. the Mother of harlots and the abominations of the earth."

Note: Babylon is not alone; she has daughters. They are the religious institutions which sprang from her. It does not matter if some of those daughters do not love their Mother; they are still her offspring, passing on her basic qualities, her spiritual DNA, so to speak, and like their Mother, they are honored by men and hated by God.

6a. And I saw the woman drunk on the blood of the saints, on the blood of the martyrs of Jesus.

Note: Committing spiritual whoredom led God's people (Israel first, and then the body of Christ) to hate righteous souls and to persecute them cruelly. The law of Moses empowered leaders of Israel to carry out physical punishments against those who were evil, but when those leaders drifted from the law of Moses, they began to abuse their authority and to persecute the righteous. Israel's leaders grew so perverse that if anyone dared to depart from evil and live a righteous life, he became prey for them (Isa.

59:15).   There is something about turning from truth that causes fallen saints to despise the faithful and, if they possess earthly authority, to abuse and even to kill them.   Such backslidden people become "adulteresses, with blood on their hands" (Ezek. 23:45), who can even boast of their evildoing. "Woe to the bloody city [Jerusalem] whose filthiness has not gone out of her!   Her blood-guilt is in her midst.   She put it on an exposed, high rock!   She did not pour it out on the ground to cover it with dust!" (Ezek. 24:6a, 7). "You have the forehead of a whorish woman!" God said to her. "You refuse to be ashamed!" (Jer. 3:3b).

Likewise, once the apostate body of Christ had given herself to the world the way Israel did, she lost her ability to blush, just as Israel did (Jer. 6:15; 8:12).   She, too, became too proud to heed the prophets' pleas for her to repent.   The subsequent horror stories of her cruel abuse of righteous souls has spanned almost two millennia, earning her the ignoble title God once gave Jerusalem: "the bloody city".[33]

6b. And when I saw her, I marveled with great wonder.

Note: John marveled because he never imagined the body of Christ would become such an abomination. John and the other apostles saw the beginnings of the apostasy of the body of Christ (cf. 1Jn. 2:18; 4:3; 3Jn. 9), but that did not prepare John for the revelation of what the body would eventually become.

7.   **And the angel said to me, "Why do you marvel?   I will tell you the mystery of the woman and of the Beast that carries her, that has seven heads and ten horns.**
8.   **The Beast that you saw was, and is not, and will ascend out of the Abyss, and he is headed for damnation.   And the inhabitants of the earth will marvel, whose names**

---

[33] God did not grant the body of Christ civil or military authority in this world; believers had to reach out to the world and blend with it in order to attain to such power, and this they did when they began to blend with the Roman Empire in AD 321. The emperor Constantine began the wicked process, but the consummation took place about seventy-five years later, when the emperor Theodosius outlawed all religions except the one proclaimed by the Whore.

are not written in the Book of Life from the foundation of the world, when they see the Beast that was, and is not, and yet, will be.

Note 1: Those whose names are written in the Book of Life and who walk after the Spirit will not marvel with the world because the Spirit will have prepared them for this man.

Note 2: The Beast "was, and <u>is not</u>, and will be." But God, on the other hand, "was, <u>and is</u>, and will be" (Rev. 1:8; 4:8). There has never been a time when God was not. But there have been rulers who died, but whose bodies have never been found.

Note 3: The world will marvel at the Beast because people around the world will recognize him as having lived on earth before. Without photographic evidence, however, it is difficult to see how the world will recognize the Beast, which suggests that he did not rule on earth before the mid-nineteenth century.

Note 4: We were told in Revelation 12 that Satan hates the Jews and those who have the Spirit of Christ. When he gives his power and authority to the Beast (Rev. 13:2), the Beast will use that power against the nation of Israel and bring it to the brink of destruction, as we will see. The Beast will be, like Satan, a supreme hater of the Jews.

9. **Here is the mind that has wisdom: The seven heads are seven hills upon which the woman sits.**

Note: As noted previously, these seven hills refer to Rome, capitol of the ancient Roman Empire.

10. **And they are seven kings; five have fallen, one is, and another has not yet come, and when he comes, he must continue a little while.**
11. **And the Beast who was, and is not, even he himself is the eighth, but he is one of the seven, and he is headed for damnation.**

Note 1: The Beast is one of the seven kings on Satan's heads, as well as the eighth king, because he reigns twice.

Note 2: We do not know which of the seven kings the Beast is; indeed, we do not know who any of the seven kings are. All that John is told is that five of the seven kings had already reigned by John's time, and that one was then in power, and that the last one was still to come.

12. **And the ten horns that you saw are ten kings who have not yet received a kingdom, but they receive authority as kings one hour with the Beast.**

Note: In visions, Daniel saw these ten kings as ten horns (7:24[34]) and then as ten toes on the image in Nebuchadnezzar's dream (Dan. 2:41–42).

13. **These are of one mind, and they give their power and authority to the Beast.**

Note: These kings follow the spirit of Satan, for he, too, had given his power and authority to the Beast.

14. **These will make war against the Lamb, but the Lamb will conquer them because he is Lord of lords and King of kings, and those with him are called, and chosen, and faithful."**

Note: This war is the Battle of Armageddon, and this is the third time it has been mentioned (Rev. 14:17–20; 16:12–16), but again, the battle is not fought until Revelation 19.

15. **Then he said to me, "The waters that you saw, where the Whore sits, are peoples, and multitudes, and nations, and languages.**

---

[34] When Daniel prophesied of these kings, calling them horns, he repeatedly used the dual form of the word "horns", which should be translated as "sets of horns".

Note: Again, the religious institution God calls the Great Whore and Babylon the Great is multi-national in scope.

The Beast Will Turn against the Whore Who Sat on His Back

16. **And the ten horns that you saw, and the Beast, these will hate the Whore, and they will make her desolate and naked, and they will eat her flesh and consume her with fire.**

Note: By "eat her flesh", the angel meant that the Beast and his ten kings will plunder Babylon's enormous wealth, as is later revealed to John. Jeremiah also prophesied that Babylon "will become plunder; all who plunder her will be satisfied, says the LORD" (Jer. 50:10).

17. **For God put it in their hearts to carry out His plan, to have one mind, and to give their kingdom to the Beast until the words of God be fulfilled.**

Note 1: Jeremiah foretold of the nations of the world, "the sea", attacking the Whore and destroying her: "The sea has come up over Babylon with its roaring billows, and she is overwhelmed" (Jer. 51:42). Regardless of how great Babylon thinks she is, or even how great she actually becomes in this world, God will utterly destroy her. "Though Babylon ascend to the heavens, and though she fortify her lofty stronghold, destroyers from me will enter in to her, says the LORD" (Jer. 51:53).

Note 2: Babylon's destruction will be "the vengeance of the LORD" (Jer. 50:15; 51:11, 53; Isa. 47:3; etc.); it will not be the vengeance of the Beast. God determined long ago that the Beast and his armies would destroy Babylon the Great: "I have commanded my consecrated ones [the Beast and his armies]. Yea, I have summoned my mighty ones to accomplish my wrath, my proudly exulting ones. The sound of a tumult in the mountains like that of many people, the sound of an uproar of kingdoms, of nations being gathered! The LORD of Hosts is mustering an army for battle! They come from the far reaches of the earth, from the end of heaven – the LORD and the instruments of His indignation – that

He might destroy the whole land! Howl! For the day of the LORD is near! It will come as destruction from the Almighty. Because of this, all hands will become feeble, and every man's heart will melt, and they will be terrified. Pangs and agony will grip them; they will be in anguish like a woman giving birth. Each man will look in astonishment at his fellow, all their faces flushed. I will shake the heavens, and the earth will move out of its place in the wrath of the LORD of Hosts and in the day of His fierce anger" (Isa. 13:3–8, 13).

Note 3: Even though God abhors Babylon the Great, He has used her, just as He has used Satan, and as He will use the Beast, to fulfill His purposes. Jeremiah revealed this: "Babylon has been a golden cup in the hand of the LORD, making all the earth drunk. The nations have drunk of her wine" (Jer. 51:7). So, while Babylon holds a golden cup in her hand (Rev. 17:4), she herself has been a golden cup in the hand of the LORD. God uses all His creatures, both good and evil ones, to accomplish His purposes.

18. And the woman whom you saw is the great city that reigns over the kings of the earth."

Note 1: Rome is the only city in John's time that could be de-scribed as reigning over the kings of the earth.

Note 2: After the body of Christ blended with mighty Rome and became Babylon the Great, it became, as Daniel described it: "dreadful, and terrifying, and exceptionally strong! And it had great iron teeth, devouring and breaking in pieces, and it trampled the rest with its feet" (Dan. 7:7). Trusting in the Beast's power, the fallen Whore not only "sinned against the LORD" (Jer. 50:14), but she also grew insolent toward Him (Jer. 50:29, 31–32), and even-tually, even strove against Him (Jer. 50:24). When the fallen virgin of Christ abandoned reliance upon the power of the Spirit, relying instead on the power of Rome, she became a hammer that brought destruction to the whole world (Jer. 50:23; 51:25); and yet, the whole world still praises her (Jer. 51:41) as the height of beauty (Isa. 13:19) and the "madam of kingdoms" (Isa. 47:5). She is a shrewd woman who presents herself as "tender and delicate" (Isa. 47:1) while drinking the blood of the martyrs of Jesus from her lovely, golden cup (Rev. 17:6; 18:24).

By blending with the Roman Empire, the fallen body of Christ enabled Rome to become a kingdom "different from all kingdoms" (Dan. 7:23), an astonishingly powerful empire that is still a mystery to fallen man.

Revelation 18

Note: John has now been told how the fallen Whore will be destroyed, but it still has not happened.

¶1. **After these things, I saw another angel coming down out of heaven, having great authority, and the earth was made bright with his glory.**

2. **And he cried out with a powerful voice, saying, "She has fallen! Babylon the Great has fallen, and has become a dwelling place of demons, and a prison for every unclean spirit, and a prison for every unclean and loathsome bird.**

3. **For all nations have drunk of the wine of her whorish passion, and the kings of the earth have committed fornication with her, and the merchants of the earth have become rich on the strength of her luxury."**

Note 1: This is Babylon in her fallen state, before the Beast and his kings destroy her. What makes her a mystery is that men do not see her as fallen. She is admired by the world, though she is home to the most dangerous of wicked spirits, the spirits that think they are good and acceptable to God and that inspire sinners to think the same about themselves. Jesus gave this blistering rebuke to the leaders of Israel, the Old Testament version of the Great Whore: "Hypocrites! *You* make the outside of the cup and dish clean, but inside, they are full of greed and injustice. You blind Pharisee! Clean first what is inside the cup and dish so that the outside of them may also be clean. Hypocrites! *You* are like whitewashed tombs, which outwardly appear to be so very lovely, but inwardly are full of dead men's bones and all uncleanness. And so are *you*! Outwardly, *you* appear very righteous to men, but inwardly, *you*'re full of hypocrisy and lawlessness. *You* snakes! *You* offspring of vipers! How can *you* escape damnation?'" (Mt. 23:25–28, 33).

Note 2: Nobody but Jesus possessed sufficient knowledge of God to judge these very devout men to be evil. To men, they looked and sounded good. They were honored leaders of the Old Testament version of the Whore. Leaders of the New Testament Whore are just like them.

¶4a. Then I heard another voice from heaven, saying, "Come out of her, my people,

Note 1: God's people are in a fallen thing, not a destroyed thing. If Babylon's fall, first mentioned in Revelation 14, was the same as her destruction, then she would be gone, and God's people could not be within her, and God would then have no reason to call them out. Babylon's fall was a spiritual event which began to take place long before the Rapture, while her destruction will be a physical event which takes place during this time of the Seventh Vial.

Note 2: The uniqueness of this supremely wicked institution is that God's people feel obligated to join it. With her claim of divine ordination, her wealth, her appearance of sanctity, and her time-honored traditions, Babylon can appear to be the right place for God's people, and many of God's children join her because they believe it pleases God for them to do so. But Babylon is not holy, and her traditions and doctrines are her own, not God's.

Note 3: Timewise, this heavenly call went out prior to the Rapture in Revelation 14. It is repeated here as a warning to all believers, including us, who live before the time of the Rapture. This is a call for God's children to separate themselves from the Whore before God's final, awful judgment comes upon her, a warning that was sounded first by the ancient prophets: "Get out of Babylon!" (Isa. 48:20a). "Flee from the midst of Babylon, and each of *you* deliver his soul! Do not be destroyed because of her iniquity!" (Jer. 51:6a). "O Zion! You who are living with the daughter of Babylon! Escape!" (Zech. 2:7).

Note 4: In the Scriptures, there is no other religious institution out of which God calls His people.

4b. so that *you* will not participate in her sins, and receive of her plagues!

Note: If God's people do not obey Him and come out of Babylon, they will be left behind to share in Babylon's awful judgment. Jeremiah said, "Come out of her, my people, and let each one save his soul from the fierce anger of the LORD!" (Jer. 51:45).

5. Her sins are piled up to heaven, and God has remembered her unrighteous deeds.
6a. Reward her just as she has rewarded *you,*

Note: That last word, "you", is added to the text. A word needed to be added, but John does not tell us what word to use. It could be "as she has rewarded others", or even (based on Jeremiah 51:35) "as she has rewarded me and my kinsmen". However, I added "you" because of the implied you's in the following verses.

6b. and repay her double, twice the amount of her works. In the cup that she mixed, mix for her a double portion.
7a. As much as she has glorified herself and lived in luxury, give her just that much torment and grief.

Note: The Father is not the one being called upon to repay Babylon for her evil deeds, for the verbs in verses 6 and 7 are all plural: "[*You* plural] reward her . . . [*you* plural] repay her . . . [*you* plural] mix for her . . . [*you* plural] give her torment and grief." This heavenly voice gave the same commands through Jeremiah, and there, the Hebrew verbs are plural as well: "[*You* plural] raise a shout against her on every side. . . . [*You* plural] avenge *yourselves* upon her! Just as she has done, [*you* plural] do to her! [*You* plural] repay her according to her deeds! According to all she has done, [*you* plural] do to her" (Jer. 50:15, 29b).

Regardless of who is being called upon to punish Babylon, God will be responsible for her destruction, for He will be the One to avenge His people: "I will recompense Babylon . . . for their evil which they have done in Zion before *your* eyes. For thus says the LORD: Behold, I will plead your cause, and I will fully avenge you. I will make her sea desolate, and dry up her fountain" (Jer. 51:24, 36; see also 51:6, 11).

7b. She says in her heart, 'I sit as a queen, and I am not a widow, and I will never know sorrow.'

Note 1: Clues to the identity of the mysterious Whore, Babylon the Great, are found in her own words:

- Babylon the Great calls herself a queen (because she claims to be the Bride of the King, the Lord Jesus).

- Babylon the Great claims that she is not a widow (because a widow's husband is dead, and the Whore tells the world that Jesus is alive).

- Babylon the Great claims that she will never know sorrow (because the Bride of Christ is promised eternal life and peace, and she believes she is the Bride).

Note 2: In essence, the Great Whore is saying, "I am not a fallen woman. I am blessed, and shall be blessed forever." Likewise, fallen Israel refused to believe that she had gone astray (Jer. 6:15) and rejected all of God's correction. "This is a nation that does not obey the voice of the LORD their God, nor receive correction. Truth has perished, and it is cut off from their mouth" (Jer. 7:28). God warned her, "You say, 'Since I am innocent, His anger is surely turned away from me.' Watch me! I will bring you to judgment for saying, 'I have not sinned'" (Jer. 2:35), but Israel would not hear.

Isaiah revealed before John did that the Whore would boast, "I shall be queen forever", and, "I shall not sit as a widow, nor shall I know the loss of children" (Isa. 47:7–8). But God will not be confused by her grand delusions. "These two things will come to you in a moment, in one day: loss of children and widowhood.[35] They will come upon you in their full measure because of your many sorceries and because of your great charms. Evil will come upon you that you will not know how to charm away, and sudden destruction will fall upon you for which you cannot provide atonement, and devastation will come upon you suddenly, of which you know nothing. Stand now with your charms and with the multitude of your sorceries with which you have toiled from your youth. Maybe you can prevail! Maybe you will frighten me!" (Isa. 47:9, 11–12).

Note 3: God describes Babylon's power over people as sorcery because false doctrine has a delusive effect on people, blinding them to the truth and hardening their hearts toward God. Even the heathen knew, as Plato once said, "Whatever deceives bewitches."[36] That is why Paul asked the Galatians when they were persuaded to forsake his gospel, "Who has bewitched *you*, that *you* should not obey the truth?" (Gal. 3:1).

8. **Therefore, in one day will come her plagues – death, and grief, and famine – and she will be consumed by fire, for the LORD God who has passed judgment on her is mighty.**

Note: Again, this concerns Babylon's destruction, not her fall.

---

[35] The only children the Whore is said to have are the harlots mentioned in 17:5, and they will be destroyed with their mother. Babylon's destruction will also prove that her claims of being the Bride of Christ were false all along. It is difficult to justify the term "widowhood" to a whore because whores have no husband. However, in this case, the Whore has claimed to have a Husband for so long that God uses the term to expose her as a fraud.

[36] *The Republic of Plato*, chapter 19. Another ancient philosopher, Gorgias of Leontini, agreed with Plato in his "Encomium on Helen": "The power of speech over the constitution of the soul can be compared with the effect of drugs on the bodily state. . . . By means of a harmful kind of persuasion, words can drug and bewitch the soul." Kathleen Freeman, translator, *Ancilla to the Pre-Socratic Philosophers* (Cambridge, MA: Harvard University Press, 1948), p. 133.

9. **And the kings of the earth who committed fornication and lived in luxury with her will cry and mourn over her when they see the smoke of her burning,**

Note: The Beast and his ten kings will not be among those mourning Babylon's destruction. The kings who mourn for Babylon are the kings to whom she brought great benefit; their wealth was in large part connected with her well-being.

10. **saying as they stand far off for fear of her torment, 'Alas! Alas! The great city! Babylon, the mighty city! For in one hour has your judgment come!'**

Note: It is God's judgment of Babylon, her *destruction*, that will come suddenly. The *fall* of Babylon took more than a single hour; it developed over centuries.

11. **The merchants of earth also will cry and mourn over her because no one will buy their merchandise any longer:**
12. **merchandise of gold, and silver, and of precious stone, and pearl, and of fine linen, and purple, and silk, and scarlet; and every kind of fragrant wood, and every ivory object, and every object made of precious wood, and of copper, and of iron, and of marble;**
13. **and cinnamon, and incense, and myrrh, and frankincense, and wine, and olive oil, and fine wheat flour, and grain, and cattle and sheep; and *merchandise* of horses, and of carriages, and of slaves; and souls of men.**

Note: Babylon the Great is a worldly power as well as a spiritual power, as the above list of her merchandise shows.

14. **And the fruits your soul lusted after have departed from you, and all precious things and splendid things are perished from you, and you shall never again find them. Never!**

15. The merchants of these things who grew rich from her shall stand far off for fear of her torment, weeping and mourning,

16. and saying, 'Alas! Alas! The great city that was arrayed in fine linen, and purple, and scarlet, and adorned with gold, and precious stone, and pearls!

17. For in one hour is such great wealth come to nothing!' And every shipmaster, and all who sail anywhere, and sailors, and as many as do business on the sea, stood far off,

18. and as they watched the smoke of her burning, they kept crying out, saying, 'What city is like the great city!'

19. And they cast dust on their heads, and they kept crying out, weeping and mourning, and saying, 'Alas! Alas! O great city, by which all who have ships on the sea grew rich through her magnificence! In one hour, she has come to nothing!'

Note 1: Wealthy merchants have been associated with Babylon from her earliest days, but in the end, none of them will be able to help her: "Your merchants [shall be no help] to you, for whom you have labored from your youth. They will wander off, each to his own way. There will be no one to save you" (Isa. 47:15).

Note 2: Multitudes of businesses would fail today were it not for sales of merchandise associated with the Whore's enterprises, holidays, and ceremonies. When the Beast and his ten kings destroy the Whore, sales of the Whore's religious merchandise will cease, and the profits of millions of merchants around the world will be greatly diminished. This is why merchants will grieve over the destruction of Babylon. Nevertheless, heaven will rejoice:

20. Rejoice over her, O heaven, and *you* saints and apostles and prophets, for God has judged *your* case against her!"

Note: Every righteous soul in heaven and earth will rejoice at Babylon's destruction; however, no rejoicing followed Babylon's fall. The fall of the body of Christ into spiritual whoredom was a tragic event; if anything, God would have called for great weeping for that. It is only the destruction of the Whore that gives cause for celebration.

¶21. **Then, one strong angel took up a stone like a great millstone and threw it into the sea, saying, "Thus shall Babylon the great city be violently thrown down, and it will never be found again!**

22. **And the sound of harpists, and musicians, and flutists, and trumpeters will never be heard in you again, and no craftsman of any craft will ever be found in you again, and the sound of a millstone will never be heard in you again,**

23. **and the light of a lamp will never shine in you again, and the voice of bridegroom and bride will never be heard in you again, though your merchants were the prominent men of earth because all the nations were deceived by your sorcery.**

24. **And in her was found the blood of prophets, and of saints, and of all who have been slain upon the earth."**

Note 1: God's condemnation in verse 24 of this whorish religious institution, Babylon the Great, is not explained, but Jesus made a similar judgment against the whorish religious institution of his day. He judged the Whore of the Old Testament as guilty of "all the righteous blood shed on earth, from the blood of Abel the righteous to the blood of Zacharias the son of Barachias" (Mt. 23:35; see also 2Chron. 24:20–21). But Babylon's blood-guiltiness is far greater because Babylon is guilty not only of "the blood of prophets, and of saints" but also "of all who have been slain upon the earth." Jeremiah foretold of this judgment of Babylon when he said, "At Babylon will the slain of all the earth fall" (Jer. 51:49).

Note 2: John is never actually shown Babylon's destruction; the angel only described it to him. When Revelation 19 begins, however, heaven is rejoicing because Babylon has been destroyed.

Revelation 19

Great Rejoicing in Heaven

¶1. **After these things, I heard as it were a loud sound of a great multitude in heaven, saying, "Hallelujah! Salvation and power and glory belong to our God!**

Note 1: Jeremiah, too, prophesied that "heaven and earth and all that is in them will shout with joy over Babylon" (Jer. 51:48a).

Note 2: Babylon's destruction will thrill the heart of every holy creature everywhere because it will mean that no one will ever be deceived by her again. It seems remarkable, at first, that no such rejoicing follows the destruction of the Beast (Rev. 19:20–21), but in the big scheme of things, the Beast is not that important. It is Babylon, not the Beast, who deceives God's children and holds them captive. The Beast will be an obvious enemy of God's people; Babylon has been much craftier – and thus, deadlier – robbing God of His saints by winning their hearts.

2. **His judgments are true and just, for He has judged the Great Whore who corrupted the earth with her whoredom, and He has avenged the blood of His slaves at her hand."**
3. **And a second time, they said, "Hallelujah! And her smoke is going up forever and ever!"**

Note: Jeremiah spoke of this curious element of Babylon's destruction as well: "Her judgment has reached to heaven. Yea, it has risen to the clouds" (Jer. 51:9b).

4. **And the twenty-four elders and the four living things fell down and worshipped God who sits on the throne, saying, "Amen! Hallelujah!"**
5. **And a voice came out of the throne, saying, "Praise our God, all His slaves and those who fear Him, both small and great!"**
6. **Then I heard something like the sound of a large multitude, or like the sound of many waters, or like the**

sound of mighty peals of thunder, saying, "Hallelujah! For the LORD our God, the Almighty, reigns!

7. Let us rejoice and be glad! And let us give Him glory! For the marriage of the Lamb has come, and his Bride has made herself ready."

Note: After the Whore's destruction, John's attention is turned to the Bride of Christ, that is, the members of the body of Christ who were faithful to the Lord and did not give in to the Whore's ways while on earth. Paul said that Christ would have a Bride "without spot, or wrinkle, or any such thing" (Eph. 5:27), and the Bride, through the trials described in Revelation 6–13, thus prepared herself for him. The Father sent His Son to fetch his Bride in Revelation 14; she met the Father in Revelation 15; she waited in heaven for the Seven Vials to be poured out in Revelation 16; she waited for Babylon to be destroyed in Revelation 18. Now, in Revelation 19, she will return from heaven with the Bridegroom to rescue and bless Israel and to reign with him on earth for a thousand years.

8. And it was given to her to be clothed with fine linen, bright and clean, for the fine linen is the righteous deeds of the saints.

9. Then one said to me, "Write: 'Blessed are they who are called to the Marriage Supper of the Lamb.'" And then he said to me, "These are the true words of God."

Note: The Millennial Reign is "the Marriage Supper of the Lamb". This marriage is mentioned only twice, here and in verse 7, above, which is just before Jesus comes from heaven with his saints to reign on earth for a thousand years.

10. And I fell at his feet to worship him, but he said to me, "Do not do that! I am your fellow slave and one of your brothers who have the witness of Jesus. Worship God!" (The witness of Jesus is the Spirit of prophecy.)

Note 1: The speaker here is unknown. It cannot be an angel because he has "the witness of Jesus", the holy Spirit of God, which angels do not have.

Note 2: Between this verse and the next one, much takes place, but for a description of those events, we must turn to the prophets, for John tells us nothing about them. The nature of the material from the prophets necessitates a format different from that which has been employed to this point. We will return to the format used heretofore when we reach Revelation 21.

Chapter 7
The Second Coming of Jesus
Revelation 19:11 – 20:3

The End from the Beginning

Surely, the Lord GOD will do nothing
except He reveal His secret to His servants, the prophets.
Amos 3:7

From the beginning, God has spoken through His prophets and told men of things to come, even to the end. No one but God can do that, and His doing that reveals Him to be infinitely wise and powerful. He repeatedly called upon Israel to acknowledge that no other god had such knowledge or power. "To whom will *you* liken me, or make me equal, or compare me, as though we were alike? I am God, and there are no other gods. There is none like me, revealing the end from the beginning, and from ancient time what has not yet happened. I have spoken; I will also bring to pass! I have planned; I will also do!" (Excerpts, Isa. 46).

God even challenged the heathen gods to prove that they were real by foretelling events as He had done: "Tell what is coming in the future, and let us know that *you* are gods! Yea, do good! Or do evil, that we may be in awe, and fear! Behold, *you* are nothing and *your* work is nothing. Whoever chooses *you* is an abomination. Who has declared it from the beginning, that we might know, or beforehand, that we might say he is righteous?" (Isa. 41:23–24, 26a). "Who spoke this long ago? Who declared *it* of old? Was it not I, the LORD? There is no other god besides me, a righteous God and a Savior![37] There is no one but me!" (Isa. 45:21b). "Listen to me, Jacob! And Israel, whom I named! I am He! I am the

---

[37] Or, "and a Messiah".

beginning and the end. . . . My hand founded the earth, and my right hand spread out the heavens! Come together, all of *you*, and listen! Who among [the heathen gods] has declared these things?" (Isa. 48:12–13a, 14a).

God told His people Israel, when they began pursuing other gods, "I revealed past events before they happened. Yea, they went forth from my mouth, and I caused them to be heard. I acted suddenly, and they came to pass. Knowing that you are stubborn, and that your neck is sinew of iron, and that your brow is brass, I told you *of them* ahead of time. Before it came to pass, I made you hear *of them*, lest you should say, 'My own effort brought those things about' or 'My graven image and my molten image ordained them'" (Isa. 48:3–5). "Bring evidence!" God demanded (Isa. 45:21a). "Present *your* case! Bring *your* proofs! . . . Let [those gods] approach and tell us what will happen! Let them reveal former things, what they were, that we may wonder, and acknowledge their fulfillment. Or declare to us things to come!" (Isa. 41:21–22). "Thus says the LORD, King of Israel, and his Redeemer, the LORD of Hosts: I am first, and I am last, and besides me, there is no god. And who is like me? Let him proclaim, and let him declare future events, and let him explain to me who created people in ancient times. And let him declare to them what will come about! Do not fear. Oh, do not be afraid! Did I not cause you to hear this long ago? I certainly declared it, and you are my witnesses!" (Isa. 44:6–8a).

Although God spoke often through the prophets concerning the Jews' future, He so well hid the meaning of those prophecies that no one in Israel could clearly see what the future held. "The vision of all this is to *you* like words in a sealed book, which men give to one who is literate, saying, 'Please read this,' and he says, 'I cannot, for it is sealed.' And then the book is given to one who is illiterate, saying, 'Please read this,' and he says, 'I can't read'" (Isa. 29:11–12). Even we who now serve Christ Jesus in the Spirit do not completely understand all that God has spoken about the future, but thankfully, by the Spirit, we can peer through the darkened glass and make out the shape of things to come. And John's vision of the end tells us that God's obedient children will understand it, for He promised them that "in the latter days, *you* will fully understand this" (Jer. 30:24b).

As early as the beginning chapters of Genesis, God glorified Himself by telling of end-time events,[38] and in the Old Testament scriptures can be found much information concerning the end times. It is God's glory to hide such things, and it is an honor for us to seek His wisdom and search out the hidden things of God (Prov. 25:2). It honors God for us to search and find His hidden treasures and then proclaim what we have found. The following contains some of the riches we have found by digging through the prophecies of old concerning what John saw.

The Beast Attacks

Blow a trumpet in Zion! Sound an alarm on my holy mountain!
Let all the inhabitants of the land tremble,
for the day of the LORD is coming. It is near!
Joel 2:1

The Beast's attack on Israel will culminate with the Battle of Armageddon, at the conclusion of which, Jesus will come down from heaven to rescue the Jews. The majesty of that event can be fully appreciated, however, only if we know the thrilling details which the prophets, not John, add to the story. So, we take the time now to examine some of what the prophets said about this momentous time.

The Consequences of Unfaithfulness

As early as the time of the Exodus, God was warning Israel of the consequences of unfaithfulness. "I swore to them in the wilderness that I would scatter them among the Gentiles and disperse them among the nations because they did not execute my judgments, but rejected my statutes and polluted my sabbaths, and their eyes followed after their fathers' idols" (Ezek. 20:23–24). In equi-

---

[38] God foretold Jesus' defeat of Satan when He cursed the serpent in Genesis 3:15, and Enoch, who is mentioned in Genesis 5:18, foretold the Second Coming (Jude 1:14–15, quoting the Book of Enoch 1:9).

table response to Israel's pollution of His law, God polluted Israel, saying, "I was furious with my people; I polluted my heritage" (Isa. 47:6a). God polluted His people, in part, by giving her over to those who hated her. "I forsook my house; I abandoned my heritage. I gave the dearly beloved of my soul into the hand of her enemies" (Jer. 12:7). "I profaned the princes of the sanctuary, and I gave Jacob over to destruction, and Israel to revilings" (Isa. 43:28).

As far back as when Israel was camped around Mount Sinai, God warned them that He would do this to them if they were unfaithful to Him: "I will scatter *you* among the nations, and I will draw out a sword after *you*, and *your* land will be a desolation, and *your* cities will be a waste. And as for those among *you* who are left *alive*, I will cause faintness to come into their hearts in the lands of their enemies. And they that are left of *you* will pine away in their iniquity in *your* enemies' lands, and also in the iniquities of their fathers will they pine away with them because they despised my judgments and their soul abhorred my statutes" (excerpts, Lev. 26).

God sent prophet after prophet to warn Israel, but because she would not hear them, God said, "I will deceive and forget *you*, and I will cast *you* out from my presence, along with the city that I gave to *you* and *your* fathers. And I will bring upon *you* everlasting disgrace and everlasting ignominy, which shall not be forgotten" (Jer. 23:39–40). The Spirit expressed through David the anguish Israel would feel when the heavy judgment of God came upon her: "As when one plows and breaks up the earth, our bones have been scattered at the mouth of Sheol!" (Ps. 141:7). Isaiah summed up the history of Israel's relationship with God by saying, "In His love and in His pity, He redeemed them, and lifted them up, and carried them all the days of old, but they rebelled and grieved His holy Spirit, and He was turned to be their enemy. He Himself fought against them" (Isa. 63:9b–10).

Lest anyone question the justice of such retribution, God provided this defense: "I dealt with them according to their uncleanness and according to their transgressions" (Ezek. 39:24a). "I judged them as their ways and as their deeds deserve" (Ezek.

36:19b). When Israel condemned God's judgments as unfair (e.g., Ezek. 18:25, 29), He indignantly defended Himself, saying, "I wounded you with the wound of an enemy, chastisement by a cruel foe, because of the greatness of your iniquity. Your sins are many! Why do you cry out over your affliction? Your bellyaching is in-curable. I have done these things to you because of the greatness of your iniquity and your many sins!" (Jer. 30:14b, 15).

Israel's Final "Sifting"

God has been scourging and purging Israel throughout their millennia-long Dispersion among the Gentiles, sifting out unwant-ed souls while preserving others, as He said He would do: "I will sift the house of Israel among all the nations as if sifted in a sieve; yet, not a kernel[39] will fall to the ground" (Amos 9:9b). "I will scatter you among the Gentiles and disperse you among the coun-tries" (Ezek. 22:15a), God said, "but I will allow some of *you* to live, escapees from the sword of the Gentiles, while *you* are dis-persed among the countries" (Ezek. 6:8). "*You*, my flock, the flock of my pasture, *you* are men. I will judge between one sheep and another" (Ezek. 34:31a, 22b), "and I will purge your uncleanness from you" (Ezek. 22:15b). "I will be relieved of my [Jewish] ad-versaries and avenge myself of my enemies. I will cause my hand to come upon you again, and I will smelt away your dross as with lye, and I will remove all your alloy" (Isa. 1:24b–25).

This is what the Jews have been going through for thousands of years because of their rebellion against their God. But there will be a final, brutal sifting of the Jews within the land of Israel as well, and God will use the Beast and his armies to carry it out.

The prophecies of punishment notwithstanding, whenever God said to Israel things like, "I also will purge from among *you* the rebels and those who transgress against me" (Ezek. 20:38a), He was implicitly promising that some Jews will survive His sifting.

---

[39] Literally, "a pebble". Amos is saying that not a soul God wants will be lost; only those whom God considers worthless chaff will be sifted out of Israel. In Isaiah 66:20, God again refers to the Jews who survive this sifting as grain, when He says that the nations who bring them back to Israel will be making a "grain offering" to the LORD.

Sometimes, He plainly added that promise, as at the end of His stern warnings in Leviticus 26: "Yet for all that, when they are in the land of their enemies, I will not reject them; neither will I abhor them, to destroy them utterly and to break my covenant with them, for I am the LORD their God. But I will for their sakes remember the covenant of their ancestors whom I brought forth out of the land of Egypt in the sight of the heathen, that I might be their God" (Lev. 26:44–45). And the promise is also found in the prophets, such as this, from Isaiah: "Zion will be redeemed by judgment, and those of her who repent, by righteousness, but all the sinful rebels will be crushed, and those who forsake the LORD will be consumed" (Isa. 1:27–28). And this, from Zephaniah: "I will remove from your midst those who rejoice in your pride, and you will not again be haughty on my holy mountain" (Zeph. 3:11b). And this, from David: "Those blessed by Him will inherit the land, but those cursed by Him will be cut off. The righteous will inherit the land, and dwell on it forever. But transgressors will be destroyed altogether" (Ps. 37:22, 29, 38a).

In those verses, God stated plainly that the goal of all His dealings with Israel, both the blessings and the curses, is to compel Israel to submit to Him as their God indeed, which He is absolutely determined they will do. Explicit or not, however, every warning of a purging of Israel contains at least an implied promise that some of Abraham's seed will be spared. It is a precious promise to Israel that "the arrogant and every evildoer will be stubble, and He will set them on fire" and that "the day is coming . . . which will leave them neither root nor branch" (Mal. 4:1). After all, the complete removal of wickedness, not only from Israel but also from the whole world, is what every godly person wants.

"Who Has Given Jacob Over to the Spoilers?"

In Revelation 17, we saw that it was God's wrath which the Great Whore suffered, although the Beast was the one whom God sent to deliver the blow. Likewise, it will be God's wrath which Israel suffers when the Beast invades their land. Isaiah cried out, "Who has given Jacob over as plunder, and Israel to spoilers? Is it not the LORD, against whom we have sinned? For they would neither walk in His ways, nor obey His law, and so, He poured out His furious anger on him, even a fierce battle which set him on fire on every side" (Isa. 42:24–25a).

John was told that Satan will elevate the Beast to the heights of worldly success by giving him "his power, and his throne, and great authority" (Rev. 13:2), but neither Satan nor the Beast will know that for the Beast to have Satan's power was part of God's plan from the beginning. And as we read in Revelation 16, when "three unclean spirits like frogs went out to the kings of all the inhabited earth to gather them for the battle of the great day of God Almighty" (Rev. 16:13–14), that, too, will only be according to God's plan, for God sent an angel from heaven to see that it was done (Rev. 14:17–19). Moreover, God plainly stated through Zechariah, "I will gather all the nations against Jerusalem for battle" (Zech. 14:2a). So, only by God's design will the three unclean spirits succeed in persuading the nations that the Jews are a useless burden to humanity, for God said long ago, "I will make Jerusalem a burdensome stone to all the nations . . . and all the nations of the earth will be gathered against her" (Zech. 12:3). Those three unclean spirits will turn the world's attention to some sort of signal that God will put into their minds to call the nations to come against Israel: "He will raise a signal to nations far away, and He will hiss for them to come from the ends of the earth. Quickly, swiftly, they will come" (Isa. 5:26). God will also give those demons the idea of promoting the war as a holy enterprise, requiring all available men and material. "Proclaim this among the nations: Declare holy war! Stir up the mighty men! Let all the men of war draw near and come up! Beat *your* plowshares into swords and *your* pruning knives into spears! Let the weak say, 'I am a mighty man!' Come and help, all nations from every side!" (Joel 3:9–11a).

Ezekiel confirms all this in a telling prophecy. In it, God claims complete responsibility for the Beast's attack on Israel, saying, "I, the LORD, have said it is coming, and I will bring it about! I will not hold back! I will show no pity, and I will not relent!" Then He concludes by saying to Israel, "They [the Beast and his armies] will judge you as your ways and as your deeds deserve" (Ezek 24:14). So, God will be the only One truly responsible for

Israel's horrible suffering, even though His agents, the Beast and his armies, will be the ones inflicting it.

It is true that "[God] does not willfully afflict and grieve the children of men" (Lam. 3:33), but it is also true that He is an "austere" God (Lk. 19:21). He is nobody's fool, and He holds men accountable for their actions (Gal. 6:7), especially those who are in covenant with Him, as He warned Israel: "Of all the families of the earth, I have known only *you*. Therefore, I will visit all *your* iniquities upon *you*" (Amos 3:2).

Conditions in Nature when the Beast Attacks

When the Beast's armies move in for the final sifting of Israel, God will cause an unnatural darkness to envelop the land. "And He looked at the land, and behold, darkness and distress, and by its clouds was the light darkened" (Isa. 5:30b). "Is not the day of the LORD darkness and not light, and gloom with no brightness in it? It will be darkness and not light!" (Amos 5:20, 18b). "The mighty man will cry aloud bitterly. That day will be a day of wrath, a day of distress and affliction, a day of devastation and desolation, a day of darkness and gloom, a day of clouds and thick darkness" (Zeph. 1:14b–15). Twice, in speaking of this time, Joel cried out in terror at the vision, "The sun and the moon are dark, and the stars gather in their light!" (Joel 2:10; 3:15). "O dark and gloomy day!" he said. "A day clouded with thick darkness, like blackness spreading out over the mountains!" (Joel 2:2a). And in addition to the darkness, "the earth will quake, and the heavens tremble" (Joel 2:10a), but it will be God, not the Beast, whose fury will make heaven and earth shiver (cf. Hag. 2:21b).

The Beast and His Armies Are Unstoppable

At the beginning of the war, God will bless the Beast with uninterrupted victory, and his merciless armies will flood the land of Israel. It will be a military force "vast and powerful, the likes of which has never been, and after them will not be again for many generations!⁴⁰   Before them, a fire devours, and behind them, a flame burns; the land before them is like the garden of Eden, but behind them, it is a desolate waste, and there is no escaping them. Their appearance is like horses, and they run like steeds. They run like mighty men; they scale the wall like men of war; they march, each in his own path, and they do not break rank. They do not encroach upon one another; they go, each man, in his course. When surrounded by weapons, they are not impeded. They rush about the city; they run on the wall; they climb up on houses; they come in through the windows like a thief" (Joel 2:2b–4, 7–9). "Violent spoilers are come upon all the bare heights in the wilderness because the sword of the LORD is devouring from one end of the land to the other. There is no safety for anyone" (Jer. 12:12). Ezekiel agreed with Jeremiah in calling these violent spoilers a "sword" (Ezek. 21:28b–32), and as representatives of God's wrath, "not one among them is weary; not one stumbles. They do not grow drowsy, and they do not sleep, nor is their waistband loosed, nor is the strap of their sandal broken. Their arrows are sharpened, and all their bows drawn; their horses' hooves are like flint, and their wheels are like the whirlwind. Their roaring is like a lion; yea, they roar like young lions. They growl and seize prey, and they safely carry it away, and there is no rescuing it. And they will growl over it on that day like the roaring of the sea" (Isa. 5:27–30a). "Ah, the thunder of many peoples! They thunder like the thundering of the seas! Oh, the roar of nations! They roar like the roaring of mighty waters. Nations will roar like the roar of many waters!" (Isa. 17:12–13a). Then, when the attacking armies have overwhelmed all Jewish defenses, they will overrun Jerusalem, brutalizing the populace, murdering, raping, plundering as they go, certain of completing their cruel mission. "And the city will be taken, and the houses plundered, and the women ravished" (Zech. 14:2).

It will be the most horrific of Israel's many horrible sufferings. Jesus appears to have been talking of this time when he told his

---

⁴⁰ That is, until the end of the Millennial Reign, when Satan will lead another massive international attack against Israel.

disciples on the Mount of Olives, "When *you* see Jerusalem surrounded by armies, then know that her desolation is near" (Lk.
21:20), "for there will be at that time a great tribulation such as has
not been from the beginning of the world until now, nor ever will
be" (Mt. 24:21; Mk. 13:19). Adolf Hitler's "final solution" for rid-
ding Europe of the Jews will pale in comparison to the effort of
these nations, led by the Beast, to annihilate the Jews once and for
all.

"*The Goodness and the Severity of God*"

To punish Israel so severely will tear at God's heart, and
punishing her has always moved Him to compassion: "Isn't [Israel]
my precious son? Isn't he a delightful child? Whenever I speak
against him, I earnestly remember him still, and my insides groan
for him. I will show him great compassion, says the LORD" (Jer.
31:20). "Israel has not been forsaken by his God," said Jeremiah,
"though their land has been full of sin against the Holy One of
Israel" (Jer. 51:5). "Thus says the LORD: If the heaven above be
measured, and the foundations of earth below be searched out, then
will I reject all the seed of Israel because of all that they have
done" (Jer. 31:37). "You must bear your wickedness and your
abominations, says the LORD. . . . I will certainly do to you as you
have done who have despised the oath and broken the covenant.
Yet, I will remember my covenant with you in the days of your
youth, and I will establish with you an everlasting covenant. Then,
you will call to mind your ways and be ashamed. And I will
establish my covenant with you, and you shall know that I am the
LORD, so that you will remember and be ashamed and never open
your mouth again because of your disgrace, when I am pacified
concerning you for all that you have done, says the Lord GOD"
(Ezek. 16:58–61a, 62–63).

Once, God was so frustrated with Israel that He told the
prophet Hosea to father a child and to call his name "Not-My-
People" as a sign to Israel, saying to them, "*You* are Not-My-
People, and I will not be *your* God!" But then, in the next sentence
came this tender promise from His lips: "Yet, the number of the
sons of Israel shall be like the sand of the sea, which cannot be

measured nor numbered, and it shall come to pass in the place where it was said to them, '*You* are not my people,' it will be said to them, '*You are* sons of the living God'" (Hos. 1:9–10). Isaiah gave us this remarkable example of God's strong desire to forgive and to heal Israel after He sorely chastened him: "I was angry, and I struck him. I hid myself and was angry, but he went on rebelling in the way of his own heart. I have seen his ways, and I will heal him. And I will lead him and restore comforts to him and to those who mourn for him" (Isa. 57:17–18).

God was always open with Israel about both His great love and His great wrath because He wanted Israel to believe in both. "For a brief moment, I forsook you, but in great compassion will I gather you. In a wave of rage, I hid my face from you for a moment, but in eternal lovingkindness will I have compassion on you, says your Redeemer, the LORD" (Isa. 54:7–8). It is not unusual at all for the prophets' blistering condemnations of Israel to be softened by loving promises of restoration and healing. "That day will be so dreadful that none will be like it," Jeremiah said. "It is the time of Jacob's distress. However, by it, he will be saved" (Jer. 30:7). "For thus says the LORD: Just as I have brought upon this people all this great destruction, so will I bring upon them all the good that I have spoken concerning them" (Jer. 32:42). "I will make my holy name known in the midst of my people Israel, and I will not cause my holy name to be polluted any longer" (Ezek. 39:7a).

There is no inconsistency with God. Prophecies like these are not self-contradictory; they only show us both "the goodness and the severity of God" that Paul taught (Rom. 11:22). It can be a difficult truth to comprehend and can lead to a misjudgment of God's actions, as is demonstrated by Israel's condemnation of God as unjust (Ezek. 18:25, 29; 33:17, 20). Sometimes God's own prophets could not see it, or did not want to. For example, when the Ninevites repented and God turned from severity to goodness toward them, "it was evil to Jonah, a great evil, and his anger was kindled" (Jon. 4:1). But as God did with Jonah (Jon. 4:4–11), He humbled Himself to explain His actions to Israel: "At some point, I may speak concerning a nation that I will pluck it up, or tear it down, or destroy it, but if that nation repents of its evil concerning which I spoke, then I will repent of the evil which I intended to do to it. Or at some point, I may speak concerning a nation that I will build up or plant it, but if it does what is evil in my sight, not heeding my voice, then I will repent of the good that I had thought to do to it" (Jer. 18:7–10).

God is good. His desire is to bless, not to curse, but He demands that sinners repent in order to receive His blessing and escape His curse. In the book of Acts, when the elders of Jerusalem learned that the Gentiles had received the holy Spirit, they responded by saying, "Then, God has granted repentance to the Gentiles!" (Acts 11:18), for they knew that God does not forgive unless the ungodly repent. This is an oft-overlooked element of God's promises of blessing to Israel in the last days. He will certainly rescue and forgive the Jews, but only after they have sincerely repented of their rebellion against Christ Jesus. And to compel them to sincerely repent will be God's principal purpose for sending the Beast and his armies against them.

For His Name's Sake

God will grant repentance and will rescue Israel from the Beast, but He will also let it be known that He is saving them not because they deserve it, but for His name's sake: "I will not do this for *your* sake, O house of Israel, but for my holy name, which *you* have dishonored among the nations where *you* have gone. And I will sanctify my great name which was profaned among the Gentiles, which *you* profaned in their midst, says the Lord GOD" (Ezek. 36:22–23a).[41] And He also let it be known that they would repent before He would come to rescue them: "*You* will remember *your* evil ways and *your* deeds that were not good, and *you* will be loathsome in *your* own sight because of *your* sins and because of *your* abominations. I will not do this for *your* sake, says the Lord GOD. Be it known to *you*! Be ashamed and confounded because of *your* ways, O house of Israel!" (Ezek. 36:31–32). "You are very treacherous," He told them. "From the womb, you were named,

---

[41] The way the Jews have dishonored God around the world is by rejecting and dishonoring His Son, and by continuing in their own, self-willed religion.

'Rebel'. For my name's sake will I defer my anger, and for the sake of my praise will I restrain it for you, lest I cut you off. For my own sake – for my own sake! – will I do it" (Isa. 48:8b–9, 11a). Throughout Israel's history, as the biblical record shows, most of the nation of Israel has wanted to be like the Gentiles, but God was, and is, determined that Israel will be a people apart from the Gentiles, no matter what He has to do to them to bring about that happy result. "What has come up in *your* mind will never happen! For *you* think, 'We will be like the Gentiles, like the families of the nations . . . .' As I live, says the Lord GOD, *I will damn myself*[42] if I will not be King over *you* with a strong hand, and outstretched arm, and poured-out wrath" (Ezek. 20:32–33).

The Chosen Third of Israel

The Beast's intention will be to destroy the Jews altogether, but God will not allow that, for He has determined that a third of the Jews living in the Promised Land at that time will survive.[43] "It shall come to pass that throughout the land, says the LORD, two parts in it will be cut off and die, and a third in it will remain. And I will put the third part through fire, and I will refine them as silver is refined, and I will try them as one tries gold" (Zech. 13:8–9a). "Just as new wine is obtained from a cluster, and one says, 'Don't destroy it, for there is good in it,' so will I do for the sake of my servants, lest he [the Beast] destroy them all" (Isa. 65:8). And "there will be gleanings left in it, as when an olive tree is beaten – two or three berries on the highest bough and four or five on its fruit-bearing branches, says the LORD, God of Israel" (Isa. 17:6). Shepherds of the time made their flocks "pass under the rod" when the flocks were being counted or divided (Lev. 27:32); in like manner, God told Israel, "I will cause *you* to pass under the rod, and then bring *you* into the bond of the covenant" (Ezek. 20:37).

---

[42] See footnote 31, page 121.

[43] Jeremiah 24 provides a clear example of God determining who will live and who will die, and God, through Moses, bluntly told Israel, "I kill, and I make alive" (Dt. 32:39). Moreover, that God makes such choices is also evidenced by the fact that before the world began, God wrote in His Book the names of those who would believe and live (Dan. 12:1; Rev. 13:8; 17:8; 20:15).

When God has done this, He will tell them, "I have refined you, but not the way silver *is refined*; I have chosen you in a furnace of affliction" (Isa. 48:10). The chosen third will be "an afflicted and lowly people, and they will seek refuge in the Name of the LORD.[44] The remnant of Israel will not act perversely, and they will not tell a lie; nor will a deceitful tongue be found in their mouth" (Zeph. 3:12b–13a).

Before the world began, God chose this third of Israel to be humbled by the Beast and be prepared for Jesus to return. An angel told Daniel that their names were written in heaven's Book of Life: "At that time, your people will be delivered, everyone who is found written in the Book" (Dan. 12:1b). These chosen Jews will likely not yet understand that they are safe from death because their names are in the Lamb's Book of Life. It may even be that some of them still do not, as yet, believe in either the Lamb or his Book. Unless God's Two Witnesses had explained these things to them, the chosen Jews will not yet know that God is using the Beast to purge Israel of souls He does not want, and to save those He does.[45]

Elijah Will Prepare the Chosen Third to Survive

Despite suffering continual and sometimes severe chastisement from God since the days of the prophets, the Jews have stubbornly persisted in their own way. Even after God cast them out of the Promised Land and dispersed them among the nations, they

---

[44] Paul referred to Christ as the Power of God and the Wisdom of God (1Cor. 1:24), and even the Spirit of God (2Cor. 3:17). The aged prophet Simeon called him the Salvation of God (Lk. 2:30). John called him the Word of God (Jn. 1:1; Rev. 19:13) and the Word of Life (1Jn. 1:1). Jesus called himself the Way of God, the Truth of God, and the Life of God (Jn. 14:6). In short, Christ Jesus is "the reflection of God's glory and the exact representation of His being" (Heb. 1:3).

The prophets often referred to Christ as the Name of God. Of course, they could not have known that the Name of the LORD of which they often spoke was a living being whose existence God was keeping secret until "the fullness of time" (Eph. 1:10). But the Son was brought out of hiding two thousand years ago, and all believers should know by now who the Name of the LORD is.

[45] The Two Witnesses would have known who Israel's Messiah is, and it is difficult to imagine them not giving that information to Israel.

rebelled and grieved God's heart. He complained bitterly through Ezekiel that "when they came to the Gentiles, wherever they came, they profaned my holy name" (Ezek. 36:20a). Seeing this self-destructive stubbornness in his fellow Jews, the prophet Jeremiah cried out, "O LORD, you have stricken them, but they have not grieved; you have consumed them, but they have refused to receive correction. They have made their faces harder than a rock! They refuse to repent!" (Jer. 5:3). However, the Beast, the fiercest chastening rod ever wielded by God,[46] will inflict such unprecedented agony on Israel that the chosen third, the promised "remnant of Israel" (e.g. Isa. 10:20; Jer. 31:7; Zeph. 3:13), will call on the name of the LORD, under the lingering influence of God's Two Witnesses, who will have been murdered about three years earlier.

To say, as both Malachi and Jesus did, that Elijah will appear and prepare Israel for the Second Coming (Mal. 4:5–6; Mt. 17:11) is to say that Elijah will prepare Israel for the coming of the Beast as well, for the Beast must come first. A significant part of Elijah's preparation of Israel will be to warn them to humble themselves under that chastening rod of God, and live. That stern message will play a critical role in the salvation of the chosen remnant, though for the rest of the Jews, that message may provoke the same animosity toward God's Witnesses that the world will feel. Malachi was referring to this remnant when he prophesied that "those who feared the LORD spoke, each one with his neighbor, and the LORD gave ear and listened, and a book of remembrance was written before Him for those who feared the LORD and thought on His name. And they shall be mine, says the LORD of Hosts, in the day that I make up my peculiar treasure, and I will spare them as a man spares his own son who serves him. And *you* will repent, and *you* will discern the difference between the righteous and the wicked, between him who serves God and him who does not serve Him" (Mal. 3:16–18).

---

[46] The Bible contains many examples of God using foreign invaders as His chastening rod for Israel (e.g., Judg. 2:14; Isa. 10:5–6).

Chastisement in Measure

God promised Israel, "I will not contend forever, nor will I be angry forever, for the spirit before me would faint away, and the souls that I have made" (Isa. 57:16). Though He warned Israel, "I will by no means leave you unpunished," He also promised, "I will chastise you in measure" (Jer. 46:28c). It was in speaking of Israel that God said His eyes "are on the sinful kingdom, and I will destroy it from the face of the earth; however," He mercifully added, "I will not completely destroy the house of Jacob" (Amos 9:8). And He repeated that promise many years later through Jeremiah, saying, "The whole land will be a waste; yet, I will not make a complete end *of it*" (Jer. 4:27b).

The Cup of God's Wrath

Only when God is satisfied that Israel is sufficiently purged of rebellious souls will He take His cup of wrath away from the lips of the Jews and give it to the nations, "for in the hand of the LORD is a cup with wine that has foamed and is fully mixed. When He pours out this wine, all the wicked of the earth will surely drink; they will drain it to the dregs!" (Ps. 75:8). To the chosen remnant, God will say, "Arise, O Jerusalem, who have drunk from the hand of the LORD the cup of His wrath, who have drunk the dregs of the cup of staggering, and drained it. Hear this now, you who are afflicted and drunk, but not from wine! Thus says your Master, the LORD, and your God, who pleads the cause of His people: Behold, I have taken from your hand the cup of staggering, the dregs of the cup of my wrath. You will never drink it again. But I will put it in the hand of your tormentors, who said to your soul, 'Bow down that we may walk over you!' And you have made your back like the ground, like the street, for them to walk over" (Isa. 51:17, 21–23). It was God's intention all along, He said, "to gather the nations so that I might pour my fury out on them, all my burning anger," but only "when the whole land is consumed by the fire of my jealousy" (Zeph. 3:8b).

Jews and Gentiles Will Both Be Judged

Until the Battle of Armageddon, the final battle of the Beast's war against Israel, God will be punishing the Jews exclusively. But the Battle of Armageddon will be the end of God's judgment upon Israel and the beginning of God's judgment upon the Beast and his Gentile armies. No one involved in this war, Jew or Gentile, will escape the judgment of God, as He said: "I will punish all who are circumcised along with the uncircumcised. For all the nations are uncircumcised, and all the house of Israel are uncircumcised in heart" (Jer. 9:25b, 26b).

Paul once pointed out that the saving grace of God had to be offered to the Jews first, and only then to the Gentiles (Acts 13:46; Rom. 1:16), and it will be the same with God's wrath. For Paul also said that "indignation and wrath" will be poured out "upon every soul of man who does evil, first to the Jew and then to the Gentile" (Rom. 2:8b–9). Peter, too, warned the saints that judgment begins in the household of God (1Pet. 4:17).

It was of this war against the Beast that God said to Israel, "I will destroy your cities, and then, in anger and in fury, I will execute vengeance upon the heathen nations" (Mic. 5:14b–15). "I have lifted up my hand. *I will damn myself*[47] if the heathen that are around *you* do not bear their own reproach!" (Ezek. 36:7). "I will surely make a complete end of all the nations to which I have driven you, but I will not make a complete end of you" (Jer. 46:28b), "for I am with you to save you. Yea, I will make a complete end of all the nations where I scattered you; howbeit, I will not make a complete end of you" (Jer. 30:11a).

Humbled to the Dirt

After the Beast's armies have slain two thirds of the nation, it will look as if Israel's complete destruction is imminent. With Jewish blood and tears flowing together throughout the land of Israel, and now in Jerusalem as well, the helpless remnant will pray with an urgency that none but the most desperate can feel.

---

[47] See footnote 31, page 121.

"Zion will think, 'The LORD has abandoned me, and my Lord has forgotten me!'" (Isa. 49:14). The Jews not yet slain by the Beast will not make seeking God their *chief* priority; they will make it their *only* priority: "Blow a trumpet in Zion! Sanctify a fast! Call a meeting! Gather the people! Sanctify the congregation! Assemble the elders! Gather the children, even the nursing infants! Let the bridegroom come out of his chamber, and the young bride from her bridal-chamber!" (Joel 2:15–16).

Just as God had to crush young Joseph in Egypt with many cruel sufferings before He could trust him with the great authority and power He planned to give him, so God will have to crush these chosen Jews before He can trust them with the very great authority He has planned for them. This is what the Spirit meant when it said through David, "The meek will inherit the earth" (Ps. 37:11). To cause the chosen third to inherit the earth with Christ is God's intention, but they will be made extraordinarily meek before He will crown them with that blessing.

The helpless and terrified survivors in Israel will be pleading with God: "As a woman at the point of giving birth writhes and cries out in her travail, so have we been in your sight, O LORD!" (Isa. 26:17). With all their remaining, ebbing strength, the trembling remnant of Israel will beg for heaven's intervention, just as God, through Isaiah, told them they would do on the day He unleashed His great wrath on the nation: "I will bring distress upon *Jerusalem*[48], and there will be mourning and moaning. And I will encamp against you and lay siege against you with palisades, and I will raise siegeworks against you. And when you are abased, you will speak from the ground, and your talk will be humbled in the dirt; your voice will be like one who has a familiar spirit from out of the ground,[49] and your speech will squeak from the dirt" (Isa. 29:2a, 3–4). "And they shall know that I, the LORD, did not say in vain that I would bring this evil upon them" (Ezek. 6:10). But

---

[48] Here, the Hebrew word "Ariel" ("lioness of God") is a reference to Jerusalem.

[49] People who are overwhelmed in spirit or demon-possessed may make abnormal sounds. Isaiah 8:19, for example, mentions "the mediums and the soothsayers, who squeal and growl."

Jesus will pray for them, as he once prayed for Peter, that their faith would lead to their salvation (Lk. 22:32). Up in heaven, Jesus, their Messiah whom their fathers rejected, will ask the Father to show them mercy: "O LORD, in distress they have sought you. They have poured out a whispered prayer, for your chastisement has been upon them" (Isa. 26:16).

God's Secret Plan

Moses gave this warning and comfort to Israel: "The LORD will certainly judge His people, but He will have pity on His servants when He sees that their strength is gone" (Dt. 32:36). The end of Israel's strength is the place where God will meet them; it is, indeed, the place to which He had sent the Beast to drive them. In that place is nothing but God's mercy in which to hope – no tradition, no ceremony, no knowledge of the scriptures, no claim of righteousness. And in that place, "They will call on my name, and I will answer them. I will say, 'This is my people!'. And they will say, 'The LORD is my God!'" (Zech. 13:9b).

The Beast and his armies will be supremely confident of a swift victory because God will have, to this point in the war, given them no reason to think otherwise. As the prophets said, "On that day, the glory of Jacob will be brought low, and the fatness of his flesh will be made lean" (Isa. 17:4), and "The whole land will be a waste" (Jer. 4:27a).

Sensing the overwhelming power of the Beast's cruel multi-national force, the prophet Joel cried out, "O LORD, send down your warriors!" (Joel 3:11b). Joel was no doubt thinking of angels when the Spirit pleaded through him for God's warriors to come down from heaven. He did not know that the Spirit was calling through him for God to send His warrior Son with his army of saints to rescue the chosen remnant of Israel. Nor did Joel know that the Son had already promised, long before Joel's time, that he and God's saints would one day come to save Israel, saying through David, "I will come with mighty ones of the Lord GOD!" (Ps. 71:16a). Moreover, even long before David, Enoch had prophesied that "the Lord is coming with ten thousands of his saints" (Jude 1:14).

Nor will the chosen Jews know God's plan when they cry out to God, "Oh, that you would tear heaven open, that you would come down, that the mountains would quake at your presence, to make your Name known to your adversaries, that the nations might tremble at your presence!" (Isa. 64:1–2b). But soon after Jesus comes, they will be shouting, "You did astonishing things we did not expect! You did come down, and the mountains did quake at your presence!" (Isa. 64:3). But for the moment, the chosen third of Israel will only be crying out for God's help against the Beast.

Jesus Comes[50]

Christ will appear a second time to bring salvation
to those who earnestly look for him.
Hebrews 9:28

At this point in John's Revelation, the time for the Jews to drink of the cup of God's wrath has passed, and the Gentiles' time to drink of that cup has come. The Father will grant His Son's petition for mercy and will "be jealous over His land, and He will pity His people. The LORD will hear, and He will say to His people, 'Here I am! I will remove the northerner [the Beast] far from you and drive him into a dry and desolate place, and his foul odor will go up. His stench will rise, though he was doing great things.' Do not be afraid, O land! Shout for joy and be glad, for the LORD Himself will do great things!" (Joel 2:18–19a, 20–21).

The Father will then send an angel out from heaven who will shout a command for the Son to go and trample the Beast and his armies: "Put in the sickle, for the harvest is ripe! Go and start treading, for the winepress is full; the vats overflow, for their wickedness is great!" (Joel 3:13; cf. Rev. 14:17–20). Jesus will then "put on righteousness like a breastplate, with a helmet of salvation on his head. He will put on garments of vengeance and

---

[50] The first time Jesus came, he said plainly that the Father had sent him only to the Jews (Mt. 15:24; cf. Rom. 15:8). The second time he comes (Rev. 19), he will again come only to the Jews, but this time with all his saints, to rescue them from the nations and to reign from Jerusalem over the whole earth.

wrap himself in zeal like a robe. He will come like a rushing river, the Spirit of God driving him on. The Redeemer will come to Zion, even to those in Jacob who repent of *their* transgression, says the LORD" (Isa. 59:17, 19b–20), "and to *you* who fear my name will the Sun of righteousness rise with healing in his wings" (Mal. 4:2).

¶11a. Then I saw heaven opened, and there was a white horse!

"The LORD will appear over them," said Zechariah, "and the LORD their God will save them as the flock of His people, as precious crown jewels glittering on His land" (Zech. 9:14a, 16).

11b. And the one sitting on it is called "Faithful and True", and he judges and makes war in righteousness.

12. His eyes were a flame of fire, and on his head were many crowns, and he has names written, and a name written which no one knew except himself,

13. and he was clothed with a blood-stained garment, and his name was called "the Word of God".

"Behold, the Name of the LORD will come from far away, burning with his anger and a heavy burden. His lips will be full of indignation, and his tongue will be like a devouring fire, and his breath will be like a flooding torrent reaching up to the neck, to sift nations in a sieve for worthlessness"[51] (Isa. 30:27–28a). "He sent me against the nations who plundered *you*," said the Son through Zechariah, "for he who touches *you* touches the apple of His eye" (Zech. 2:8).

14. And the armies that are in heaven, clothed in fine linen, white and clean, were following him on white horses.

Zechariah also prophesied of the saints returning with Jesus: "Then will the LORD go out and do battle with those nations . . . and all the saints with you" (Zech. 14:3a, 5b). And Jude quoted the

---

[51] That is, to remove those whom God considers worthless.

even more ancient prophecy of Enoch: "Enoch, the seventh from Adam, prophesied, saying, 'Behold! The Lord is coming with ten thousands of his saints'" (Jude 1:14).

The Mount of Olives

While here among us the first time, Jesus was submissive and quiet as he stood before his enemies, but not this time. When Jesus returns to earth to save Israel, he "will roar from Zion; from Jerusalem will he lift up his voice, and heaven and earth will shake" (Joel 3:16a). "He will not be silent! Fire will devour before him, and around him, it will be very tempestuous" (Ps. 50:3b). When Jesus comes down, "his feet will stand on that day on the Mount of Olives, which is on the east side of Jerusalem" (Zech. 14:4a), and when his feet touch the mountain, his fury will be so great that "the Mount of Olives will be split in two, *making* a very large valley from east to west. Half the mountain will move to the north, and half to the south" (Zech. 14:4b). But that earthquake will be good news to Israel and fulfill Nahum's prophecy: "Behold upon the mountains the feet of the one bringing good news, pro-claiming peace!" (Nahum 1:15a) – peace, that is, to Israel.

Finished now with using the Beast, God will "change the sovereignty of the kingdoms [by giving it to His Son] and bring to an end the power of the Gentiles' kingdoms" (Hag. 2:22a; Dan. 7:11–14). "On that day, I will set about to annihilate all the nations that come against Jerusalem" (Zech. 12:9), "and it shall come to pass that everyone who calls on the Name of the LORD will be saved, for there shall be deliverance on Mount Zion and in Jerusalem, as the LORD has said, even among the survivors whom the LORD will call" (Joel 2:32).

15. **And out of his mouth went a sharp, double-edged sword, that with it, he may strike down the nations, and he will rule them with a rod of iron, and he himself will tread the winepress of the furious wrath of God Almighty.**

16. **And on his garment and on his thigh, he had a name written: "King of kings and Lord of lords".**

Did the Two Witnesses Tell Them?

The surviving third of the Jews in Israel will be so broken and feel so forsaken at this point that when they see an army coming down from heaven, they may wonder if that army is coming to help the Beast finish them off. Unless God's Two Witnesses had told them that Jesus would come down from heaven to save them, they will not be aware of the ancient promise which the Son of God made to them when he said, "Behold, I will wave my hand over them [the Beast and his armies], and they will become plunder for their own slaves [Israel], and *you* shall know that the LORD of Hosts has sent me" (Zech. 2:9). We do not know how much information about Jesus will be given to Israel by God's Two Witnesses, but we do know that when he comes, the Jews will not immediately know who he is, as we will soon see.

The Son, Not the Father, Will Come

The Father Himself will not be the one who comes down from heaven to rescue the Jews; it will be the Son coming in the Father's name, that is, by His authority. In the prophets, the Son often spoke in the name of the Father using the pronoun "I" because the message was from the Father, though it came through him. The prophets also used "I" in their prophecies when God was speaking through them. In a few such prophecies, after the Son delivered a message from the Father, the Son would speak for himself. Here is one example from Zechariah:

[The Son speaking the Father's words] "Shout and rejoice, O daughter of Zion, because I will surely come, and I will dwell in your midst, says the LORD" (Zech. 2:10).

[The Son speaking for himself] "And many nations will be joined to the LORD in that day, and they will become my people, and I will dwell in your midst. And you shall know that the LORD of Hosts has sent me to you" (Zech. 2:11).

God's Great Banquet

Throughout ancient history, animals were sacrificed for men. Now, God will offer a sacrifice of men for animals.

¶17. And I saw one angel standing in the sun, and he cried out with a loud voice, saying to all the birds that fly in the midst of heaven, "Come! Gather together for God's great banquet,

18. that *you* may eat the flesh of kings, and the flesh of commanders, and the flesh of mighty men, and the flesh of horses and those who sit on them, and the flesh of all men, free as well as slaves, both small and great!"

Ezekiel revealed more of what God will command this angel to say: "Thus says the Lord GOD: Tell every sort of bird and every wild beast, 'Assemble and come! Gather from all around to my sacrifice that I am making for *you*, a great sacrifice on the mountains of Israel! And *you* will eat flesh and drink blood. *You* will eat the flesh of mighty men, and *you* will drink the blood of princes of the earth, all of them. And at my sacrifice which I am making for *you*, *you* will eat fat until *you* are full, and *you* will drink blood until *you* are drunk. And at my table, *you* will be filled with horse and charioteer, mighty men, and all men of war'" (Ezek. 39:17–20). God even told the Beast himself that He would do this to him, though the Beast will not know it: "I will cause you to come against the mountains of Israel, and then I will strike your bow out of your left hand, and make your arrows drop from your right hand. Upon the mountains of Israel will you fall, you and all your hordes, and the peoples who are with you. I will give you as food to predatory birds of all kinds and to the beast of the field. You will fall in the open field, for I have spoken, says the Lord GOD. I will send a fire upon Gog [Ezekiel's name for the Beast and his army], and upon those who inhabit the isles, for a sacrifice, and they shall know that I am the LORD" (Ezek. 39:2b–6).

The Battle of Armageddon

¶19. Then I saw the Beast, and the kings of the earth, and their armies gathered to make war against him who sat on the horse, and against his army.

20a. And the Beast was taken, and with him the False Prophet who performed the miraculous signs in his

**presence, by which he deceived those who had re-
ceived the mark of the Beast and who worshipped his
image.**

Three times previously (Rev. 14:17–20; 16:12–16; 17:12–14),
John spoke of the Battle of Armageddon as if it will be a major
event, but here, when it finally takes place, John says very little
about it. Again, we find much more information about an end-time
event from Israel's prophets than we do from John.

According to Isaiah, the Beast will at first exalt himself and act
bravely toward the man coming down from heaven, but then he
will realize he has no hope of victory and will flee in terror:
"Though he curse at him, yet he will take flight for a distant place,
but he will be chased like chaff on the hills before the wind, and
like whirling dust before a tempest" (Isa. 17:13b). "And it shall
come to pass in that day that the LORD will punish the army of the
exalted one by the Exalted One, and *punish* the kings of the earth
on the earth" (Isa. 24:21).

The battle is over quickly. Of the swiftness of Jesus' victory,
Isaiah prophesied: "The multitude of your intruders will become
like fine dust, and the multitude of ruthless men like chaff drifting
away. And it will happen in an instant – suddenly! You will be
visited by[52] the LORD of Hosts with thunder, and an earthquake,
and a loud noise of wind, and a tempest, and the flame of a devouring fire. And the multitude of all the nations that wage war against
[Jerusalem] will be like a dream, a vision in the night. . . . So will
the multitude of all the nations be that wage war against Mount
Zion" (Isa. 29:5–7, 8b). "In the evening, behold, terror! Before
morning, he is no more! This will be the portion of those looting
us and the lot of those plundering us" (Isa. 17:14).

The Beast Will Not Go to Hell

**20b. Those two [the Beast and the False Prophet] were
thrown alive into the Lake of Fire that burns with sulfur.**

---

[52] Or, "from *one* with".

Since the beginning of time, sinners have gone to hell when they die instead of to the Lake of Fire. There in hell, they languish in torment, awaiting the Final Judgment when they will be cast into the burning Lake. The Beast and the False Prophet are unique in that God will cast them into the Lake of Fire without them first dying and going to hell, and they will be the first of all God's creatures to be cast into that horrible place.

A River of Blood

21. And the rest were slain by the sword of him who sat on the horse, which *sword* came out of his mouth, and all the birds were gorged with their flesh.

"And this is the plague with which the LORD will strike all the nations who make war against Jerusalem: He will make their flesh rot away while they are standing on their feet, and their eyes to rot away in their sockets, and their tongue to rot away in their mouth. And the plague of the horse, the mule, the camel, the ass, and every animal in those camps will be like this plague" (Zech. 14:12, 15). The slaughter of men and animals will be so great that blood will flow approximately four feet deep for two hundred miles across the land (Rev. 14:20). "All who are angry with you will be ashamed and confounded. They will be as nothing, and the men who contend with you will perish. You will seek them, but you will not find them. The men who strove with you shall be as nothing, and the men who made war against you, as though they had not been" (Isa. 41:11–12).

An Unpleasant Surprise

Up to the moment Jesus comes down and intervenes, the invaders' victory will appear to be assured. Ignorant of God's ultimate purpose, the Jews will be greatly surprised at the turn of events. Through Micah, God told Israel, "Many nations will have assembled against you who were saying, 'Let her be defiled, and let our eyes look on Zion!' But they will not know the LORD's thoughts, and they will not understand His purpose, that He has gathered them like a sheaf to the threshing floor" (Mic. 4:11–12).

Habakkuk glorified the LORD for His victory over the Beast. "In fury, you marched through the land. In anger, you threshed nations. You went forth to save your people, to save them with your Messiah" (Hab. 3:12–13a).

In veiled language, God promised that He would "gather all nations and tongues, and they will come and see my glory" (Isa. 66:18b), but the glory which the nations see will not make them happy, for the glory will be Jesus' sudden and bloody triumph over them. Nevertheless, according to God's enigmatic promise, those nations will see it.

From the South

At some point in this brief battle, for reasons unknown to us, Jesus will go toward the south, but then return (Zech. 9:14). His return northward is mentioned a few times by the prophets: "God came from Teman, and the Holy One from Mount Paran. His majesty covered the heavens, and his praise filled the earth, and *his* brightness was like the dawn. Before him went a plague, and a flame went before his feet. He stood still and shook the earth;[53] he looked and dispersed the nations" (Hab. 3:3–4a, 5–6a). And in the book of Deuteronomy, we find this prophecy from Moses: "The LORD came from Sinai, and appeared to them from Seir. He shone forth from Mount Paran. From His right hand came the Holy One with myriads; fire was his mandate" (Dt. 33:2).

The Father will then playfully give Jesus an opportunity to boast of his triumph by asking His Son, "Who is this coming from Edom, from Bozrah in red-stained garments, this man glorious in his apparel, marching in his mighty strength?" (Isa. 63:1a).

To which Jesus will gleefully respond, "It is I, who speaks in righteousness, mighty to save!" (Isa. 63:1b).

The Father, again: "How is it that there is red on your apparel, like a treader in a winepress?" (Isa. 63:2).

Jesus: "I have trodden the winepress. I trod them down in my anger and trampled them in my rage; their lifeblood spattered on my garments, and all my raiment was sullied. For the day of

---

[53] Possibly, "surveyed the land". Hebrew uncertain.

vengeance was in my heart, and the year of my redeemed ones had come. I trampled down the nations in my anger; I made them drunk with my rage, and I brought down their lifeblood to the earth" (Isa. 63:3a, 4, 6).

Then the Father and the Son will probably laugh together.

The Jews Join the Fight

Jesus will not only thrash the armies of the Gentiles throughout the land of Israel (Isa. 27:12a), but he will also surprise the Jews by calling on them to join him in thrashing them, and Jesus will give the weary Jews renewed strength to do it: "O daughter of Zion, rise and thresh! For I will make your horn iron, and I will make your hooves brass, that you might crush many peoples" (Mic. 4:13a). "On that day will I make the leaders of Judah like a furnace among trees, and like a flaming torch among sheaves. To the right and to the left, they will devour all the encircling nations. He who is feeble among them will be like David, and the house of David will be like gods, with the likeness of the angel of the LORD before them" (Zech. 12:6a, 8b). "The least one will become like a thousand, and the insignificant one, like a mighty nation" (Isa. 60:22a). "They will be like the mighty in battle, trampling *the enemy* in the mud of the streets. They will wage war because the LORD is with them" (Zech. 10:5a). God will further facilitate the victory of the Jews by causing confusion and fear among the Gentiles. "In that day, there will be great turmoil among them from the LORD; each man will seize his neighbor's portion, and his hand will rise up against his neighbor's hand" (Zech. 14:13).

As Joel said, the Beast's soldiers will be powerful "like horses, and they run like steeds" (Joel 2:4), but Zechariah said that the Jews "will make the horsemen ashamed" (Zech. 10:5b). "*You will* tread down the wicked; they will be ashes under the soles of *your* feet in the day that I am preparing, says the LORD of Hosts" (Mal. 4:3). "Yea, Judah will do battle at Jerusalem, and the wealth of all the surrounding nations will be gathered: gold, and silver, and clothing, very much" (Zech. 14:14), "and I will devote their unjust gain to the LORD, and their wealth to the Lord of all the earth" (Mic. 4:13b).

The Land of Israel Is Cleansed of All Evildoers

When Jesus has destroyed the Beast and his armies, he will have completed a thorough cleansing of the land of Israel, a cleansing of both the Beast and the ungodly among the Jews: "For the terrifying man will have come to nothing, and the scorner will have come to an end, and all will have been cut off who look for wickedness, who make a man a sinner because of a word, and lay a trap for the judge in the gate, and by false pretense defraud the righteous man" (Isa. 29:20–21).

Jesus Reveals Himself to the Jews

At the conclusion of the Battle of Armageddon, the Jews will humbly draw near their mysterious, mighty Deliverer from heaven. Someone among them will notice, with great wonder, that the Deliverer's hands have deep scars in them. Who could have inflicted a wound on such a supernatural being? "And one will say to him, 'What are these wounds in your hands?' And he will answer, 'Those with which I was wounded in the house of my friends'" (Zech. 13:6). The wounds are marks from Jesus' crucifixion, and upon hearing his answer, any doubts about who the Deliverer is will disappear. Moreover, the Jews will realize that the wounds in his hands are proofs of his profound love for them. He may even repeat what he said to them through Isaiah, "I have engraved you upon the palms of *my* hands" (Isa. 49:16a), and explain to them that it was God, not the Romans, who had him crucified so that their sins could be washed away. Speaking through Zechariah, the Father plainly took credit for Jesus' crucifixion scars, saying, "I will engrave *his* engraving, and I will take away the iniquity of that land in one day" (Zech. 3:9).

Young Joseph: A Figure of Jesus

The story of Joseph is a prophetic shadow of this holy moment. From it, we learn what the rest of this conversation between Jesus and the Jews will be like. Joseph's envious brothers sold him into slavery when he was just seventeen years old, thinking to be forever rid of him. Jesus was likewise envied by his kinsmen (Mk.

15:9–10), and when he was killed, they, like Joseph's brothers, thought they were rid of him forever.   God miraculously raised Joseph up from prison, and Pharaoh made him ruler over Egypt, under himself.   Pharaoh told Joseph, "Without you, no man will lift his hand or his foot in all the land of Egypt" (Gen. 41:44).   Likewise, God miraculously raised Jesus up from the dead and made him ruler of all creation, under Himself.   Without Jesus, no one can so much as move a finger; indeed, without him, the universe would collapse into turmoil, for "all things are held together by him" (Col. 1:17).   When Joseph's brothers saw him again, many years after they thought they were rid of him, they did not recognize him (Gen. 42:8), and when the Jews see Jesus again, they will not recognize him, either (Zech. 13:6).   Nor did Joseph's brothers know how much Joseph loved them and wanted to take them under his wing; likewise, the surviving Jews will not know how much Jesus loves them and wants to take them under his wing (cf. Mt. 23:37; Lk. 13:34).

After Joseph rescued his brothers and their families from certain death, he told them who he was.   At that, they were terrified because (1) they knew beyond all doubt that they were worthy of death, and (2) they knew beyond all doubt that their lives were altogether in Joseph's hands (Gen. 45:3).   Likewise, after Jesus rescues Israel from certain death, he will tell the Jews who he is, and they, too, will know that they are worthy of death and that their lives are altogether in his hands.   Joseph responded kindly to his terrified brothers and asked them to please come near him, "and he kissed all his brothers and wept over them" (Gen. 45:15), and Jesus will speak kindly to the surviving Jews, and will no doubt weep again for them as he did the first time the Father sent him to Israel (Lk. 19:41).

Joseph explained to his brothers that God was responsible for all the things that he suffered, and he pleaded with them, "Don't be sorry, and don't be angry with *you*rselves, that *you* sold me here. God sent me ahead of *you* to preserve a remnant on the earth for *you* and to bring about a great deliverance for *you*" (Gen. 45:5, 7). Jesus likewise said that his sufferings had been determined for him by God (Mt. 16:21–23; Jn. 18:11).   Joseph tried to comfort his brothers by assuring them that although they "meant to do evil to me, God meant it for good, in order to save the lives of many people, as it is this day" (Gen. 50:20). Jesus will need to say such comforting things to the Jews, for they will be deeply grieved with themselves and with their fathers for the blindness of their heart.

After his resurrection, Jesus opened the eyes of his disciples to the scriptures so they could see that the ancient prophets spoke of him (Lk. 24:27; cf. Lk. 1:69–70). Now, at his Second Coming, he will open the eyes of the surviving Jews, and they will see that God sent Jesus to suffer and die to save them from sin, just as He had sent him now to rescue them from the Beast and to bring about the promises spoken by the prophets.

Israel Repents

With their hearts now in awe of the Son of God whom their nation had long rejected, the Jews will be granted repentance. This is the day Jeremiah saw coming, when "the people who survived the sword found grace", for Jesus will come "to give Israel rest" (Jer. 31:2). "And I will pour out on the house of David and on the inhabitant of Jerusalem the spirit of grace and of supplication, and they will look upon me whom they pierced. And they will mourn for him as one mourns for an only son, bitterly crying out for him as one would bitterly cry out for a firstborn. The wailing in Jerusalem that day will be great" (Zech. 12:10–11a). "The children of Israel will repent and seek the LORD their God and David their King.[54] Yea, in the latter days, they will come in fear to the LORD and to His Good One" (Hos. 3:5).

Washed from Blood-Guiltiness

To the Jews' terror and desperate cries for help against the Beast, God's response had been to send Jesus from heaven to save them. Now, to their remorse and submission to His Son, God's response will be to pour out His Spirit on them and cleanse their souls from sin. "In that day, there will be a fountain opened for the

---

[54] In prophecies related to the end times, Jesus is often referred to as "David" instead of "the son of David".

house of David and the inhabitants of Jerusalem for sin and un-cleanness" (Zech. 13:1), "and I will forgive their blood-guiltiness which I had not forgiven" (Joel 3:21a).

The blood-guiltiness of which Joel the prophet spoke is the blood-guiltiness for which Israel asked when they demanded that the reluctant Pontius Pilate crucify Jesus, saying, "His blood be on us and on our children!" (Mt. 27:25b). Pilate resisted the Jews' call for Jesus' execution because he perceived that Jesus was innocent and that the Jews were accusing Jesus because they envied him (Mt. 27:18; Mk. 15:10). However, at length, he caved in to pres-sure from them and granted their demand – but only after he "took water and washed his hands before the crowd, saying, 'I am inno-cent of the blood of this righteous man!'" (Mt. 27:24b).

The kind of water Pilate used that day to wash his hands of Jesus' blood can never wash away the guilt of Jesus' blood from the hands of the Jews, but God's kind of water can, and after He pours out from heaven the living water of the holy Spirit upon the surviving Jews, "he who is left in Zion and he who remains in Jerusalem will be called holy, everyone who is written among the living in Jerusalem, when the Lord has washed away the filth of the daughters of Zion and cleansed the blood-guiltiness of Jerusalem from her midst" (Isa. 4:3–4a). After this glorious event, Jesus will say to the Jews, "I have blotted out your transgressions as with a cloud, and your sins as with a thick cloud. Return to me, for I have redeemed you!" (Isa. 44:22). And then he will invite all of creation to rejoice with him: "Shout for joy, O heavens, for the LORD has done it! Shout, O lower parts of the earth! Break out in praise, O mountains! Forest, and every tree in it! For the LORD has redeemed Jacob and glorified Himself in Israel!" (Isa. 44:23).

The Aftermath of Armageddon

Jesus' destruction of the armies of the Beast will leave an enormous amount of debris that will have to be cleaned up. Body parts and pieces of military equipment will be so widely strewn in the valleys and on the hills that the Jews will have to labor seven months to clean up their land: "It shall come to pass on that day that I will give to Gog a place for burial there in Israel, the valley of those who pass by, east of the sea, and it will stop those who pass by.[55] And they will bury Gog and all his multitude there, and they will call it 'The Valley of Hamon-Gog' "[56] (Ezek. 39:11). "Their dead will be cast out; the stench of their corpses will rise; and the mountains will be drenched with their blood" (Isa. 34:3). "And for seven months, the house of Israel will be burying them to purify the land, and all the people of the land will do the burying. And the day I glorify myself will be a memorable day for them, declares the Lord GOD" (Ezek. 39:12–13).

After those seven months, workers will be appointed to complete the cleanup, and it will take them seven years to find and pick up all the remains of the Beast's army: "They will designate men who will pass through the land on a regular basis, burying the trespassers that remain on the face of the land, to purify it. At the end of the seven months, they will begin to search. And when those who pass through the land go over it and see a human bone, one will put up a marker beside it until the buriers bury it in the Valley of Hamon-Gog. Thus will they cleanse the land" (Ezek. 39:14–15, 16b). So much equipment will be left by the slain soldiers that it will provide fuel for fires in Israel for the duration of those seven years: "Those who live in the cities of Israel will go out and make fires with the weaponry and will burn it: bucklers and shields, bows and arrows, clubs and spears. And they will make fires with them seven years. They will not pick up wood from the fields nor cut wood out of the forests, for they will make fires with the weaponry. And they will spoil those who were spoiling them, and they will plunder those who were plundering them, declares the Lord GOD" (Ezek. 39:9–10).

---

[55] Isaiah 34:3 and Joel 2:20 imply that what stops those who pass that way is the stench of rotting corpses.

[56] Or, "Multitude of Gog".

A New Covenant with Israel[57]

This will be a very happy day, for the precious promises God made to Israel long ago will be fulfilled, such as this: "I will pour out my Spirit on your seed, and my blessing on your offspring" (Isa. 44:3b). And this: "I will make a new covenant with the house of Israel and with the house of Judah, not the kind of covenant that I made with their fathers in the day I took their hand to lead them out of the land of Egypt, my covenant which they broke, even though I was their Husband, says the LORD. For this is the covenant that I will make with the house of Israel after those days, says the LORD: I will put my law within them, and I will engrave it on their heart. And I will be their God, and they will be my people. And they will no longer teach, each his fellow and each his brother, saying, 'Know the LORD!' For they will all know me, from the least of them even to the greatest, says the LORD. For I will forgive their iniquity, and I will remember their sin no more" (Jer. 31:31–34). "And from that day forward shall the house of Israel know that I, the LORD, am their God" (Ezek 39:22), for "I will no longer hide my face from them when I have poured out my Spirit upon the house of Israel, says the Lord GOD" (Ezek. 39:29). "In those days and at that time, says the LORD, the iniquity of Israel will be sought, but it will not be there, and the sins of Judah will not be found, for I will forgive those whom I spare" (Jer. 50:20). "Behold, it is coming, and it shall be done, declares the Lord GOD, this day of which I have spoken" (Ezek 39:8).

The Jews Will Forget Moses' Law

"And it shall come to pass in those days, says the LORD, that they will no longer say, 'The ark of the covenant of the LORD!' It will not come to mind, neither will they remember it, nor will they miss it, nor will it be made again. At that time, they will call

---

[57] God did not make a New Covenant with the Gentiles; the New Covenant was made with Israel to replace the old one that God had made with Israel at Mount Sinai. When the Jews rejected the New Covenant, God offered it to the Gentiles instead. Now, in John's vision, God calls Israel back to the New Covenant that their fathers once rejected.

Jerusalem, 'The LORD's throne', and all the nations will be gathered to it, to Jerusalem, to the Name of the LORD, and they will no longer walk after the stubbornness of their evil heart" (Jer. 3:16–17). The Jews will finally understand that for their fathers to have continued practicing the law after the Son of God suffered and died for their sins was to commit sacrilege, as Isaiah boldly foretold: "Slaughtering one of the herd *will be like* killing a man; sacrificing one of the flock, *like* breaking a dog's neck; offering up a gift, *like offering up* blood from a pig; burning incense, *like* blessing an idol" (Isa. 66:3a).

When the Jews rejected the Son of God, they were turned over by God to bondage to the very law He had given them for their blessing. God had warned them that He would curse their blessings and smear filth on their faces if they rejected the truth, explaining that He was speaking of the filth of the sacrifices which the law commanded: "I will curse your blessings. Behold, I will smear dung on *your* faces, the dung of your festival sacrifices, and one will lift up *your* faces to it" (Mal. 2:2a, 3). And when the resurrected Son returned to heaven and made his sacrifice for sin, he asked the Father to do just that: "Let their table [in the temple] be a snare before them, and the things they are content with [the law], a trap" (Ps. 69:22). But after Jesus pours out the Spirit on them, Israel will no longer be proud of the law God gave them; instead, they will leave it behind and humbly worship God as He demands to be worshipped, that is, in spirit and in truth (Jn. 4:23–24).

The Jews in those days will feel just as Paul felt after he came to know the glory of Christ: "I consider all things but loss for the surpassing value of the knowledge of Christ Jesus my Lord, for whose sake I have suffered the loss of everything. But I consider *it all* garbage, that I might gain Christ" (Phip. 3:8). Compared to Christ, all earthly things, including Moses' law, is worthless trash, and the Jews of that time will come to know that.

The Jews Will Never Turn from God Again

With Israel purged of every ungodly soul, her union with God will endure. "I will betroth you to me forever," God said. "Yea, I will betroth you to me in righteousness, and in judgment, and in lovingkindness, and in compassions. I will betroth you to me in faithfulness, and you will come to know the LORD" (Hos. 2:19–20). "My Spirit that is upon you, and my words that I put in your mouth, will not depart from your mouth, nor from the mouth of your children, nor from the mouth of your children's children, says the LORD, from that time, and forever" (Isa. 59:21b). "And I will make a covenant of peace with them. It will be an everlasting covenant with them, and I will establish them and multiply them, and I will put my sanctuary in their midst forever. Then my tabernacle will be with them, and I will be their God, and they will be my people" (Ezek. 37:26–27). "For this is as the waters of Noah to me, concerning which I swore, 'The waters of Noah will *never* again overflow the earth.' Likewise do I swear that I will be angry no more with you, nor rebuke you. For the mountains may depart, and the hills may be shaken, but my lovingkindness will not depart from you, and my covenant of peace will not be shaken, says the LORD, the One who pities you" (Isa. 54:9–10).

Micah exulted in God's promised blessing of Israel: "Who is a God like you, taking away iniquity and passing over the transgression of the remnant of His inheritance! He will not retain His anger forever because He delights in kindness. He will relent; He will have compassion on us; He will subdue our iniquities" (Mic. 7:18–19a). But Micah then stopped speaking *about* the Father, and spoke directly *to* Him: "You will cast all their sins into the depths of the sea! You will show truth to Jacob and kindness to Abraham, as you swore to our fathers in days of old!" (Mic. 7:19b–20).

Revelation 20[58]

Satan is Bound in the Abyss

¶1. And I saw an angel coming down out of heaven, having the key to the Abyss and a great chain in his hand.

---

[58] For the next few verses, we return to our previous format of adding explanatory notes after the verses.

Note: Since this angel comes down from heaven, he cannot be Apollyon, the fallen angel who opened the shaft of the Abyss in Revelation 9, for Apollyon had already been cast out.

2. **And he seized the Dragon, that ancient serpent, who is the Devil, and Satan, who deceives the whole world, and he bound him a thousand years.**
3. **And he threw him into the Abyss and locked it, and set a seal upon it so that he would no longer deceive the nations until the thousand years were ended. Afterward, he must be released for a short time.**

Note 1: Satan is thrown neither into hell nor into the Lake of Fire, but into the Abyss because creatures in the Abyss come back to earth again, and God is not at this point finished using Satan.

Note 2: Throughout man's history, Satan and his angels have ruled over the kingdoms of man (cf. Dan. 10:20–21; 12:1). When Satan is thrown into the Abyss for a thousand years, we are not told that Satan's angels are removed from their earthly offices and thrown into the Abyss with him. During the Millennial Reign, the saints will rule over the earth with Jesus, which means that if the angels that rule over the nations now are not thrown into the Abyss with Satan, they will be under the authority of the saints. This will not present the saints with a problem, for being in spiritual bodies, they will be able to see all the angels, both the good and the bad, and will have authority with Christ to deal with them as their masters. This may be what the apostle Paul was referring to when he said that the saints will not only rule over the world but will also rule over angels (1Cor. 6:2–3).[59]

It stands to reason that if the ruler of demons is kept in prison until God visits him and releases him for a short time, then his followers will be imprisoned, too. That scenario seems consistent with this prophecy from Isaiah concerning the end of the world: "It shall come to pass in that day that the LORD will punish the army

---

[59] God's children have a higher rank in His kingdom than all the angels, whether fallen or faithful. The apostle Paul spoke as if this was common knowledge among believers.

of the exalted one [the Beast] by the Exalted One [Christ] and punish the kings of the earth on the earth. And they shall be gathered together as a prisoner in the Pit, and they shall be shut up in prison, and after many days, they will be visited" (Isa. 24:21–22).

Still, we are not told plainly what will happen to Satan's angels when he is cast into the Abyss. If they remain in their offices over the nations of earth, they will be compelled by the power of Christ to do as he commands. And at the end of the thousand years, when Satan is released from the Abyss, his angels will welcome his return and eagerly join the world's rebellion against Christ.

Chapter 8
The Millennial Reign
Revelation 20:4–10

Behold, a King will reign in righteousness,
and princes will rule justly.
Isaiah 32:1

Jesus Will Reign on Earth a Thousand Years

¶4. And I saw thrones, and they sat on them, and judgment was given to them, and *I saw* the souls of those who were beheaded because of the testimony of Jesus and because of the word of God, and those who had not worshipped the Beast or his image and had not received the mark on their forehead or on their hand. And they came to life and reigned with Christ a thousand years.

5. (But the rest of the dead did not come to life until the thousand years were ended.) This is the first resurrection.[60]

6. Blessed and holy is he who has part in the first resurrection; over these, the Second Death[61] has no power, but they will be priests of God and of Christ, and they will reign with him a thousand years.

---

[60] The first resurrection took place in chapter 14 when Jesus appeared on a cloud and harvested the saints from the earth. John is referring to that event. Here, he is only saying that those who are in the first resurrection will reign with Christ.

[61] See footnote 7, page 27.

The Father's Joy

The Father's joy at giving His Son rule over the earth is evident in what He said about it through the prophets: "I will bring to pass the good word which I have declared concerning the house of Israel and concerning the house of Judah. I will cause David's righteous Branch to come up, and he will execute justice and righteousness on earth" (Jer. 33:14–15). "In righteousness will he judge the poor and reprove with equity on behalf of the oppressed of the earth. He will smite the earth with the rod of his mouth, and with the breath of his lips will he slay the wicked. Righteousness will be a girdle for his loins, and faithfulness, his waist belt" (Isa. 11:4–5). "He will judge the poor among the people; he will deliver the children of the needy and crush the oppressor. All kings will bow down before him. All nations will serve him" (Ps. 72:4, 11). "He will deal wisely and will execute justice and righteousness in the earth" (Jer. 23:5). "He will bring forth justice to the nations. He will not fail, nor be discouraged, until he has established justice on the earth, and the isles will wait for his law" (Isa. 42:1b, 4).

Princes Will Rule with Christ

In a message to one of the pastors in Asia, Jesus promised that faithful saints would reign with him (Rev. 2:26–27a). The princes whom Isaiah said will reign with Christ (Isa. 32:1) are the believers who were caught up to heaven in the first resurrection and who later returned to earth with him when he came to save the Jews from the Beast. The Psalmist foretold this when he said, "He [is coming] to judge the earth. He will judge the world in righteousness, and with upright men will He judge the nations" (Ps. 98:9). He went on to describe the saints' authority this way: "To execute vengeance among the Gentiles, reproofs among the nations; to bind their kings with chains and their nobles with fetters of iron; to execute upon them the judgment written – this honor belongs to all His saints" (Ps. 149:7–9).

An Eternal Dominion

In his vision of the end-times, Daniel saw that the reign of Christ will continue forever, after his thousand-year reign on earth. "In the visions of the night, I was there, watching, and behold, one like a son of man [Jesus] was coming with the clouds of heaven, and he approached the Ancient of Days [the Father], and they ushered him in before Him. And dominion was given to him, and majesty, and a kingdom. And all peoples, nations, and languages will serve him. His dominion will be an eternal dominion that shall not pass away, and his kingdom shall not be destroyed" (Dan. 7:13–14). Then Daniel was told that the saints will reign forever with him: "The saints of the Most High will receive the kingdom. And the sovereignty, and dominion, and greatness of the kingdoms under the whole heaven was given to the people, the saints of the Most High. And they will take possession of the kingdom forever, even forever and ever" (Dan. 7:18a, 27, 18b).

Authority According to Ability

Jesus emphasized in a parable that the authority given to individual saints during the Millennial Reign, and beyond, will be determined by the ability each has demonstrated in this life. "A certain nobleman was going to a distant country to receive a kingdom for himself, and then return. And he called ten of his servants and gave them ten minas, and he told them, 'Take care of things until I come.' And it came to pass that when he returned from receiving the kingdom, he commanded that those servants be called to him, the ones to whom he had given the money, to find out who had gained what by trading. And the first arrived and said, 'Master, your mina has earned ten minas.' And he said to him, 'Well done, good servant! Since you have been faithful with a little, you are to have authority over ten cities.' Then the second came and said, 'Master, your mina has made five minas.' And he said to him, 'You are to be over five cities'" (Lk. 19:12–13, 15–19).

All the saints who return to earth to reign with Jesus will be appointed to their stations around the world; however, very little is written about their specific activities during the Millennial Reign.

On the other hand, the prophets said much about what Jesus will do in Israel. From that, it seems reasonable to conclude that God's principal focus will be on restoring and blessing the Jews.

Jews from All Nations Will Come to Israel

The Son of God will spare some of the Beast's army and send them back home to tell their respective countries about his triumph over the mighty Beast: "I will send some of the survivors to the nations, the distant coasts that have not heard the news about me and who did not see my glory, and they will proclaim my glory among the Gentiles" (Isa. 66:19). But in addition to reporting his triumph, these messengers will also carry a command from King Jesus for the nations to bring the Jews who live in their countries home to Israel. "Hear, O Gentiles, the word of the LORD! Let them proclaim it in the distant isles and say, 'He who scattered Israel will gather him, and He will watch over him as a shepherd does his flock,' for the LORD has ransomed Jacob and has redeemed him from the hand of him that was stronger than he" (Jer. 31:10–11). "I will say to the north, 'Give them up!' and to the south, 'Do not withhold them! Bring my sons from afar and my daughters from the ends of the earth – each one who is called by my name, and whom I created for my glory! I formed him! Yea, I made him!'" (Isa. 43:6–7). "And they will bring all *your* brothers from all the nations as a grain offering to the LORD, on horses, and by chariots, and in wagons, and on mules, and on camels to my holy mountain, Jerusalem, says the LORD" (Isa. 66:20a).

The Third Aliyah

An aliyah is a "going up" of the Jews to the land which God promised to Abraham and his descendants. Israel's first aliyah took place when Moses led the Israelites up out of Egypt to go to the land of promise. Israel's second Aliyah took place in the early twentieth century and resulted in the re-establishment of Israel as a nation in 1948. Israel's third aliyah will take place at the beginning of the Millennial Reign, and it will be far greater than the first. "The Lord will extend his hand a second time to redeem the remnant of his people that is left, from Assyria, and from Egypt, and from Pathros, and from Ethiopia, and from Elam, and from Shinar, and from Hamath, and from the coastlands of the sea" (Isa. 11:11). After the massive aliyah that Jesus will bring about, "it will no longer be said, 'As the LORD lives, who brought up the children of Israel from out of the land of Egypt,' but 'As the LORD lives, who brought up the children of Israel out of the land of the north and out of all the countries into which He had driven them.' And I will bring them back to their land which I gave to their fathers" (Jer. 16:14–15).

"For thus says the Lord GOD: I myself will search for my sheep and seek them out. As a shepherd seeks his own flock on a day when he is in the midst of his sheep that are scattered, so will I seek out my sheep and rescue them out of all the places where they were scattered" (Ezek. 34:11–12). "I will seek that which is lost, and bring back that which is cast out, and I will bind up that which is injured, and I will make the weak strong" (Ezek. 34:16a). "I will bring them out from the nations and gather them from the lands, and will bring them to their own land, and I will feed them on the mountains of Israel, by the streams and in all the dwelling places of the country. I will feed them in a good pasture, and their fold will be on the high mountains of Israel; there will they lie down in a good fold, and they will feed in rich pastures upon the mountains of Israel. I myself will feed my sheep, and I will cause them to lie down, says the Lord GOD" (Ezek. 34:13–15). "I will gather them from all the countries to which I banished them in my anger, and in my wrath, and in my great indignation, and I will bring them back to this place and cause them to dwell safely, and they will be my people, and I will be their God" (Jer. 32:37–38).

God Will Give a Signal

The prophets spoke of a signal that God will give to the nations: "He will lift up a signal for the Gentiles, and He will gather the banished men of Israel and assemble the dispersed women of Judah from the four corners of the earth" (Isa. 11:12). God repeatedly said He would do this: "I will lift up my hand to the Gentiles and raise up my signal to the nations, and they will bring your sons in their bosom, and your daughters will be carried on their shoulder" (Isa. 49:22), "and *you* will live in the land that I gave to *your* fathers, and *you* will be my people, and I will be *your* God" (Ezek. 36:28). "I will whistle[62] for them and gather them because I ransomed them. Though I sowed them among the nations, yet in those distant places will they remember me, and they will live and return with their children" (Zech. 10:8a, 9). God's "whistle for them" will be a trumpet blast, probably from one of His angels. Isaiah first mentioned it: "A great trumpet will be sounded, and those who were perishing in the land of Assyria and those who were banished in the land of Egypt will come and worship before the LORD on the holy mountain at Jerusalem" (Isa. 27:13).

God spoke often through the prophets concerning His miraculous gathering of the Jews: "I will rescue my people from the land of the rising sun and from the land of the setting sun. I will cause them to come, and they will dwell in the midst of Jerusalem" (Zech. 8:7–8a). "I will take the children of Israel from among the nations where they have gone, and I will gather them from every direction and bring them into their own land" (Ezek. 37:21). "The isles will gather *them* for me, with ships of Tarshish in the lead, to bring your children from afar, their silver and gold with them, to the Name of the LORD your God, even to the Holy One of Israel, because He will have honored you" (Isa. 60:9).

The Returning Jews Will Repent

The Jews who survive God's sifting among the nations will be as grieved for their former blindness as were the chosen third who survived in the land of Israel and who will have already received the Spirit. Once the Jews in foreign nations hear that Jesus saved Israel and conquered the Beast, said God through Ezekiel, "They will remember me among the nations where they are taken captive, how I was crushed by their whorish heart that turned away from me and by their wanton eyes *that followed* after their idols. And they will loathe themselves because of the evils that they did, and for all their abominations" (Ezek. 6:9). "They will no longer defile

---

[62] Hebrew: "hiss".

themselves with their idols, or with their abominations, or with any of their transgressions, but I will rescue them from all the places they have lived and where they have sinned, and I will purify them. And they will be my people, and I will be their God" (Ezek. 37:23). "I will bring them from the north country, and I will gather them from the far reaches of the earth; a great company will return. With weeping and with supplications will they come" (Jer. 31:8–9a). And knowing now that Jesus is their Messiah, "the children of Israel will come, weeping as they go, and they will seek the LORD their God. They will ask the way to Zion, their faces turned toward it, saying, 'Come! We will join ourselves to the LORD in an eternal covenant that will not be forgotten'" (Jer. 50:4b–5).

The Returning Jews Will Receive the Spirit

When God sent John the Baptist to Israel, he commanded the Jews to prepare to meet the Lord by doing deeds that demonstrated repentance (Mt. 3:8; Lk. 3:8). The Jews returning from the nations will earnestly do such deeds. If anything, they will be even more zealous for righteousness than the Jews who survived the war with the Beast, for these will rid the country of elements of false religion that the chosen third of the Jews in Israel had allowed to remain. "When they arrive, they will take away from the land all its detested things and all its abominations" (Ezek. 11:18).

In response to the sincere repentance of the returning Jews, Jesus will wash them of their sins as he already washed their brethren from theirs who lived within the borders of Israel. "I will cleanse them from all their iniquity whereby they sinned against me, and I will pardon all of their iniquities whereby they have sinned against me and whereby they have transgressed against me" (Jer. 33:8). "I will take *you* from among the Gentiles and gather *you* out of all countries, and I will bring *you* to *your* land and sprinkle clean water upon *you*, and *you* will be clean. And I will cleanse *you* from all *your* uncleanness and from all *your* idols. I will also give *you* a new heart, and I will put a new spirit within *you*. And I will remove the heart of stone from *your* flesh, and I will give *you* a heart of flesh. And I will put my Spirit within *you*, and I will enable *you* to walk according to my statutes and my judgments, and *you* will diligently keep them" (Ezek. 36:24–27).

Christ Will Institute Righteous Government in Israel

"I will restore your judges as at the first, and your counselors as at the beginning.[63]   After that, you will be called, 'The City of Righteousness', a faithful town" (Isa. 1:26). "Though the Lord has given *you* the bread of distress and the water of affliction, your Teacher[64] will no longer hide himself, but your eyes will see your Teacher" (Isa. 30:20). "I will raise up shepherds for them, and they will feed them, and they will no longer be afraid, nor be dismayed, nor will any be missing, says the LORD" (Jer. 23:4). "The voice of your watchmen! They lift up their voice! They cry out as one, for they will see eye to eye when the LORD comes back to Zion" (Isa. 52:8). "And I will make them one nation in the land, on the mountains of Israel. And there will be one King over them all" (Ezek. 37:22a). "Hear, *you* who are far away! And acknowledge my might, *you* who are near. Your eyes will see the King in his beauty" (Isa. 33:13, 17a), "and the LORD will be King over all the earth" (Zech. 14:9a).

God Will Quickly Answer the Jews' Prayers

"O people in Zion, dwelling in Jerusalem, you will never weep again! He will be very gracious to you at the sound of your cry. When He hears it, He will answer you. And your ears will hear a voice behind you, saying, 'This is the way; walk in it,' when *you* go to the right or when *you* go to the left" (Isa. 30:19, 21). "And it shall come to pass that before they cry out, I will answer. While they are yet speaking, I will hear" (Isa. 65:24).

---

[63] God first gave Israel such men after they came out of Egypt, putting His Spirit on seventy leaders of Israel so that they could help Moses (Num. 11:16–17).

[64] Literally, "Teachers". Most translators understand the word "teachers" in this verse to be a "plural of majesty", referring to Jesus as the Teacher of Israel.

Righteousness Will Be Enforced in Israel

When God has cleansed all the Jews from sin by His Spirit, false religion will become a capital offense within the borders of Israel. "I will drive the prophets and the spirit of uncleanness out of the land. And it shall come to pass that if a man prophesies again, then his father, and his mother who bore him, will say to him, 'You shall not live, for you have spoken lies in the name of the LORD!' And his father, and his mother who bore him, will pierce him through while he is prophesying. And it shall come to pass in that day that every one of the prophets will be ashamed of his vision when he tells it. And they will not put on a shaggy cloak to deceive" (Zech. 13:2b–4).

The Son foretold of this purging of the ungodly from the land of Israel: "A perverse heart will depart from me; I will not know an evil person. I will destroy him who slanders his neighbor in secret; him whose eyes are haughty and who has a proud heart, I will not endure. My eyes are on the faithful of the land, that they may dwell with me; he who walks in a perfect way, he will minister to me. The worker of deceit will not dwell in my house; he who speaks lies will not remain in my sight. Morning by morning, I will destroy all evildoers of the land, that I may cut off from the city of GOD all those who do wickedness" (Ps. 101:4–8).

Such will not be the case outside of the land of Israel. Many among the nations will choose to continue worshipping their own way, and they will be allowed to do so. "For all the nations will walk, each one, in the name of its god, but we will walk in the name of the LORD our God forever and ever" (Mic. 4:5).

God's New Covenant with Israel Will Last Forever

"I will make an eternal covenant with them" (Isa. 61:8b), "and I will give them one heart and one way, that they might fear me always, for their good and for the good of their children after them. And I will make an everlasting covenant with them, that I will not turn away from them and cease to do them good, and I will put my fear in their heart so that they do not turn away from me" (Jer.

32:39–40). "And they will walk in my judgments and keep my statutes, and they will do them" (Ezek. 37:24b).

God Will Bless the Jews as Much as He Had Cursed Them

"Because their [65] shame *has been* double, and humiliation was decreed their lot, they will possess double in their land. For I, the LORD, love justice, and I will give them a true recompense" (Isa. 61:7a, 8). "This day," He will say to Israel, "I declare, I will restore to you double!" (Zech. 9:12b), "and it shall come to pass, O house of Judah and house of Israel, that as much as *you* were a curse among the nations, so will I deliver *you*, and *you* will become a blessing. Do not fear! Let *your* hands be strong! For thus says the LORD of Hosts: As much as I purposed to do *you* harm when *your* fathers provoked me to wrath – and I did not relent – so have I purposed to do good in these days to Jerusalem and to the house of Judah. Do not fear!" (Zech. 8:13–15). "As I have watched over them to root out, and to tear down, and to overthrow, and to kill, and to bring evil, so will I watch over them to build up and to plant, says the LORD" (Jer. 31:28). "And I will rejoice over them, to do them good, and in faithfulness will I plant them in this land with all my heart and with all my soul" (Jer. 32:41), "and they will be my people, and I will be their God, in truth and righteousness" (Zech. 8:8b). "In that day you will say, 'I will praise you, O LORD! Though you were angry with me, your anger has turned away, and you are comforting me. Behold, God is my salvation. I will trust, and I will not be afraid, for the Lord GOD is my strength and my song, and He has become my salvation!'" (Isa. 12:1–2).

The Jews Will Be Healed Physically

"No inhabitant will say, 'I am sick.' The people who live in [Zion] will be forgiven of *their* sin" (Isa. 33:24). "I will bring it restoration and healing; I will heal them and reveal to them an abundance of peace and truth" (Jer. 33:6). "The eyes of the blind will be opened, and the ears of the deaf will be unstopped" (Isa. 35:5). "The deaf will hear words of a scroll, and out of dimness

---

[65] Literally, "*your*".

and out of darkness, the eyes of the blind will see. The meek will increase *their* joy in the LORD, and the poor among men will rejoice in the Holy One of Israel" (Isa. 29:18–19). "The lame man will leap like a stag, and the tongue of the dumb man will sing" (Isa. 35:6a). "In that day, says the LORD, I will gather the lame, and gather her who was cast out, and her whom I afflicted, and I will transform the lame into a remnant and her who was scattered afar into a mighty nation, and the LORD will reign over them in Mount Zion from that time and forever" (Mic. 4:6–7).

"There will no longer be an infant there that lives but a few days or an old man who does not fulfill his days. If the young man, even the sinner, dies at a hundred years old, he will have been cursed at a hundred years old. As the days of a tree will be the days of my people" (Isa. 65:20, 22b), "for I will bring you health, and I will heal you of your wounds, says the LORD, because they have called you, 'Outcast Zion, whom no one wants'" (Jer. 30:17).

The Jews Will Be Healed Spiritually

"Those who erred in spirit will come to understanding, and those who grumbled will take in instruction" (Isa. 29:24). "The eyes of those who see will not look away, and the ears of those who hear will give heed. The heart of the hasty will understand and know, and the tongue of stammerers will speak readily and clearly" (Isa. 32:3–4). "All your people will be righteous; they will possess the land forever, the plant of His planting, the work of my hands, that I might glorify myself" (Isa. 60:21).

Jews Will Be Honored by the Gentiles

"I will bring *you* in! And when I gather *you*, I will assuredly give *you* renown and praise among all the peoples of the earth, when I return *your* captivity before *your* eyes, says the LORD" (Zeph. 3:20), "and nations that do not know you will run to you because of the LORD your God, the Holy One of Israel, for He has honored you" (Isa. 55:5b). "And the children of those who are afflicting you will come to you bending low, and all who despise you will bow at the soles of your feet, and they will call you, 'The City of the LORD, Zion of the Holy One of Israel'. Instead of you being forsaken and hated, I will make you an everlasting excellency, a joy from generation to generation" (Isa. 60:14–15).

"Thus says the LORD, the One who ransomed Abraham, to the house of Jacob: Jacob will no longer be ashamed, nor will his face turn pale, for when he sees his children, the work of my hands, in his midst, they will sanctify my name, and they will sanctify the Holy One of Jacob, and will stand in awe of the God of Israel" (Isa. 29:22–23). "Their seed will be of repute among the Gentiles, and their offspring among the nations; all who see them will acknowledge them, that they are the seed that the LORD has blessed" (Isa. 61:9), and "I will cause them to be honored, and they will not be disdained" (Jer. 30:19b).

God Will Never Abase Israel Again

"Thus says the LORD: I will return to Zion, and I will dwell in the midst of Jerusalem. Jerusalem will be called 'The City of Truth', and 'The Mountain, the Holy Mountain, of the LORD of Hosts'" (Zech. 8:3). "You will no longer be thought of as forsaken, and your land will no longer be considered a desolation, but you will be called Hephzibah[66], and your land, Beulah[67]. For the LORD delights in you, and your land will be married. And they will call them 'the holy people, redeemed of the LORD', and you will be called 'Wanted', a city not forsaken" (Isa. 62:4, 12). "Do not be afraid, for you will not be ashamed, nor will you be humiliated. You will not be disgraced! On the contrary, you will forget the shame of your youth, and the reproach of your estrangement will you remember no more" (Isa. 54:4). "I will deliver *you* from all *your* uncleanness, and I will summon the grain and multiply it, and I will not give *you* famine. I will make the fruit of the tree and the produce of the field abundant, so that *you* no longer bear the reproach of famine before the Gentiles" (Ezek. 36:29–30).

---

[66] Literally, "My delight is in her."

[67] Literally, "Married".

"Cry out and shout for joy, O inhabitant of Zion, for the Holy One of Israel is exalted in your midst" (Isa. 12:6). "Never again will the destroyer pass through you. He has been utterly cut off!" (Nah. 1:15c). "Be glad and rejoice forever for what I am creating, for behold, I am creating Jerusalem a joy, and her people a delight. And I will rejoice in Jerusalem and delight in my people, and no one will ever hear in her a sound of mourning or a sound of crying" (Isa. 65:18–19). "For as the earth brings forth its shoot, and as a garden causes its seed to sprout, so will the Lord GOD cause righteousness and praise to spring up before all the Gentiles" (Isa. 61:11). "And He will take away the reproach of His people from the whole earth, for the LORD has spoken. And it will be said on that day, 'Behold, this is our God! We have waited for Him, and He has saved us. This is the LORD! We have waited for Him! Let us rejoice and be glad in His salvation!'" (Isa. 25:8b–9).

Israel Will Have Peace and Security

"It shall come to pass on that day, says the LORD of Hosts, that I will break his yoke off your neck, and I will tear apart your fetters" (Jer. 30:8a). "Violence will no longer be heard in your land, nor devastation and destruction within your borders, and you will call your walls 'Salvation' and your gates 'Praise'" (Isa. 60:18). "Foreigners will no longer enslave him, and they will serve the LORD their God and David their King, whom I will raise up for them. Do not be afraid, O Jacob my servant, says the LORD, nor be dismayed, O Israel! I am going to deliver you out of distant places, and your seed from the land of their captivity. Jacob will return and have quiet, and be at ease, and no one will make him afraid" (Jer. 30:8b–10). "And they will dwell in the land that I gave to my servant Jacob, where *your* fathers dwelt; they will dwell in it, they, and their sons, and their son's sons forever, and David my servant will be their prince forever" (Ezek. 37:25). "And they shall know that I, the LORD their God, am with them, and that they, the house of Israel, are my people, says the Lord GOD" (Ezek. 34:30).

"Thus says the Lord GOD: When I have gathered the house of Israel out of the nations where they were scattered, I will sanctify them in the sight of the Gentiles, and they will dwell in their own land, which I gave to my servant Jacob. Yea, they will safely dwell in it and build houses and plant vineyards, and they will dwell safely while I execute judgments upon all those around them who despise them, and they shall know that I am the LORD their God" (Ezek. 28:25–26). "They will rebuild and inhabit cities that were laid waste, and they will plant vineyards and drink their wine, and plant gardens and eat their fruit. And I will plant them in their land, and they will never be uprooted again from their land that I gave them, says the LORD your God" (Amos 9:14b–15). "They will sit, each one, under his vine and under his fig tree, and none will make afraid, for the mouth of the LORD of Hosts has spoken" (Mic. 4:4). "They will build houses and live in them, and they will plant vineyards and eat their fruit. They will not build and another dwell; they will not plant and another eat. My chosen will enjoy the work of their hands" (Isa. 65:21–22). "They will not labor for nothing, and they will not give birth for trouble, for they are the seed blessed of the LORD, and their offspring with them" (Isa. 65:23). "They will be safe on their own land, and they shall know that I am the LORD when I break the bars of their yoke and snatch them out of the hand of those who enslaved them" (Ezek. 34:27b).

"Cry aloud, O daughter of Zion! Shout, O Israel! Be glad and rejoice with all *your* heart, O daughter of Jerusalem! The LORD has done away with your judgments; He has turned away your enemy! The King of Israel, the LORD, is in your midst! You shall not fear evil again! In that day, it shall be said to Jerusalem, 'Do not fear, O Zion! Let not your hands be weak! The LORD, your God in your midst, is mighty. He will save! He will rejoice over you with gladness! He will make *you* quiet in His love! He will rejoice over you with a shout!'" (Zeph. 3:14–17).

A Protective Covering over Jerusalem

Jesus will set above Jerusalem a pillar of a cloud by day and a pillar of fire by night, as God did for the Israelites in the wilderness. He "will create over the whole site of Mount Zion and over her Assemblies a cloud by day and the smoke and brightness of a flaming fire by night, for over all the glory will be a canopy. And it will be a pavilion for shade from the heat by day, and a refuge and shelter from storm and rain" (Isa. 4:5–6). "I, myself, says the LORD, will be a wall of fire all about her, and I will be the glory in her midst" (Zech. 2:5). God will joyfully call out to Israel, "Arise! Shine! For your light has come, and the glory of the LORD has risen upon you! Darkness may cover the earth, and thick darkness the nations, but upon you will the LORD rise, and His glory will be seen over you" (Isa. 60:1–2). "Your eyes will see Jerusalem, an untroubled habitation, an unmoved tent whose stakes will never be pulled up, nor will any of its cords be broken" (Isa. 33:20b).

Jesus Will Rid the Land of Dangerous Beasts

"In that day, I will make a covenant for them with the beasts of the field, and with the birds of the sky, and things that creep on the ground" (Hos. 2:18a). "And I will make for them a covenant of peace so that I rid the land of dangerous beasts, and men will live in the wilderness in safety, and sleep in the woods. They will no longer be a prey for the Gentiles, neither will the beast of the land devour them, but they will live in security, and nothing will make *them* afraid" (Ezek. 34:25, 28). "My people will dwell in a peaceful meadow, and in secure dwellings, and in tranquil resting places" (Isa. 32:18). "The wolf will dwell with the lamb; and the leopard will lie down with the kid; and the calf and the young lion and the fatling will be together; and a little boy will lead them. And the cow and the bear will graze, and their young will lie down together. . . . And the nursing infant will play over the hole of an asp, and the weaned child will put his hand in a viper's den" (Isa. 11:6–8). "The wolf and the lamb will feed together, and the lion will eat straw like the ox, and dust will be the serpent's food.[68] They will neither do harm nor destroy in all my holy mountain, says the LORD" (Isa. 65:25), "for the earth will be filled with the knowledge of the LORD, as the waters cover the sea" (Isa. 11:9b). But God went beyond promising to make dangerous animals harmless; He promised Israel that He would "make them, and the areas around my hill, a blessing" (Ezek. 34:26a).

---

[68] Cf. Genesis 3:14.

The Land Will Be Repopulated

Jesus will pray to the Father for the land of Israel to be repopulated, and his prayer will be heard: "Thus says the Lord GOD: I will be asked this for the house of Israel, to do for them; I will multiply them like a flock of men, like a flock of holy men, like the flock of Jerusalem during her appointed feasts. Thus will desolate cities be filled with a flock of men, and they will know that I am the LORD" (Ezek. 36:37–38). "I will gather the remnant of my sheep out of all the countries to which I drove them, and I will bring them back to their fold, and they will be fruitful and multiply" (Jer. 23:3), "and they will be as many as they used to be" (Zech. 10:8b). "I will bring them back from the land of Egypt and gather them from Assyria, and I will bring them to the land of Gilead and Lebanon until there be found no room for them" (Zech. 10:10).

"Enlarge the place of your tent, and let the curtains of your habitations be stretched! Do not hold back! Lengthen your ropes and strengthen your stakes! For you will break out to the right and to the left, and your seed will possess the nations and populate abandoned cities" (Isa. 54:2–3). "I will cause all the cities to be inhabited, and the waste places will be built" (Ezek. 36:33b), and "Jerusalem will be inhabited *like* unwalled villages because of the abundance of men and animals within her" (Zech. 2:4b). "Thanksgiving and the sound of celebrating will come forth from them, and I will multiply them, and they will not be few" (Jer. 30:19a).

The Land Will Be Healed

"The LORD will comfort Zion; He will comfort all her ruins and make her wilderness like Eden, and her dry plain like the garden of the LORD" (Isa. 51:3a). And like the garden of Eden before the curse, God will make the whole country free of briars and thorns (Ezek. 28:24). "He will give rain for your seed that you sow in the ground, and grain, the produce of the ground, and it will be rich and full, and in that day, your cattle will feed in large pastures, and the oxen and young asses that work the ground will eat seasoned provender that has been winnowed with a winnowing shovel and fork" (Isa. 30:23–24). "Instead of the thornbush will come up the cypress; instead of the nettle will come up the myrtle" (Isa. 55:13a). "The wilderness and the dry place will rejoice, and the desert will shout for joy and bloom like a rose. It will bloom abundantly and shout, for waters will break forth in the wilderness, and streams in the desert. The parched ground will become a pool, and the thirsty land, springs of water" (Isa. 35:1–2a, 6b–7a). "Jacob will take root; Israel will blossom and send out shoots, and they will supply the whole world with produce" (Isa. 27:6).

"And *you*, O mountains of Israel, *you* will put forth *your* branches and yield *your* fruit for my people Israel when they are about to come. For, behold, I am for *you*, and I will turn to *you*, and *you* will be tilled and sown. And I will multiply men upon *you*, all the house of Israel – all of it! – and the cities will be inhabited, and the desolate places will be built. I will certainly multiply man and beast upon *you*, and they will multiply and bear fruit. And I will settle *you* as in *your* former times, and I will do *you* more good than at the first, and *you* will know that I am Jehovah. I will cause men to walk over *you*, even my people Israel, and they will possess you, and you will be their inheritance, and you will never again be bereaved of them. Thus says the Lord GOD: Because they say to *you*, 'You, *O land*, are a devourer of men and a bereaver of your own nation.' Therefore, you will no longer devour men or again bereave your own nation, says the Lord GOD. Neither will I cause the invective of the heathen against you to be heard any longer, nor will you bear the reproach of the nations, nor will you bring ruin to your nation again, says the Lord GOD" (Ezek. 36:8–15).

"And I will send down the rain in its season. There will be showers of blessing, and the tree of the field will yield its fruit, and the land will yield its increase" (Ezek. 34:26b–27a). "I will send *you* the grain, the wine, and the oil, and *you* will overflow with it. And I will not make *you* a reproach among the Gentiles again" (Joel 2:19b). "I will cause acclaimed crops to come up for them so that they no longer waste away with famine in the land and never again bear the reproach of the Gentiles" (Ezek. 34:29), "and the fruit of the land will be the pride and glory of the survivors in Israel" (Isa. 4:2b). "I will open up rivers in high places, and fountains in the midst of valleys. I will make the wilderness a pool of water, and the dry land, springs of water. I will plant cedar, acacia, and myrtle, and olive trees in the wilderness. I will set in the desert plain the cypress, the plane-tree, and the box tree together, that they may all see, and realize, and consider, and understand that the hand of the LORD has done this, and the Holy One of Israel has brought it to pass" (Isa. 41:18–20). "And it will be for the LORD's acclaim, an everlasting sign that shall not be cut off" (Isa. 55:13b).

"I will rebuke the devourer for *your* sakes, and he will not destroy the fruit of *your* ground. Neither will *your* vine in the field lose its fruit. All nations will call *you* blessed, for *you* will become a delightful land, says the LORD of Hosts" (Mal. 3:11–12). "The land that was made desolate will be worked instead of being the desolation that it was. And they will say, 'This land that was made desolate has become like the garden of Eden! And the cities that were laid waste, and made desolate, and left in ruins are unassailable and inhabited!' And the nations around *you* that are left will know that I, the LORD, have rebuilt the places that were thrown down, and I have planted the desolated place. I, the LORD, have spoken, and I will do it!" (Ezek. 36:34–36). Those living in Israel at that time will rejoice at the fulfillment of David's prophecy: "Mercy and truth have met. Righteousness and peace have kissed each other. Truth will spring up from the earth, and righteousness will look down from heaven. Yea, the LORD will grant prosperity, and our land will yield its increase" (Ps. 85:10–12).

The Dead Sea Will Be Healed

God showed Ezekiel a vision of fresh water flowing eastward from the threshold of the temple of God in Jerusalem (Ezek. 47:1), through the valley Jesus made when he descended upon the Mount of Olives. As Ezekiel watched the water flow toward the Dead Sea, an angel spoke to him and said, "These waters are going out toward the eastern region, and they descend to the Arabah, and then they will enter the sea when they have been brought forth to the sea, and *its* waters will be healed. And it shall come to pass that every creature that swarms will live; wherever the streams go,

they will live. And there will be very many fish because these waters went there, and they were healed. Everything lives where the
stream goes in. And it shall come to pass that fishermen will stand
on its *shore*; from En-gedi to En-eglaim will be a place for the
spreading of nets. Their fish will be of very many kinds, like the
fish of the Great Sea" (Ezek. 47:8–10). This fresh water from
Jerusalem will become two streams, one flowing west toward the
Mediterranean, and one toward the Dead Sea: "In that day, living
waters will go out from Jerusalem, half of them to the eastern sea
and half of them to the western sea" (Zech. 14:8a).

The Jews Will Rejoice because of Their Blessings

"The redeemed of the LORD will return and enter into Zion
with singing and eternal joy on their heads. They will obtain gladness and joy, and sorrow and sighing will flee away" (Isa. 35:10).
"They will come forth and shout for joy on the height of Zion, and
they will flow to the goodness of the LORD, for the grain, and new
wine, and fresh oil, and flocks and herds. Their souls will be like a
watered garden, and they will never languish again. Then the virgin, together with the young and old men, will rejoice in the dance,
for I will have turned their mourning into joy, and I will comfort
them and give them joy for their sorrow. And I will satiate the soul
of the priests with abundance, and my people will be sated with my
goodness, says the LORD" (Jer. 31:12–14). "And *Jerusalem* will
give me a reputation for joy, for praise, and for glory before all the
nations of the earth who hear of all the good that I will have done
for them, and they will fear and tremble because of all the good
and because of all the prosperity that I will provide to that *city*"
(Jer. 33:9). "Joy and gladness will be found in her, thanksgiving
and the voice of singing" (Isa. 51:3b).

Even nature will be called upon to rejoice for the superabun-
dant goodness of God that is poured out on His people. "Shout for
joy, O heavens, and rejoice, O earth! Break forth with a shout of
praise, O mountains! For the LORD has comforted His people, and
He will have compassion on His afflicted" (Isa. 49:13). "*You will
come out with joy and be led forth in peace; the mountains and the*

hills will burst out before *you* into singing, and all the trees of the field will clap their hands" (Isa. 55:12).

The Nations Will Serve God

It has been mentioned that God allowed some of the Beast's army to escape death. He did this for at least two reasons: (1) so that the surviving soldiers could return home with the news of Jesus' victory and to deliver to their countries Jesus' command to bring the Jews home, and (2) to give the survivors the opportunity to serve the true God and His chosen people. After the Battle of Armageddon, Jesus will summon the survivors and say, "Assemble and come! Gather *yourselves* together, *you* survivors of the nations! They have no knowledge who raise up their carved image of wood and pray to a god who cannot save. Turn to me and be saved, all ends of the earth! I am God, and there is no other!" (Isa. 45:20, 22). Then the nations will be given a choice: "If they will diligently learn the ways of my people, to swear by my name, 'As the LORD lives', the way they taught my people to swear by Baal, then they will be established in the midst of my people. But if they will not listen, I will utterly pluck up and destroy that nation, says the LORD" (Jer. 12:16–17). Any nation that refuses to serve Jesus and his people will perish; "those nations will be utterly laid waste" (Isa. 60:12).

When the nations hear this, many of them will fear God and humble themselves to Him, as the prophets said: "O LORD! My strength and my stronghold! My refuge in the day of trouble! To you will come nations from the farthest reaches of earth, and they will say, 'Our fathers inherited nothing but falsehood and vanity, and nothing in them is worthwhile'" (Jer. 16:19b). "Nations will come to your light, and kings to the brightness of your rising" (Isa. 60:3). "All nations whom you have made will come and bow down before you, O Lord, and they will glorify your name" (Ps. 86:9).

"My righteousness *will come* near *them*, my salvation will go forth, and my arms will bring justice to the nations. The isles will yearn for me, and they will put their hope in my strength" (Isa. 51:5). "From the rising of the sun until its going down, my name shall be great among the Gentiles! And in every place, incense and a pure offering will be offered to my name" (Mal. 1:11a), "for the earth will be filled with the knowledge of the glory of the LORD, as the waters cover the sea" (Hab. 2:14), "and his dominion will be from sea to sea, and from the river to the ends of the earth" (Zech. 9:10c).

Of the Son, the Father said, "I have appointed him a leader and commander for the peoples" (Isa. 55:4), and "he will rule from sea to sea, and from the river to the ends of the earth. Those who dwell in the desert will bow down to him, and his enemies will lick the dust. Kings of Tarshish and of the isles will render tribute; kings of Sheba and Seba will offer a gift. All kings will bow down before him; all nations will serve him. By him will all nations be blessed, and they will call him blessed" (Ps. 72:8–11, 17b). Then the Father said to the Son, "You will call a nation that you do not know, and nations that do not know you will run to you because of the LORD your God, the Holy One of Israel, for He has honored you" (Isa. 55:5). "Nobles will come from Egypt," said the Psalmist; "Ethiopia will quickly stretch out his hands to God" (Ps. 68:31).

Wars on Earth Will Cease

"A law will go forth from me," the Son of God said through Isaiah, "and my justice, as a light. I will give rest to the nations" (Isa. 51:4b). The "rest" which Jesus will bring to the nations is a rest from the strife and wars which have always existed among them. He will "speak peace to the nations" (Zech. 9:10b) and make "wars to cease to the end of the earth. He will break the bow and cut the spear in pieces; the wagons will He burn with fire" (Ps. 46:9), and in gratitude for this peace, the nations will honor the Lord (Ps. 46:10).

The prophet Micah also foretold of the peace that Jesus will impose upon the world: "The mountain of the house of the LORD will be established as head of the mountains, and it will be exalted above the hills, and nations will stream to it. Many nations will go, and they will say, 'Come, and let us go up to the mountain of the LORD, to the house of the God of Jacob! And He will teach us His ways, and we will walk in His paths.' For from Zion will the law go forth, and the word of the LORD from Jerusalem. And He will judge between many nations, and He will reprove mighty nations that are far off, and they will beat their swords into plowshares and their spears into pruning hooks. Nation will not lift up sword against nation; neither will they learn war any more" (Mic. 4:1–3; cf. Isa. 2:2–4).

The Nations Will Also Serve Israel

"The nations will take [the Jews] and bring them to their place, and the house of Israel will possess them in the LORD's land as slaves, male and female, and they will take them captive whose captives they were, and they will rule over those who oppressed them" (Isa. 14:2). "Strangers will stand and tend *your* flocks, and the children of foreigners will be *your* plowmen and *your* vine-dressers, but *you* will be called priests of the LORD; *you* will be addressed as 'ministers of our God'" (Isa. 61:5–6a). "Sons of the foreigner will build your wall, and their kings will serve you, for in my wrath, I struck you down, but in my favor, I have had mercy on you" (Isa. 60:10). "Kings will be your attendants, and their queens, your supporters. They will bow before you, face to the earth, and lick the dust of your feet" (Isa. 49:23a). "They will follow you in chains. They will pass over and bow down to you. They will en-treat you, saying, 'God is with you, and there is no other God! No other!'" (Isa. 45:14b). "Then you shall know that I am the LORD. Those who wait for me will not be disappointed!" (Isa. 49:23b).

Many Gentiles Will Voluntarily Come to Israel

"Many people will come, even mighty nations, to seek the LORD of Hosts in Jerusalem and to seek the LORD's face. In those days, ten men from every language and nation will seize upon the skirt of a Jew, saying, 'Let us go with *you*! For we have heard that God is with *you*'" (Zech. 8:22–23). "For the LORD will have mer-cy on Jacob, and He will yet choose Israel and make them to rest in their land, and the foreigner will join himself to them and be united with the house of Jacob" (Isa. 14:1). The foreigners who come to

Israel to serve the Lord will find rest under his wing. For when Jesus organizes the land after his victory over the Beast, he will command the leaders of the Jews, "*You* shall divide this land among *yourselves* . . . as an inheritance for *yourselves* and for the foreigners who sojourn among *you* who have come and begotten children among *you*. And they shall be to *you* as native sons of Israel; they shall be apportioned an inheritance with you, among the tribes of Israel. And it shall be that within the tribe in which the sojourner sojourns, there shall *you* assign his inheritance, says the Lord GOD" (Ezek. 47:21–23). These foreigners will not be heathen slaves to Israel; they will voluntarily come to Israel to serve the Lord, and they will share in all the blessings that come upon the land and its people.

Gentiles Who Join Israel Will Be Given the Spirit

Jesus will welcome the Gentiles who come to Israel to serve him with the Jews, and he will accept their worship. "As for the children of the foreigner who join themselves to the LORD, to minister to Him and to love the name of the LORD, and to be His servants, every one who keeps His Sabbath rather than profane it, and who holds fast my covenant, them will I also bring to my holy mountain, and I will make them joyful in my house of prayer. Their burnt offerings and their sacrifices will be acceptable on my altar, for my house will be called a house of prayer for all peoples" (Isa. 56:6–7). These Gentiles, like the humble Canaanite woman whom Jesus called a dog (Mt. 15:22–28), will admit their inferiority to the Jews, and because of their submissive attitude, God will pour out His holy Spirit on them, just as He poured it out on the Jews on the day of Pentecost. On that day, long ago, those who received the Spirit began to speak in new languages, and when God pours out His Spirit on the Gentiles in the last days, He "will turn to the nations a pure language so that they may all call on the name of the LORD, to serve Him in one accord" (Zeph. 3:9).

As was explained in Revelation 10, when Jesus spoke of the time of the Gentiles coming to an end, he did not mean that Gentiles could no longer be forgiven and washed from their sins by the Spirit. He only meant that after "the times of the Gentiles", if a

Gentile wants to receive forgiveness and cleansing from sin, he will have to go to Israel to receive it. At this present time, which is the time of the Gentiles, Jews have been welcome to come to Christ if they would believe the gospel and repent, the same way Gentiles do. But during the Millennial Reign, forgiveness and cleansing from sin appear to be available only within the borders of Israel, and Gentiles must submit to the Jews and travel to the land of Israel in order to receive it. God's covenant during the Millennial Reign will only be with Israel; it will not exist among the nations any longer. The time of the Gentiles will have ended.

The Nations Will Bring Their Wealth to Israel

"You will suck the milk of the Gentiles and suck the breasts of kings, and you shall know that I, the LORD, am your Savior, and your Redeemer, the Mighty One of Jacob" (Isa. 60:16). "Your gates will always be open; they will not be closed day or night so that the wealth of the Gentiles may come in to you, their kings led in procession" (Isa. 60:11). "The goods of Egypt and the merchandise of Ethiopia and the Sabeans (men of stature) will pass over to you, and they will be yours" (Isa. 45:14a). "The glory of Lebanon will come to you, the cypress, the plane-tree, and the box tree together, to beautify the place of my sanctuary, and I will glorify the place of my feet" (Isa. 60:13). "I will shake all the nations, and they will come with the treasure of all the nations, and I will fill this house with glory, says the LORD of Hosts. The silver is mine, and the gold is mine" (Hag. 2:7–8). "A multitude of camels will cover you, camels of Midian and Ephah. All those of Sheba will come, carrying gold and incense, proclaiming the praises of God. All the flocks of Kedar will be gathered to you; the rams of Nebaioth will be at your service. They will be offered up with favor on my altar, and I will magnify the house of my glory" (Isa. 60:6–7).

"You will consume the wealth of the Gentiles and boast in their riches" (Isa. 61:6b). "Instead of brass, I will bring gold; and instead of iron, I will bring silver; and instead of wood, brass; and instead of stones, iron. And I will make peace your overseer, and righteousness your taskmaster" (Isa. 60:17). "Then you will see, and you will beam, and your heart will be in awe and swell because the multitude of the sea[69] will be changed toward you, and the wealth of the Gentiles will come to you" (Isa. 60:5). "I will pour forth prosperity to her like a river, and the abundance of the Gentiles like an overflowing stream. And *you* will nurse, *you* will be borne on the hip, and *you* will be dandled on knees. As one whom his mother comforts, so will I comfort *you*, and *you* will be comforted in Jerusalem" (Isa. 66:12–13).

The Nations Will Sing for Joy

The psalmist often spoke of the nations rejoicing in God during the wonderful reign of Christ on earth, as in Psalm 67, which speaks of God blessing Israel and reaching out to the Gentiles with mercy and truth: "God will show us favor and bless us. Let His face shine on us – Selah! – so that your way might be known on earth, your salvation among all nations! Let the nations praise you, O God! Let all the nations praise you! Nations will rejoice and sing for joy when you judge the nations with equity and guide the nations on earth. Selah. Let the nations praise you, O God! Let all the nations praise you! The land will yield her produce. God, our God, will bless us. God will bless us, and all the ends of the earth will fear Him" (Ps. 67:1–7).

Egypt

Egypt is mentioned favorably in Isaiah's prophecies dealing with the Millennial Reign. "On that day, there will be five cities in the land of Egypt that speak the language of Canaan and swear by the LORD of Hosts. One will be called, 'City of the Sun'.[70] On that day, there will be an altar to the LORD in the midst of the land of Egypt, and a monument to the LORD at its border. And it will be for a sign and a testimony to the LORD of Hosts in the land of Egypt. When they cry out to the LORD because of oppressors, He will send them a savior, and he will contend for and deliver them.

---

[69] The sea represents the nations of earth, as John said in Revelation 17:15.

[70] Hebrew text has "City of Destruction". The Dead Sea Scrolls (4q56) has "City of the Sun" (Greek: Heliopolis).

And the LORD will reveal Himself to the Egyptians, and the Egyptians will know the LORD in that day, and they will bring sacrifices and offerings, and make vows to the LORD and perform them" (Isa. 19:18–21).

"The LORD will strike Egypt," Isaiah went on to say, "but strike to heal, for they will turn to the LORD, and He will be entreated of them and will heal them. On that day, there will be a highway from Egypt to Assyria, and the Assyrians will come into Egypt, and the Egyptians, into Assyria, and the Egyptians will serve *God* with the Assyrians. On that day, Israel will be a third with Egypt and Assyria, a blessing in the midst of the earth, for the LORD of Hosts will bless them, saying, 'Blessed be Egypt, my people, and Assyria, the work of my hands, and Israel, my heritage'" (Isa. 19:22–25).

To make the way for the highway from Egypt to Assyria, God will change the geography of Egypt. "The LORD will completely destroy the tongue of the sea of Egypt" (Isa. 11:15a); "all the depths of the Nile will be dried up" (Zech. 10:11b). "And He will wave His hand over the river[71] with His mighty wind and strike it into seven streams, enabling *men* to cross over in sandals. And there will be a highway for the remnant of His people from Assyria who remain, as there was for Israel on the day they came up out of the land of Egypt" (Isa. 11:15b–16). "And a highway will be there, and a way, and it will be called, 'The Way of Holiness'. No un-clean man will travel over it, but it belongs to him who walks the Way, and fools will not wander about on it. No lion will be there; indeed, no ferocious beasts will go up on it. Such will not be found there. But the redeemed will travel on it" (Isa. 35:8–9). This miraculous peace on a highway stretching for over five hundred miles is a wonderful example of the blessings of Israel extending beyond Israel's borders during the Millennial Reign.

Occasional Rebellions Will Break Out among the Nations

As has been pointed out, many Gentiles will not humble them-selves to join Israel, and they will all be allowed the liberty to walk

---

[71] That is, the Euphrates River.

in the name of his own god (Mic. 4:5a). But when those nations use that liberty to disobey the commands that Jesus issues for them from Jerusalem, there will be swift and severe repercussions. A case in point will be when a nation refuses to obey Jesus' command to come to Israel to celebrate the Feast of Tabernacles. This Feast of Tabernacles will not be the ceremony commanded in the law of Moses. The Old Testament Feast of Tabernacles commemorated the forty years that Israel spent in tents of animal skins before they entered the Promised Land (Lev. 23:39–43), but the Feast of Tabernacles during the Millennial Reign will commemorate the years that believers spent in tents of their own skin before the first resurrection, before Jesus gave them glorified bodies like his.

"And it shall come to pass that everyone who is left of all the nations that came against Jerusalem will come up from year to year to worship the King, the LORD of Hosts, to make pilgrimage for the Feast of Tabernacles. And it shall come to pass that there will be no rain on those from among the families of the earth who do not come up to Jerusalem to worship the King, the LORD of Hosts. If the family of Egypt does not go up, and does not come, then on them will there be none. This is the plague with which the LORD will strike the nations who do not come up to observe the Feast of Tabernacles. This will be the punishment for Egypt's sin, and the punishment for all the nations that do not come up to observe the Feast of Tabernacles" (Zech. 14:16–19).

Some Believers May Be Cast Out of God's Kingdom during the Millennial Reign?

Another observation from the Scriptures is that it may be possible that some believers will be cast out of God's Kingdom during the Millennial reign. It is difficult to imagine that any believer would fall from righteousness during this time; yet, Jesus' Parable of the Marriage Feast compels us to leave the question open. In that parable, one of the invited guests came to the marriage feast for the king's son without wearing an appropriate wedding garment. When the king came in and saw him, he confronted him and cast him out (Mt. 22:1–13). So, the possibility appears to exist that during the thousand-year Marriage Supper of the Lamb, someone

among the invited guests (the raptured saints) may be found without the appropriate wedding garment and be cast out of the kingdom.

The Final Battle

**¶7. And when the thousand years come to an end, Satan
will be released from his prison,**

**8.   and he will go out to deceive the nations that are in the
four corners of the earth, Gog and Magog, to gather
them for the war, the number of them being as the sand
of the sea.**

**9a. And they came up upon the breadth of the earth and
surrounded the camp of the saints and the beloved city,**

Note 1: It will not be difficult for Satan to persuade the nations
around the world to rebel against the stern Ruler in Jerusalem who
has ruled them "with an iron rod" for a thousand years.

Note 2: Almost all of the information about Christ and the
saints in Jerusalem being surrounded by Satan and the armies of
the nations comes from Ezekiel, who called those armies, as John
does here, "Gog and Magog": "You will come up like a devastating *storm*; you will come like a cloud to cover the land, you and all
your hordes, and many nations with you. And you will say, 'I will
go up against the land of unprotected villages; I will come against
the quiet people, all of them living securely, dwelling without a
wall, and no gates and bars for themselves,' to take spoil and carry
off plunder, to turn your hand against the waste places now inhabited, even against the people gathered out of the nations, who have
livestock and goods, who dwell on the pre-eminent part of the
earth" (Ezek. 38:9, 11–12).

"Thus says the Lord GOD: Are you the one of whom I spoke in
former days by the hand of my servants, the prophets of Israel,
who prophesied in those days that I would bring you up against
them? But it shall come to pass on that day, the day that Gog
comes against the land of Israel, that my hot anger will come up
within me, and I will judge him with a plague, and with blood, and
an overwhelming downpour, and I will make stones of hail, fire,

and sulfur to rain upon him, and upon all his hordes, and upon the many nations that are with him. And I will magnify myself, and sanctify myself, and make myself known in the sight of many nations, and they shall know that I am the LORD" (Ezek. 38:17–18, 22–23). David, too, prophesied that God "will make it rain coals upon the wicked, fire and brimstone, and scorching wind – the portion of their cup" (Ps. 11:6). This is exactly what John saw:

9b. and fire came down out of heaven from God and devoured them.

Note: Thus ends the last battle ever to be fought, and God, the Father alone will fight it.

10. And the Devil who deceived them was thrown into the Lake of Fire and Sulfur, where both the Beast and the False Prophet are, and they will be tormented night and day forever and ever.

Note: The Beast and the False Prophet were cast into the Lake of Fire at the beginning of the thousand-year reign, but Satan is not cast into the Lake of Fire until the end.

Chapter 9
Two Advents, One Messiah

"If he is killed, then this man is definitely not the one
whom the Law promised."
Maimonides, *Hilkoth Melakhim*, XI, 4

"We preach Christ crucified, a stumbling block to the Jews."
Paul, 1Corinthians 1:23a

Determining Factors

Since the time of Abraham, one of the determining factors in
the shaping of human history has been the relationship between
God and the descendants of that very great man. God blessed nations for treating Abraham's descendants kindly, and cursed nations for abusing them; He used nations as instruments of His
wrath when Israel rebelled against Him and as instruments of His
care when they obeyed Him. The previous two chapters have
shown that this pattern will continue to the end of this age. For all
future events, the determining factors of world history will be (1)
God's resolution to redeem and bless the Jews and (2) the Jews'
stubborn refusal to believe in His Son Jesus as their Messiah.

The conduct of God's people has always played a determina-
tive role in the fulfillment of prophecy. God promised Abraham,
for instance, that his seed would depart from Egypt after 400 years
(Gen. 15:13–14), but Moses delayed that promise thirty years by
killing an Egyptian and having to flee from Egypt (Ex. 2:11–12;
12:40–41). For another example, it was only eleven days' journey
from Mount Sinai to the border of the Promised Land (Dt. 1:2), but
when Israel arrived at the border and rebelled, God angrily sent
them back into the wilderness for forty more years (Num. 13–14).
God is obligated to do nothing that He promises to do if conditions

change with those to whom He made the promise.   He said as much, you may recall, through the prophet Ezekiel: "When a righteous man turns from his righteousness and does wrong, he will die because of those *deeds*; for his wrong which he has done, he will die.   And when an evil man turns from his wickedness which he has been doing, and he does what is just and right, he shall keep his soul alive" (Ezek. 18:26–27).   A few scenes in the gospels even suggest that Christ would have fulfilled at his first Advent all that the prophets said of him if Israel had received him, such as when he lamented that because of Israel's rejection of him, he could not do for them what he would have done: "O Jerusalem! Jerusalem, who kills the prophets and stones those who are sent to her! How many times I wanted to gather your children together, the way a hen gathers her chicks under her wings, but *you* would not. Behold! *Your* house is left to *you*, desolate" (Mt. 23:37–38).[72]

We pause now from our detailed examination of Revelation to explain why Israel failed to recognize their Messiah. Then, we will explain why God's New Testament people rejected Paul's gospel, and how they became "Babylon the Great, the Mother of harlots and the abominations of the earth," which event has shaped the history of the entire world.

EXPECTATION AND DISAPPOINTMENT

Of the Messiah, God said, "No enemy will oppress him, and no wicked man will humble him, but I will crush his adversaries before him, and those who hate him will I strike down" (Ps. 89:22–23).   God even commanded His angels to stay so close to the Messiah that they could catch him if his foot tripped over a stone (Ps. 91:11–12).   Moreover, as we have seen, God promised Israel that the Messiah would deliver the nation from heathen domination, bestow upon her unprecedented blessings, and then gloriously rule the world forever from Jerusalem: "All peoples, nations, and languages will serve him," wrote Daniel. "His dominion will be an eternal dominion, and his kingdom shall not be destroyed" (Dan. 7:14).   Such promises from God were cherished

---

[72] See Appendix, "The 2000-Year Gap".

by Israel, and trusting in those promises, Israel looked for a Conqueror-Messiah whom God would protect and anoint with power to be King over the world forever and to turn the plundered land of Israel into another garden of Eden.

Nobody in Israel was expecting a meek and harmless Messiah, and when the Messiah made his appearance, and neither subdued the heathen nor exalted Israel, disappointment in Jesus was un-avoidable. His refusal to fight the Romans and bring about Israel's exaltation was the greatest test of hearts since the days of David.[73] It was regarding this fiery trial of faith that the old prophet Simeon had given his enigmatic warning to Jesus' mother: "A sword shall pierce even your own soul!" (Lk. 2:34–35).

The Expectation of the People and their Rulers

Every judge whom God had ever raised up for Israel delivered the nation from foreign oppressors; the book of Judges is full of such stories. But before any of those judges were sent to deliver the nation, the people were required to repent. Therefore, John the Baptist's thundering call for repentance was seen as a harbinger of good things to come, a sign that something wonderful was at hand.

After Jesus was baptized by John and tempted by Satan in the wilderness, he "returned to Galilee in the power of the Spirit" (Lk. 4:14). He entered his hometown synagogue, and "the scroll of Isaiah the prophet was handed to him. And when he had unrolled the scroll, he found the place where it was written, 'The Spirit of the LORD is upon me because He has anointed me to proclaim good news to the poor. He has sent me to heal the brokenhearted, to preach liberty to those held captive, and recovery of sight to the blind, to send the oppressed away free, to preach the acceptable year of the LORD.' And when he had rolled up the scroll and hand-ed it to the attendant, he sat down. And the eyes of everyone in the synagogue were fixed on him. Then he said to them, 'Today, this scripture is fulfilled in your hearing.' And they all marveled at the gracious words which proceeded from his mouth" (Lk. 4:17–22).

---

[73] God's unlawful forgiveness of David's adultery with Bathsheba and murder of Uriah led to a coup d'état and civil war.

Everyone in the synagogue that day marveled at Jesus' words because they knew that the prophecy he quoted spoke not only of the Spirit being upon the Messiah, but also of the great blessings that would come to Israel after the Spirit came upon him: "They will build again the ancient ruins; they will raise up places laid waste of old; they will repair desolate cities that have lain waste for many generations. And foreigners will stand and tend *your* flocks, and the children of foreigners will be *your* plowmen and *your* vinedressers" (Isa. 61:4–5). If this prophecy was now fulfilled, as Jesus said it was, then Israel's great day of deliverance and exaltation had come! Could it really be so? The astonishing miracles which Jesus soon began to perform answered that question for them with a resounding yes!

At the time of Jesus' birth, the rulers in Israel were aware of both where and when the Messiah would appear (Mt. 2:3–6; cf. Dan. 9:25). They also knew that Moses said the Messiah would be a man like him (Dt. 18:15–19), and part of Moses' uniqueness was that he was the only man ever ordained by God to ceremonially wash others with water (Lev. 8:5–6). That is why, when God sent John the Baptist to baptize repentant Jews in the Jordan River, "everyone was wondering in their hearts about John, whether he might be the Messiah" (Lk. 3:15b). Israel's curious rulers even "sent priests and Levites from Jerusalem to ask John, 'Who are you?' And he confessed, and did not deny it, but confessed, 'I am not the Messiah'" (Jn. 1:19–20). Later, when John was asked why he was washing people the way Moses did if he was not the Messiah, John replied that he was preparing Israel for the Messiah, who was about to appear with a baptism of his own. "The reason I came baptizing with water is so that he might be made known to Israel," he said (Jn. 1:31). "I baptize *you* with water, but he who is mightier than I is coming, the strap of whose sandals I am not worthy to loosen. He will baptize *you* with the holy Spirit and fire!" (Lk. 3:16).

When John said to those rulers that he was unworthy to loosen the sandal strap of the One coming after him, the rulers must have been mystified. John was obviously a mighty prophet – the first such prophet God had sent to Israel in centuries and the only

prophet that Israel had ever had cause to compare with Moses –
yet, John was declaring the imminent appearance of one far greater
than he! This would have confirmed for the rulers what the
prophets said about the Messiah, namely, that he would be a supernaturally powerful figure who would destroy the wicked, reward
the righteous, and set all things right in the world.

The Disappointment of the People and Their Rulers

Although the Jews were stirred up by the preaching of John the
Baptist and Jesus, other than telling the Jews to believe and repent,
neither John nor Jesus gave them anything to do. What, then, were
the people to do with their great excitement and joyous expectation, powerless as they were to liberate themselves from the Romans or to transform their land into another garden of Eden? Only
the Messiah could do that. As time passed, those who believed in
Jesus as Israel's Messiah began to wonder when he would start doing those things.

The day Jesus fed five thousand with a few loaves and fish, the
people, frustrated with Jesus' inaction, proclaimed, "This really is
the Prophet who is coming into the world!" and they decided to
"take him by force to make him king." To escape their misguided
Messianic enthusiasm, Jesus retreated to a mountain alone (Jn.
6:14b–15). The following day, some of the people, knowing that
Jesus had previously sent others out with miraculous power (e.g.,
Mt. 10:1), asked that he send them out, too, to "work the works of
God" (Jn. 6:28). But the "works of God" they had in mind were
not the works that God had sent His Son to do, and Jesus' reply to
their request only increased their frustration: "This is the work of
God," he said, "that *you* believe on the one He has sent" (Jn. 6:29).
All that God wanted of them was to trust in His Son, and to wait,
but they expected so much more of the Messiah than what Jesus
was doing that his reply to their request did not quench the zeal
which their misguided expectations produced. After all, both John
and Jesus had proclaimed that the kingdom of God was at hand
(Mt. 3:2; 4:17). So, where was it?

As has been pointed out, the rulers who believed the prophets
were curious and hopeful when John first came preaching. They

knew that the time for their Messiah had come, and they saw John as a prophet like the one Moses told Israel to look for. However, when John harshly and publicly rebuked some of them for coming to be baptized without first repenting, their attitude toward John, and then Jesus, who also rebuked them, soured. Instead of receiving the reproofs which John and Jesus gave them, the rulers condemned both John and Jesus and made every effort to persuade the people not to believe in them.

In time, most of the nation came to agree with their leaders that Jesus was only another pretender, a would-be Messiah cursed by God. "We did not value him," Isaiah prophetically confessed; "we considered him stricken, smitten by God, and afflicted" (Isa. 53:3b, 4b). To the Jews, a Messiah who did not subjugate the nations to Israel was no Messiah at all, and the harsh reality of Israel's continued servitude to Rome swayed the nation against Jesus, so that "although so many miracles had been done by him in their presence, they did not believe in him" (Jn. 12:37).

The people's disappointment in Jesus was exploited to personal advantage by the leaders of Israel. They condemned the Jews who did believe in him as ignorant, even cursed by God (Jn. 7:49), and they excommunicated anyone who openly expressed faith in Jesus (Jn. 9:22). Whenever the rulers heard someone speak well of Jesus' miracles (Mt. 9:8), they dampened that enthusiasm with the warning that Jesus was "casting out demons by the ruler of demons" (Mt. 9:34; Mt. 12:22–24). This accusation seemed plausible to the Jews for two reasons: first, they knew it was possible for demons to give men supernatural powers (cf. Mt. 8:28; Mk. 5:1–4), and second, they knew that Jesus was not doing what the prophets said their mighty Messiah would do.

The Expectation of Jesus' Relatives

While ministering to the LORD in the temple in Jerusalem, the elderly priest Zacharias, John the Baptist's father, received an astonishing visitation from heaven. The angel Gabriel appeared to him, "standing to the right of the altar of incense" (Lk. 1:11), and he told Zacharias that his aged wife Elizabeth would bear him a son, adding, "You will have joy and gladness, and many will rejoice at his birth. He will be great before the LORD, and he will be filled with the holy Spirit while in his mother's womb. It is he who will go before [the Messiah] in the spirit and power of Elijah, to make ready a people prepared for the LORD" (excerpts, Lk. 1:13–17).

On the day of the baby John's circumcision, many neighbors and relatives were in Zacharias' house when the Spirit moved Zacharias to say, "Blessed be the LORD, God of Israel, for He has visited and brought redemption to His people! And He has raised up a horn of salvation for us in the house of David His servant, as He spoke by the mouth of His holy prophets from of old, to bring us salvation from our enemies and from the hand of all who hate us" (Lk. 1:67–71). Zacharias' visitors, as well as Zacharias himself, must have been amazed and thrilled to know that God was at long last visiting Israel again! And the Spirit continued speaking glorious things through Zacharias, declaring that God was about "to perform the mercy promised to our fathers, and to remember His holy covenant, the oath which He swore to Abraham our father, that He would grant to us that we, being delivered out of the hand of our enemies, might serve Him without fear" (Lk. 1:72–74). Those who knew the prophets were, like Zacharias, aware that the Messiah's time was at hand, and they were thrilled at the prospect of seeing many wonderful promises fulfilled. And here, before their eyes, was a miraculous birth which equalled that of Isaac. It is no wonder that when Elizabeth gave birth to John, it was "talked about throughout the hill country of Judea, and everyone who heard these things laid them up in their heart, saying, 'What will this child be?'" (Lk. 1:65–66).

Not long after Gabriel appeared to Zacharias, he appeared to a virgin named Mary to tell her that she would have a child and that her child would "be called the Son of the Highest" (Lk. 1:32a). Mary knew what that meant, for "Son of the Highest" and "Son of God" were titles used by the Jews to refer to the Messiah (cf. Mt. 26:63). Then Gabriel confirmed for Mary that her son would be the Messiah by adding, "The LORD will give him the throne of David his father, and he will rule over the house of Jacob forever, and of his kingdom, there will be no end" (Lk. 1:32b–33).

At the time Gabriel visited Mary, she was engaged to Joseph, a righteous man who could have neither understood nor welcomed the pregnancy of his bride-to-be. Therefore, God sent Gabriel to Joseph, to explain that the child "which is conceived in her is of the holy Spirit, and she will bear a son, and you shall call his name Jesus, for he will save his people from their sins" (Mt. 1:20b–21). Joseph, like Mary, possessed faith sufficient to believe God's angel, and so, he went ahead with the marriage, fully persuaded that the child would be Israel's longed-for Messiah.

Gabriel mentioned to Mary that her elderly kinswoman Elizabeth was pregnant, and shortly after that angel's visit, Mary went to see her. As soon as Mary entered Zacharias' house, Elizabeth was filled with the Spirit and began prophesying about both their sons (Lk. 1:41–45). Mary was likewise filled with the Spirit, and she praised God that He had "come to the aid of Israel His son, as He said to our fathers, to Abraham, and to his seed forever" (Lk. 1:54–55). How bright and blessed Israel's future now looked!

Afterward, Joseph and Mary continued to experience the miraculous. The night Jesus was born, shepherds entered the shelter that Joseph and Mary had found, and they reported to them that angels had appeared in the night sky above them, singing about the birth of the child who was to be Israel's Savior, Messiah, and Lord (Lk. 2:11). About a month after that, in accordance with the law, Joseph and Mary took their baby to Jerusalem to present him to the Lord (Lk. 2:22; cf. Lev. 12:2–8). Waiting at the temple for them was Simeon, an old prophet who had been told by God that he would not die until he had seen the Messiah, and on this day, the Spirit had prompted him to go to the temple to see him. When he saw Mary with her baby, "he took the child into his arms, and blessed God, and said, 'Now, Master, let your slave go his way in peace, according to your word, for my eyes have seen your salvation, which you have prepared before the face of all peoples, a light for revelation to the Gentiles, and glory for your people Israel!'" (Lk. 2:28–32). With this, God again confirmed for Joseph and Mary that their child was the Chosen One whom the prophets said would compel the Gentiles to acknowledge the true God and bring to Israel great honor and wealth.

After that, Joseph managed to find a house in Bethlehem for his family, and when they had lived there a while, some Magi, observers of the stars from Mesopotamia, came to Israel and asked King Herod for help in locating "the one born King of the Jews, for we saw his star in the east, and we have come to pay him homage" (Mt. 2:2). With Herod's help, they found Jesus and "did him homage, and they opened their treasure chests and presented gifts to him" (Mt. 2:11). Then, as quickly as they had come, they went away, being warned by God in a dream not to return to Herod, but to go home by a different route (Mt. 2:12). Then, another dream from God prompted Joseph and Mary to flee to Egypt to save their son from the devious King Herod (Mt. 2:13–18), confirming for them God's promise through David: "The LORD will save His Messiah" (Ps. 20:6a). After Herod died, another miraculous dream let Joseph and Mary know that it was safe for them to return home (Mt. 2:19–21). By these events, Joseph and Mary saw how greatly God cared for their child, and though they had many questions, there is one thing of which they felt certain: God would never allow anyone to harm His Messiah.

For three long decades after Jesus' birth, Mary lived in anticipation of God sending him to proclaim liberty and healing to Israel. One can only imagine the excitement Mary felt when "God anointed Jesus of Nazareth with the holy Spirit and power," and her precious son began to travel across the land, "doing good and healing all who were oppressed of the Devil" (Acts 10:38). The incredible miracles Jesus performed, along with his proclamation that the kingdom of God was at hand (Mk. 1:15), must have skyrocketed Mary's expectation that God was finally about to "give him the throne of David his father," and that he would indeed "rule over the house of Jacob forever," and that "of his kingdom, there will be no end," just as Gabriel had told her.

The Disappointment of Jesus' Relatives

When Jesus did not drive out the Romans and bring about Israel's exaltation, Mary could only cling to her experiences, to

Gabriel's promise, and to the prophecies, both ancient and recent, which declared that the Messiah would exalt Israel and reign over the heathen. But even after Jesus was anointed by God, Mary could only wait. And the longer Jesus went without doing the things she expected, the more Mary's faith was challenged.

Months passed after Jesus was anointed, and then one year, and then two, and Mary sensed that something was wrong. But what was it? Mary knew that Gabriel was not wrong when he said that God would give her child the throne of David and make him king forever. She knew that the Spirit was not wrong when it fell on Zacharias, and Elizabeth, and on herself and said that her Son was the Messiah who would deliver Israel from all their enemies. She also knew that the prophets were not wrong in predicting un-precedented glory and power for him, and that the elderly prophet Simeon was not wrong when he saw her baby and thanked God for allowing him to see God's Messiah. And she knew that she was still a virgin when she gave birth to Jesus and that the multitude of angels were not wrong who had sung in the night sky when Jesus was born and had told the shepherds that the Messiah had been born in Bethlehem. And Mary knew that the dreams from God which saved her Son's life were not wrong. But why was he not doing what God, at many times and in many ways had said through both prophets and angels, that he would do? For those who loved Jesus, like Mary, the painful but seemingly unavoidable answer was that the "something" that was wrong was Jesus.

Mary's other children began scoffing at him (Jn. 7:3–5),[74] and in time, Jesus' kinsmen concluded that he had lost his mind and that they should take him away (Mk. 3:21). Their determination to do this was not based on a lack of miracles, for Jesus' miracles had become legendary, nor was it based on any lack of devotion in Jesus toward the law of Moses, for Jesus strictly kept the law, even commanding those he healed to keep it (e.g., Mt. 8:2–4). Their judgment that Jesus had become deranged was based entirely on the fact that Jesus was not using his miraculous power the way that

---

[74] They were putting the same pressure on Jesus that Satan put on him in the Temptation (Mt. 4:5–6; Lk. 4:9–11), that is, for him to make a show of his pow-er so that the Jews would be in awe of him and accept him as their Messiah.

they understood the Messiah should use it, that is, to liberate and exalt Israel to be head of the nations.

Jesus' troubled kinsmen decided to find him and to take him, and when they found him, he was preaching inside a house packed with listeners. Being unable to get to him because of the crowd (Lk. 8:19), they waited outside for a chance to take him. Just how deeply embedded in the psyche of the Jews was the expectation of a Conqueror-Messiah is revealed by the fact that Mary was among Jesus' relatives standing outside Jesus' crowded house, waiting to take him away, by force if necessary (Mk. 3:21, 31–32; Mt. 12:46–47; Lk. 8:19–20).

Mary and Jesus' other relatives sent a messenger through the throng, who informed Jesus that "your mother and your brothers have been standing outside wanting to speak to you" (Mt. 12:47). But he answered, loudly enough for all to hear, "Who is my mother? And who are my brothers?" (Mt. 12:48). One can only imagine what Mary and her sons thought when the messenger returned and told them that Jesus was asking the people inside to tell him who his mother and brothers were.

To the Jews at that time, there seemed to be but two possible explanations for Jesus' failure to fulfill the prophecies about the Messiah, and people leaned toward one or the other depending on whether or not they believed in Jesus. Unbelieving Jews reasoned that, since Jesus did not deliver Israel, he could not be the Messiah, and that, if he was not the Messiah, then his miracle-working power must be from an evil spirit, not from God (Mt. 12:24; Mk. 3:22; Lk. 11:15). Believing Jews, including Mary, reasoned that since Jesus was beyond all question the Messiah, his power must be from God, and if his power was from God, then he had somehow gone astray from his purpose and had become mentally imbalanced.

Nobody understood Jesus, whether they believed in him or not.

There was, of course, a third possibility, the correct one, which no one considered, namely, that the prophets had foretold of two Advents of the one Messiah, and that in the First Advent, he would suffer. But no one knew that. Had Mary and the others known it,

Jesus would not have seemed insane. But they didn't, and so, he did.

The Expectation of John the Baptist

God sent John to the Jordan River as "a voice crying in the wilderness" (Isa. 40:3), and John was fearless and fierce with his message and his baptism. He demanded that Israel repent in order to be worthy of the soon-coming Messiah, and whenever anyone, regardless of social status, dared to come to him for baptism without repenting, he gave them a blistering rebuke: "*You* brood of vipers, who warned *you* to flee from the coming wrath? Bear fruit worthy of repentance!" (Mt. 3:7–8; Lk. 3:7–8).

John spoke with such boldness because he knew – God had told him – that the Messiah was at hand, and knowing the prophets as he did, John expected him to come with supreme authority, bringing into the world the fearsome judgments of God. John said it this way: "He will gather his wheat into the storehouse, but he will burn up the chaff with unquenchable fire. Every valley shall be filled, and every mountain and hill, brought low, and the crooked *ways* shall be straight, and the rough *ways* shall be smooth roads, and all flesh shall see the salvation of God!" (Mt. 3:12b; Lk. 3:5–6). John eagerly anticipated the appearance of Israel's Messiah, a holy man of unshakable will and unconquerable power, perfect in righteousness and judgment.

John did not have to wait long, and when Jesus came to him at the Jordan, the Spirit fell on John, and he cried out, "Behold! The Lamb of God that takes away the sin of the world! This is the one of whom I said, 'After me is coming a man who is greater than I, for he was before I was'" (Jn. 1:29b–30).

The Disappointment of John the Baptist

When God sent John to preach, He told him that when the Messiah came, he would baptize with holy Spirit instead of with water (Lk. 3:16). That baptism, John very much looked forward to receiving. That is why, when John saw Jesus coming to his baptism in the Jordan River, "John tried to stop him, saying, 'I need to be baptized by you, and you come to me?' Jesus answered and said to him, 'Let it be for now, for it is right that we fulfill all right-eousness this way'" (Mt. 3:14–15a). John did not understand that Jesus would have to suffer and die to make his baptism available.

Thus it was that John's first expectation, namely, that the Messiah would appear and immediately baptize him and others "with holy Spirit and fire", was dismissed by the One whom God said would do it. Perhaps even more puzzling to John was that God continued to have him baptize with water even though the Messiah had appeared. Did John wonder why Jesus did not baptize, as God had plainly told him the Messiah would do? If so, there was no one who could have answered that question for John. John had called Jesus, "the Lamb of God that takes away the sin of the world" (Jn. 1:29), but he did not know that Jesus was to become a real sacrificial Lamb and that only by his sacrifice would the way be made for him to baptize with the Spirit and take away sins.

Not long after Jesus turned down John's request to be baptized with the Spirit, John's faith was tested again when he was arrested by Herod Antipas and thrown into prison. There he languished, and in his affliction, he began to doubt who Jesus was. With a troubled mind, John "summoned two of his disciples and sent them to Jesus, saying, 'Are you the one who is coming, or should we look for another?'" (Lk. 7:19–20). In essence, his question to Jesus was this: "Why am I here in prison if you are the Messiah?" John had been rejected and slandered by many of his fellow Jews as being demon-possessed (Mt. 11:16–19). He had expected to share in the glorious reign of God's invincible Messiah; instead, he had been rejected and slandered, and now, he lay in a dungeon, the prisoner of a heathen ruler within the borders of God's Promised Land (Mt. 11:16–19).

In reply to John's despairing question, Jesus could only point to the miracles he was performing (Lk. 7:21–22); he could point to no one he had baptized with the Spirit, nor to any desolate places in Israel that he had transformed into another Eden, nor to the repatri-ation of dispersed Jews, nor to any Gentile nation that he had com-pelled to submit to God. It is difficult to see how Jesus' reply could have comforted John, though, inasmuch as (1) he already knew about Jesus' miracles and (2) his imprisonment continued. Nevertheless, that is the only response the dejected prophet received.

Of John, Jesus said that "among those born of women, there has arisen no greater prophet than John the Baptist" (Lk. 7:28), and yet, in the end, John died alone in Herod's prison, beheaded to satisfy the spite of a wicked woman (Mt. 14:3–10).

The Expectation of the Disciples

At least two of the men who became Jesus' disciples, Andrew and Philip, were at the Jordan when John saw Jesus and proclaimed him to be the Messiah. Andrew, upon hearing John say that, immediately went to his brother, Peter, and told him, "We have found the Messiah!" (Jn. 1:41). And Philip found his friend Nathanael and told him, "We have found the one Moses and the prophets wrote about in the law, Jesus of Nazareth, the son of Joseph" (Jn. 1:45). When Nathanael met Jesus, he was moved to exclaim, "Rabbi, you are the Son of God! You are the King of Israel!" (Jn. 1:48–49).

In the ensuing years, as they followed Jesus, the disciples saw and heard many astonishing things, but certain moments especially filled them with great confidence that Jesus was about to deliver Israel from the Romans and set up his eternal kingdom. For instance, Jesus once told his disciples, "There are some standing here who will not taste of death until they see the Son of man coming in his kingdom" (Mt. 16:28). Then, just a few days later, "Jesus took Peter, and James, and his brother John, and he led them up on a high mountain by themselves. And, behold, there appeared to them Moses and Elijah, talking with him" (Mt. 17:1, 3). Everyone in Israel knew Malachi's prophecy that God would "send Elijah the prophet before the great and fearful day of the LORD comes" (Mal. 4:5). So, to Peter, James, and John, Elijah being on the mountain with Jesus was undeniable confirmation that Jesus was about to take his place on David's throne and to reign eternally over the earth.

So certain were the disciples that Jesus was about to establish an earthly kingdom that they sometimes quarreled about who should occupy the highest office in it, as happened one day when Jesus went to Capernaum and "asked them, 'What were *you* discussing among *yourselves* on the way?' But they stayed quiet, for on the way they had been arguing with one another about who was the greatest" (Mk. 9:33–34). And this dispute among the disciples continued the entire time Jesus was with them, even during the Last Supper (Lk. 22:24). Once, they even came to Jesus directly, wanting him to settle the matter once for all and tell them who would be the greatest in his kingdom. "And when Jesus had called a little child to him, he stood him in their midst and said, 'Truly, I tell *you*, unless *you* are converted and become like little children, *you* will never enter into the kingdom of heaven. Whoever humbles himself like this little child, he is the greatest in the kingdom of heaven'" (Mt. 18:2–4). The disciples did not understand him, or if they did, they did not believe him. *How could a harmless child*, they might have thought, *drive out the Romans and conquer the world?*

The Disappointment of the Disciples

Since the disciples' expectations concerning the Messiah were no different from that of other Jews, Jesus disappointed them as well; nevertheless, their hearts would not let them forsake him as so many others did. They held on until the end to God's promises of earthly glory for Israel, and, ironically, it was their faith in the one who was disappointing them which kept that fading hope alive. In the garden of Gethsemane, the disciples' wilting hope was briefly revived when Jesus, surrounded by officers sent by the high priest, declared that more than twelve legions of angels were standing by, waiting for him to give them the order to come (Mt. 26:53). Not even one Roman legion was stationed in Judea at that time, and they knew that if Jesus called for those angels, the war would be over in moments! But Jesus didn't give the order, the officers arrested him, and when his disciples realized that they were also in danger of being arrested, "they all forsook him and fled" (Mt. 26:56; Mk. 14:50).

The following day, when Jesus was hanging on the cross, his mother, Mary, the disciple John, and a few others stood nearby, heavy with sorrow. It is possible that they yet harbored some hope that Jesus would miraculously escape the cross and thus prove to everyone that he was the Messiah, but when Jesus, in great agony, cried out to God, nothing happened. One man, thinking Jesus was calling for Elijah, "ran, and filling a sponge with sour wine gave him a drink, saying, 'Let's see if Elijah comes to take him down'" (Mk. 15:34–36). But Elijah didn't come; Jesus died; and those who loved him went home, wondering why they had ever thought that he was the Messiah. Not one soul continued to believe.[75] That is why no one was at his grave on the third day after his crucifixion, waiting to greet him when he came back from the dead. In fact, on the morning of the third day when a few women who had gone to mourn at Jesus' tomb excitedly came to the disciples saying that they had seen the Lord alive again, their words seemed to the disciples to be nothing more than "idle talk" (Lk. 24:9–11).

In the afternoon of that third day, Jesus found two of his disciples dejectedly walking on the road from Jerusalem to the village of Emmaus. They were "conversing with one another about all these things that had happened. And it came to pass that while they talked and reasoned together, Jesus himself drew near and walked with them, but their eyes were kept from recognizing him. And he said to them, 'What are these things that *you're* discussing as *you* go along, looking so sad?' The one named Cleopas answered and said to him, 'Are you the only one living near Jerusalem who doesn't know what things have happened in it these *past few* days?' He said to them, 'What things?' Then they said to him, 'The things concerning Jesus of Nazareth, who was a man, a prophet [they no longer called him the Messiah], mighty in deed and word before God and all the people, and how our chief priests and rulers handed him over *to the Romans* to be condemned to death, and they crucified him. We had hoped that he was the one who was going to redeem Israel. But now, after all these things – today marks the third day since these things happened – some of the women among us utterly astounded us when, after going to the sepulcher early in the morning and not finding his body, they came

---

[75] For more on this, see my online book, *After Jesus Died*, at GoingtoJesus.com.

saying they had actually seen a vision of angels who said he was alive![76] And then some of those with us went out to the sepulcher and found it exactly as the women had said, but they didn't see him.' Then he said to them, 'O fools! So slow in heart to believe all that the prophets have spoken! Did not the Messiah have to suffer these things and enter into his glory?'" (Lk. 24:14–26).

Then Cleopas and his fellow disciple listened attentively as Jesus, still not telling them who he was, "began explaining to them the things concerning himself in all the scriptures, beginning with Moses and all the prophets" (Lk. 24:27). What Jesus pointed out to them most would have been the prophecies of his sufferings and death, since they already believed the prophecies of his glory. And not long afterward, Jesus also opened the minds of his other disciples to the prophecies concerning his sufferings, saying to them, "Thus it is written, and so, it was necessary for the Messiah to suffer and to rise from the dead on the third day" (Lk. 24:45–46).

Summary

Jews of Jesus' time trusted their prophets who said that the Messiah would deliver them from foreign oppressors and bless Israel with enduring holiness, surpassing wealth, and perfect peace. As for the few Jews whom God used to bring about or to announce the Messiah's appearing – Zacharias, Elizabeth, Mary, Joseph, the old prophet Simeon, and John the Baptist – it was beyond question that Jesus was the promised Messiah who would fulfill the ancient prophecies. And for them, that made their time the best time in Israel's history to be alive. But when Jesus died, every person who had believed in him was disillusioned and lost faith, for Jesus had accomplished none of the great things for Israel that the prophets said the Messiah would do.

To be fair to those who were disappointed in Jesus, we must say that the ancient prophecies concerning the Messiah were a

---

[76] The women did not tell these men they had seen a vision. They told them they had really seen an angel who spoke to them. Cleopas' characterization of the women as seeing a vision indicates his continuing unbelief of what they had said.

mystery which exceeded the capacity of human understanding. They are still understood only when unraveled by the Spirit of God, and it was unraveled for no one until after the Messiah's resurrection and ascension. Only when the Spirit came upon them were the eyes of Jesus' followers opened to the treasure of wisdom hidden in the Scriptures. And just as it is impossible to adequately describe the disciples' disappointment caused by Jesus' death, so it is impossible to adequately describe their joy and excitement when he rose from the dead and renewed all their expectations.

JESUS TRIED

To Jesus' followers, his death was conclusive proof that he was not the Messiah, or if he was, that he had failed miserably in his purpose. Jesus had repeatedly and plainly told them that he must die (e.g., Mt. 20:17–19; Lk. 9:22), but that the Messiah would die was such an impossibility that they could not process his words, regardless of how plain his words were. In one instance, for example, after Peter, James, and John witnessed Jesus' transfiguration, "as they were coming down out of the mountain, Jesus commanded them, saying, 'Tell the vision to no one until the Son of man rises from the dead.' And so, they kept the matter to themselves, debating with one another what it means to 'rise from the dead'" (Mt. 17:9; Mk. 9:10). Again, on his last journey to Jerusalem, knowing that he was soon to die and leave this world, he told his followers a parable about a man going on a long journey because "he was nearing Jerusalem, and they were thinking that the kingdom of God was immediately about to appear" (Lk. 19:11). But his doing that did not help; his followers still expected the promised earthly kingdom soon to be established.

Until the Spirit came on the day of Pentecost, the disciples' confusion concerning the things of God was inescapable because the Spirit alone brings the knowledge of God into man's heart (Jn. 16:13), and Jesus no doubt asked his disciples, "Are *you* still without understanding?" more than the few times it is recorded (e.g., Mt. 15:16; Mk. 8:21). Jesus even once tried to force them to face the reality of his approaching death, but they just could not take it in: "Jesus said to his disciples, 'Let these words sink down into *y*our ears! The Son of man is going to be betrayed into the hands of men!' But they did not understand this saying, and it was hidden from them so that they should not comprehend it, and they were afraid to ask him about this saying" (Lk. 9:43b–45).

Jesus tried plain speech: "The Son of man did not come to be served, but to serve, and to give his life as a ransom for many" (Mt. 20:28). He used metaphors: "The good shepherd lays down his life for the sheep. I am the good shepherd, and I lay down my life for the sheep" (Jn. 10:11, 14–15). He used parables: "Unless the kernel of wheat falls to the ground and dies, it remains alone, but if it dies, it bears much fruit" (Jn. 12:24). And the night before his death, he told his disciples, "It is better for *y*ou that I go away, for if I do not go away, the Comforter will not come to *y*ou. But if I go, I will send him to *y*ou" (Jn. 16:7). None of these things helped them to comprehend what Jesus was saying, and understandably so. When Jesus spoke of becoming a sacrifice for sin, nobody in Israel believed that he meant he would become a *real* sacrifice, for God had expressly condemned human sacrifice as an abomination "which I did not command, and did not speak, nor did it come into my mind!" (Jer. 19:5; 32:35).[77]

What God did have in mind was to sacrifice His own dear Son, who had been by His side from the beginning, for God was not subject to the law He gave to man. Moreover, He was the only One who had a Son worthy to die for the sins of the world, and it provoked Him to jealousy when humans thought their children were worthy sacrifices for sin. This is why God stopped Abraham from sacrificing Isaac (Gen. 22:10–12); Abraham was willing, but Isaac was not worthy.

The first time Jesus told the disciples that he would die, Peter rebuked him for expressing such an appalling thought: "Peter took him aside and began to rebuke him, saying, 'God forbid, Master!

---

[77] A friend of mine argued that since the imperishable Son of God who came from heaven was not human, no human sacrifice was made, technically speaking. I understand that argument; however, the Son *became* human when he took on a human body, and he took on that human body so that he could die and become a sacrifice for sin. Besides, God's command not to practice human sacrifice was for Israel, not for Himself. God is perfectly free to do as He will.

This shall never happen to you!'" But Jesus' response to Peter's rebuke was swift and harsh: "Get behind me, Satan! You're a stumbling block to me! Your mind isn't on the things of God, but the things of men" (Mt. 16:21–23). Based on that harsh reply, Peter probably figured that he needed to think more spiritually about this dying-and-rising-from-the-dead thing, especially since, after that sharp rebuke, Jesus repeated his statement that some who were there that day would not die before seeing him come in his kingdom. That declaration would have sounded right to Peter; he could understand Jesus talking about soon setting up his kingdom on earth. At least, he thought he understood him.

It was because the disciples never figured out Jesus' "parable" about rising from the dead that his death ended their hope that he was the Messiah. The time immediately following his crucifixion was the gloomiest time of their lives. There was not an ounce of faith left in them that Jesus was the Messiah. There was only fear of what the future held for them, now that he was gone. And in fear of what the rulers would do to them, they went into hiding (Jn. 20:19a).

On the evening of the day he rose from the dead, Jesus appeared to his fearful disciples and comforted them (Jn. 20:19), but Thomas, who didn't happen to be there, refused to believe it even when they told him about it, insisting that he would never believe unless he saw Jesus for himself and touched his wounds with his own hands (Jn. 20:24–25). Thus it was that, while Jesus lived among them, none of his followers believed he would die until he proved it to them by dying, and after he rose from the dead, none of his followers believed he had risen from the dead until he proved it to them by standing in their presence.

Reasons for the Jews' Disappointment in Jesus

(1) Believing Only Some of the Prophecies

The failure of Jesus' followers to believe *all* that was written concerning him, both the suffering and the glory, was a principal cause of their great disappointment in Jesus, and that same failure caused the rest of Israel to not believe in him at all. Both camps believed only in a supernaturally powerful Messiah who would appear and crush Israel's enemies, greatly bless and exalt Israel, and then reign over the earth from Jerusalem (e.g., Isa. 9:7; Dan. 7:14). Everyone in Israel knew that the law and prophets said the Messiah would live forever (Jn. 12:32–34a; cf. Lk. 1:32–33), and nobody – absolutely nobody – believed the Messiah would die.

Maimonides, a Jewish scholar of the 12th century, summed up the feelings of unbelieving Jews from Christ's time until now when he wrote:

> "If a king arises from the house of David, learned in the Torah and an observer of the commandments, as was David his father ... and if he compels all of Israel to live according to it and to reinforce breaches in it, and if he fights the wars of the LORD, then it is this man, assuredly, who is Messiah. Once he has successfully accomplished *these things*, and has rebuilt the Sanctuary in its place, and has gathered the dispersed of Israel, then this man is certainly Messiah. And he will put the world aright — all of it — to serve the Name together.... But if he does not succeed in these things, or if he is killed, then this man is definitely not the one whom Torah promised.... Jesus the Nazarite thought he was Messiah indeed, but he was executed by the Council, as was long ago prophesied by Daniel: 'Robbers among your people will lift themselves up to fulfill the vision, but they will fall.'"[78]

To unbelieving Jews, it has always seemed absurd to suggest that Isaiah was speaking of the Messiah when he prophesied of a man whom God was pleased to harm: "He was pierced for our transgressions; he was crushed for our iniquities; chastisement for our peace was laid upon him; and by his wounds, we are healed. He was oppressed, and he was afflicted, yet he opened not his mouth. He was brought as a lamb to the slaughter, and as a sheep before its shearers is dumb, so he opened not his mouth. He was taken from prison and from justice; he was cut off from the land of the living. For the transgression of my people was he stricken. He

---

[78] Maimonides, *Hilkoth Melakhim* (excerpts, XI, 4). Author's translation.

made his grave with the wicked and with the rich in his death, although he had done no violence, neither was any deceit in his mouth. Yet, it pleased the LORD to crush him; He has put him to grief. He will see the travail of his soul and be satisfied. Yet, he bore the sins of many and interceded for transgressors" (excerpts, Isa. 53). To the collective mind of Israel, to this day, the humbly and innocently suffering man of that prophecy, whom God was pleased to afflict and put to death, cannot possibly be the Messiah.

When Paul was an unbelieving Jew, he, too, thought it was absurd to suggest that a crucified man would be Israel's Messiah, for God had plainly said that anyone who was hanged on a tree was accursed by God (Dt. 21:23). But when Jesus came to Paul and showed him the truth, Paul rejoiced that Christ Jesus became a curse for us, so "that we might receive the promise of the Spirit through faith" (Gal. 3:13–14).

(2) Ignorance of the Two Advents

The Jews of Jesus' time were not wrong to believe that the Messiah will conquer their enemies and exalt Israel; we have seen in this study of Revelation that Jesus will do that when he returns. But to do those things will be the purpose of Jesus' Second Advent; the purpose for his first was to become the atonement for man's sin. That is what nobody in Israel understood, in spite of it being declared plainly by the prophets. Jeremiah, for one example, prophesied that the Messiah would be taken in a trap laid by the wicked (Lam. 4:20),[79] and Daniel, for another, famously foretold that the Messiah would be "cut off and will have nothing" (Dan. 9:26). But the Jews' strong desire for the earthly blessings of Jesus' Second Advent made them oblivious to the heavenly blessings provided by his first one. The bridge connecting those two Advents was the Messiah's resurrection, ascension into heaven, and return to earth. Being ignorant of those elements of the Messiah's story, the Jews expected the Messiah to come but once.

---

[79] This assumes that Jeremiah wrote Lamentations.

Knowing that the prophet said the Messiah would be filled with greater joy than anyone else (Ps. 45:7), the Jews did not realize that the "man of sorrows" of whom Isaiah spoke was also the Messiah (Isa. 53:3). And knowing that God promised to make the Messiah "most blessed, forever" (Ps. 21:6), the Jews did not realize that it was also the Messiah who cried through David, "They pierced my hands and my feet!" (Ps. 22:16). To the Jews, a supremely joyful and blessed Messiah would never have cried out, "I am a worm, and not a man, a reproach to men, and despised by people. Everyone who sees me ridicules me. My strength is dried up like a potsherd, and you have brought me to the dust of death" (excerpts, Ps. 22). It is ironic that, although no one in Israel believed in a suffering and rejected Messiah, by persecuting and rejecting Jesus, unbelieving Jews made the prophecies of the Messiah's suffering come true.

(3) Pride

Another principal reason that so many in Israel rejected Jesus was their great pride in who they were: God's chosen people. Had they not truly been God's chosen people, they could not have become so proud, for truth gives strength to sin when sin makes use of the truth.[80] The Jews' enormous pride in who they were was exposed on the day Jesus read Isaiah's prophecy in the synagogue in Nazareth. At first, everyone there approved of him because they thought he was saying it was time for the Jews to become masters over the Gentiles. But when Jesus went on to remind them that God had at times healed Gentiles instead of equally needy Israelites, those same people "rose up and threw him out of the city, and they led him to the brow of the mountain on which their city was built, to throw him off the cliff" (Lk. 4:22–29). Their pride in who they were blinded them to who Jesus was revealing God to be.

---

[80] This is what Paul meant when he described God's holy law as "the strength of sin" (1Cor. 15:56).

(4) Envy

When the rulers of the Jews arrested Jesus in Gethsemane and took him to Pilate, the perceptive Roman procurator quickly perceived that envy was the rulers' motivation for wanting Jesus destroyed (Mk. 15:10). But envy is always ashamed of itself, and it hides behind causes that appear noble. Before arresting Jesus and taking him to Pilate, the rulers' envy disguised itself as devotion to Moses' law. Now, standing before the Roman governor, the rulers adopted the guise of patriotic devotion to Rome. In flagrant contradiction to the law, which they claimed to represent, they cried out with great passion that they would have no king but Caesar (Jn. 19:15; cf. Dt. 17:15), adding this thinly disguised threat: "If you release this man, you are not a friend of Caesar! Every man who makes himself king opposes Caesar!" (Jn. 19:12b). That crafty tactic worked, for by it, the rulers successfully forced Pilate to prove his devotion to Caesar by crucifying the innocent man standing before him.

RENEWED EXPECTATIONS

Power!

It was an astonishing moment for Cleopas and his fellow traveller when Jesus opened their eyes to see that it was he with whom they had been speaking. When that happened, they finally understood what Jesus had meant all those times he had said that he would rise from the dead. And now, with his resurrection, their expectation of an earthly kingdom was rekindled in all the disciples' hearts, and it burned more intensely than ever. *After all*, they would have thought, *how could the Romans resist the power of a miracle-working Warrior whom they could kill but not keep dead?* This renewed excitement moved the disciples to repeatedly ask[81] the resurrected Jesus, "Is this the time you will re-establish the kingdom of Israel?" (Acts 1:6). Jesus' reply to their question intensified their fervor. He said to them, "It isn't for *you* to know

---

[81] The verb form allows for the translation, "They kept on asking."

times or seasons which the Father has reserved to His own authority. But *you* will receive power after the holy Spirit comes upon *you*" (Acts 1:8a).

Power! That was what the disciples had been waiting for all along. They remembered Jesus' promise to them: "When the Son of man sits down on his glorious throne, *you* will also sit on twelve thrones, judging the twelve tribes of Israel" (Mt. 19:28b; cf. 12:27). And now, Jesus had told them what to look for next: "the promise of the Father", that is, the holy Spirit, which they thought would bestow upon them the kind of power they were looking for.

God's Sign

The disciples watched as Jesus ascended into heaven, and when he was gone, two angels appeared and assured them that Jesus was coming back: "Men of Galilee, why are *you* standing there, staring at the sky? This same Jesus who was taken up from *you* into heaven will come again, the same way *you* watched him go into heaven" (Acts 1:11). The amazed disciples then returned to Jerusalem and waited for the Spirit to come bring them power to reign over Israel with Jesus.

When the Spirit came, about a week later, it filled the disciples' hearts with irrepressible joy (1Pet. 1:8). They emerged boldly from their hiding place, overwhelmed with the glory of God that filled their souls, and in that joy, they staggered out into the street like drunk men (Acts 2:13). Peter then addressed the gathering crowd, warning them that the end had come: "This is that which was spoken by the prophet Joel: 'It shall come to pass in the last days, says God, that I will pour out my Spirit on all flesh, and I will cause wonders to appear in heaven above and signs on earth below: blood and fire and billows of smoke. The sun will be turned to darkness and the moon to blood before the coming of the great and glorious day of the LORD'" (excerpts, Acts 2:16–20; cf. Joel 2:28–31).

The disciples now realized that God had always planned for the Messiah to heal Israel, the land as well as the people, and to reign as King over the earth *only after God poured out His Spirit,* as He said through Ezekiel: "I will put my Spirit within *you*, and I will enable *you* to walk according to my statutes and my judgments, and *you* will diligently keep them. And I will summon the grain and multiply it. And I will make the fruit of the tree and the produce of the field abundant. The land that was made desolate will be worked instead of being the desolation that it was in the sight of all who passed by. And they will say, 'This land that was made desolate has become like the garden of Eden!'" (excerpts, Ezek. 36:27–35). Isaiah, too, prophesied that Israel's land would remain poor "until the Spirit is poured out on us from on high. Then the wilderness will become a fruitful field, and the fruitful field will be deemed a forest, and justice will dwell in the wilderness, and righteousness will dwell in the fruitful field" (Isa. 32:15–16).

So, the disciples rejoiced to realize, though they had been slow to do so, that the outpouring of the Spirit had been the sign to look for all along. John the Baptist had said from the beginning that Jesus would pour out the Spirit (Mt. 3:11), and now that Jesus had done it, how foolish the disciples must have felt to have been disappointed in Jesus! Could there be a more thrilling time to be alive? With the Spirit in them now, Jesus' disciples were beginning to perceive God's long-hidden plan for all mankind! The kingdom now was at hand! Or at least, they thought that it was.

As Soon as Jesus Comes Back

For believers at that time, Jesus' soon return to reign over the earth was the real "promise of the Father". The baptism of the Spirit (which Jesus had called "the promise"), they saw only as God's sign that the salvation and exaltation of Israel was at hand. Jesus had told the disciples to go and wait for the promise. Now, they had waited, the Spirit had come, and the time for fulfilling the promise had come – just as soon as Jesus came back from heaven.

Peter knew that Jesus would remain in heaven "until the time for the restoration of all things, of which God has spoken by the mouth of all His holy prophets from time immemorial" (Acts 3:21). But he thought that time was at hand. The two angels had told the disciples when Jesus ascended that Jesus was coming back, and now, after Pentecost, they felt prepared for him to come and at last do what he was meant to do. So great was the expectation of believers that many of them sold their possessions and property, "and brought the proceeds of the sales and placed them at the feet of the apostles to distribute to each man according to his need" (Acts 2:45; 4:34b–35). What need had they of houses and parcels of land when Jesus was about to make them masters of the whole world, and fill their land with riches beyond measure? Believing Jews were ecstatic to think that they were the generation chosen by God to witness the fulfillment of all things – just as soon as Jesus came back.

RENEWED DISAPPOINTMENT

Jesus Did Not Come Back

When God's two angels told the disciples that Jesus would return, the disciples assumed that he would be back very soon. But that is not what the angels said. Their message was only that "this same Jesus will come again, the same way *you* watched him go into heaven" (Acts 1:11b). At that, the excited disciples returned to Jerusalem and waited for the Spirit to come and for all things to be fulfilled – just as soon as Jesus came back. They now realized that the prophets had prophesied of two Advents of their Messiah, one of suffering and one of glory (cf. 1Pet. 1:11), and now that the Advent of suffering was past, they assumed the Advent of his glory would not be far behind. The thousands of Jews who were converted after the outpouring of the Spirit followed the apostles in believing that Israel's deliverance and exaltation was at hand. But weeks, and then months, and then years passed, and Jesus did not come back. What were believers to think? Had the apostles taught them wrongly? Instead of conquering the nations and ruling the world with Jesus, believing Jews remained under the Roman yoke, and were even despised by many of their own nation (cf. Acts 5:40; 1Thess. 2:14). Believers were again confused and greatly disappointed, and, no doubt, mocked and embarrassed.

Skeptics in Israel were provided with a powerful argument against faith in Jesus when the sun did not turn black, the moon did not turn to blood, and no other astonishing signs occurred, as Peter had proclaimed on the day of Pentecost (Acts 2:16–20). And their criticisms could have been strengthened by using the apostles' own words to prove their point, such as Peter's declaration that the end was at hand and James' assertion that Jesus was even at the door (Jas. 5:8–9). And after decades of frustrated expectation, few Jewish believers could have offered their fellow Jews a convincing defense of faith in Jesus as the Messiah. Time itself seemed to testify against them, and many no doubt came to regret that they had sold their homes and possessions and given the money to the apostles (cf. Acts 4:34–35).

In AD 70, the skeptics' case was made even stronger when the Romans destroyed Jerusalem. Disaster had befallen Israel instead of the promised deliverance, and the Jews' great suffering now made it all but impossible for believing Jews to win unbelieving Jews to the faith. Israel had fallen upon the worst time since Nebuchadnezzar's destruction of the city; so, where was the all-conquering Messiah that believers had been proclaiming? If any one event ruined Jewish believers' hopes of winning their country-men to the Faith, that was it. Indeed, unless the apostles had prepared believers for it, Rome's destruction of Jerusalem would have been a devastating blow to their confidence in Christ. Only if those saints had abandoned hope of seeing Jesus *soon* could they have escaped the abyss of discouragement in Jesus as the Messiah.

The Outpouring of Which Spirit?

After Jesus' death, the oppression of Israel continued, and even increased, and unbelieving Jews would therefore have argued that, since the outpouring of God's Spirit was the sign that Israel's deliverance was at hand (Ezek. 36:24–30), then the Spirit which fell on Jesus' followers on the day of Pentecost must not have been God's Spirit, but an evil spirit instead. And what could believers have said in response? Jesus had not returned, and they and their land were not delivered from the heathen. Believers could testify that the Spirit they received was of God, but they could hardly convince other Jews of it, even by working miracles, as long as Rome dominated them and Israel was not exalted above the nations. The scribes and Pharisees had warned Israel while Jesus was still among them that he was working miracles by the power of the prince of demons (Mt. 9:34; Mk. 3:22), and after the fall of Jerusalem, it would have seemed to most Jews that the scribes and Pharisees had been proved right, for the true Messiah surely would never have allowed such a thing to happen to the holy city.

God does not mind making the righteous look wrong to those whom He has chosen to cut off from His grace. He takes no pleasure in the death of the wicked, to be sure (Ezek. 33:11), for He is full of compassion and willing to forgive. However, He can be provoked by stubborn rebelliousness to the point that He no more offers His grace and will let the wicked think they are the righteous. In such cases, we may see how true it is that "it is a fearful thing to fall into the hands of the living God" (Heb. 10:31). God can curse souls with such blindness that they feel blessed not to be among those who are truly righteous, and He did this to the Jews who refused His Son, even to this day. Seeing God hardening the heart of his beloved fellow Jews, the apostle Paul grieved aloud that the wrath of God had finally overtaken them (Rom. 9:1–2; 1Thess. 2:16). They were at that time descending into complete darkness. Having rejected their Messiah, many in Israel were happy, even thankful to God, that they did not believe Jesus.

The Veil

As long as the Jews are despised and persecuted around the world, it will continue to seem wrong-headed to them to believe in Jesus. To their way of thinking, life as it has been for them during the past two millennia makes no sense if Jesus was their Messiah, for they are blinded by a flawed faith, a faith that believes only in the Messiah of the Second Advent and rejects the Messiah of the First. Their hearts are covered with a thick veil of unbelief, but on the day Jesus comes from heaven to save the surviving third of the nation from the Beast and his armies, that remnant of Israel will bow before Jesus and the blinding veil will be removed, just as Paul predicted: "Whenever Moses is read, a veil lies over their heart. But if ever their heart turns to the Lord, the veil will be lifted off" (2Cor. 3:15–16). In John's vision of the end-times, he saw that wonderful day come.

No Vain Expectations: Paul's Gospel

Paul Knew

God sent Paul to the Gentiles with a new gospel that differed in two principal ways from the Jewish gospel that Jesus' apostles had been preaching since Pentecost: first, Paul's gospel for the Gentiles excluded the law of Moses, and second, it rejected the notion that Jesus would soon return and enrich the saints by making them the rulers of this world. The significance of the latter can hardly be overemphasized. Jesus' Second Coming, as we have seen, will be to fulfill all the prophecies of healing and enrichment of Israel and their land, as well as the prophecies of believers reigning with him over the earth. But Paul taught the saints of his time that that would not happen soon and that saints would have to suffer before they reigned with Christ (Rom. 8:17; 2Tim. 2:12). Indeed, Paul taught that everyone who lives a righteous life will suffer in this world (2Tim. 3:12). The Jewish gospel, which Peter and the other apostles taught, as good as it was, had an undeniable appeal to man's corrupt, fleshly nature by promising believers unprecedented earthly wealth and power – just as soon as Jesus came back, which they believed would happen in their lifetime. And that means they did not expect or prepare for the suffering which Paul's gospel insisted the righteous would experience.

We are not told when, if ever, Jesus' original apostles came to understand that Jesus would not return quickly, but Paul certainly knew it. He taught the Gentiles not to place their hope in any earthly thing, whether it be the law of Moses or the kind of worldly glory that Jesus will bring to believers when he returns. Paul understood that God has determined that His children must share in the suffering of the Messiah's First Advent in order to be counted worthy to share in the glory of his Second. He straitly warned his Gentile converts to reject the notion that Christ's return was at hand (2Thess. 2:1–3), exhorting them instead to be faithful through the unavoidable trials of this life. And he warned believers that "we must through many tribulations enter into the kingdom of God" (Acts 14:22b). Paul assured believers that they would reap all the good they had done, but he let them know that God would give them their reward only "in due time" (Gal. 6:9). In other words, "Do not look for that reward today, or any time soon."

Paul warned believers that those who desire worldly gain and glory would "fall into temptation, and a snare, and many foolish and harmful lusts which plunge men into ruin and destruction" (1Tim. 6:9), and it is for that reason that he told the Corinthian saints, "We do not look at things that are seen, but at things that are not seen, for things that are seen are temporal, but things that are not seen are eternal" (2Cor. 4:18). Paul exhorted his Colossian converts to "seek things that are above, where Christ is sitting at God's right hand" and to "keep your minds on things above, not on things on the earth" (Col. 3:1b–2). To have one's mind on earthly power and wealth, Paul said, "is death. But to be spiritually mind-ed is life and peace" (Rom. 8:6). That is why it was so important to Paul to direct the saints' desire toward spiritual things. He knew that it would be impossible for God's children *not* to have their minds on earthly things if they believed that Jesus was soon return-ing to bring them incomparable earthly blessings. The gospel that God gave to Paul, and it alone, provided believers with perfect peace, for it gave them no false hope and stirred up no vain expec-tations.

The Great Apostasy

At first, many of the elders among Jewish believers, including the apostles, acknowledged Paul's gospel as being of God (Gal. 2:9). Some of them, however, knowing that when Jesus returned, he would return to rescue and exalt Israel, were concerned that be-lieving Gentiles would be left out of that blessing unless they con-verted to Judaism. Believing that Gentile believers would be damned unless they became Jews (Acts 15:1; cf. Acts 17:5–13), and with great zeal for the souls of believing Gentiles, those men went out from Jerusalem (with no commission from God) to "en-lighten" the Gentiles as to their need to be circumcised and become a part of Israel. "They went out from us," wrote John, "but they were not of us, for if they were of us, they would have remained among us [i.e., among the Jews]" (1Jn. 2:19).

What those Jewish teachers carried to the Gentiles was the gospel that Jesus had taught and that Peter and the other apostles were still teaching, but God had given that gospel only for the Jews. Outside the Jewish community, it was a false gospel, for God did not give it for the Gentiles. Paul tried to quash the influence of that Jewish gospel among his converts, but the appeal of a gospel that promised believers supreme earthly power and wealth (as soon as Jesus came back) was just too powerful. And when Paul traveled to Jerusalem for the last time, the misinformation that those teachers had spread among the Jews about Paul almost cost him his life (Acts 21:21, 27–35).

Paul's gospel was entirely a gospel of the Spirit, and he forbade Gentile believers to follow the Jews in worshipping "in the flesh", the way Moses commanded in the law (Gal. 5:4; cf. Phip. 3:3–6). According to Paul, if Jesus circumcised a man's heart by the Spirit, then he was already a Jew (Rom. 2:28–29), a part of "the Israel of God" (Gal. 6:16), for the law of God had been engraved on his heart, "written not with ink but with the Spirit of the living God, not on tablets of stone but on tablets of human hearts" (2Cor. 3:3; Heb. 8:8–10). But Paul's gospel, which provided believers with the strength they would need to endure the unavoidable sufferings of this life, was not as attractive as a gospel which offered no suffering at all, but great riches and glory in this life – as soon as Jesus came back.

In part, the Jewish teachers won the hearts of Gentile believers because they appeared to love them, praising them for putting their faith in Jesus. But when Paul learned this was happening to his beloved converts in Galatia, he warned them, "They are making much of *you*, but not for good; they want to exclude *you* [because of *your* uncircumcision] so that *you* will make much of them" (Gal. 4:17). Paul insisted that Jesus had ushered in a new way, in which Gentiles were washed from their sins without physical circumcision, water baptism, or any other ceremony, and that the riches of God's kingdom had nothing to do with this world's wealth. But hope of supreme earthly glory overwhelmed the Gentiles' faith in Paul and his gospel.

Paul confessed that God had revealed to him "inexpressible things which are unlawful for a man to speak" (2Cor. 12:4), and Peter was forced to admit that Paul taught "some things hard to understand" (2Pet. 3:15–16). But what makes any truth hard to understand is a heart dulled by what it thinks it knows. So it was with the earliest body of Christ. The believing Jews, first, and later the believing Gentiles, were certain that Jesus was coming back soon to bring them magnificent worldly glory. But as Paul would have told them, they were attracted to that vain hope only because they were "in the flesh" instead of "in the Spirit".

As part of the astonishing gospel which God revealed to Paul, God clarified for him two of the events which Jesus said would precede his Second Coming. They were, first, a great apostasy of the body of Christ and, second, the exposing of the "man of sin, the son of damnation, who opposes and exalts himself above everything called God or that is worshipped, so that he, as God, sits in God's temple, promoting himself as being God" (2Thess. 2:1–4).[82] No one in Paul's day who believed that those two events must take place before Jesus returned would have looked for Jesus to return soon. But relatively few at that time believed Paul's gospel, and the number of those who did believe it decreased dramatically over time.

With a heavy heart, Paul wrote to the Corinthians, "The more I love *you*, the less I am loved" (2Cor. 12:15), which reflected Paul's feelings toward all his Gentile converts. To the Galatians, Paul wrote in desperation, "Who has bewitched *you*, that *you* should not obey the truth? Are *you* so foolish? Having begun in the Spirit, are *you* now perfected by the flesh?" (Gal. 3:1, 3). It broke Paul's heart to see God's Gentile saints persuaded to set their hope on earthly things, and he mourned that they were being turned into "enemies of the cross of Christ" (Phip. 3:18–19). But nothing Paul did availed, and the body of Christ everywhere embraced the gospel of the Jews. The swiftness of the Gentiles' turn to that

---

[82] Paul was speaking of a spiritual event, for in this covenant, the bodies of His saints is the place God dwells, by the Spirit (1Cor. 6:19). But after Paul's gospel was rejected by the body of Christ at large, an expectation of a rebuilt temple in Jerusalem became widespread among believers, even to this day.

gospel, once they heard it, stunned Paul (Gal. 1:6–7), and he watched helplessly as the "chaste virgin" of Christ was courted and won by unordained ministers. He had pleaded, wept, threatened, and grieved for what was happening, but nothing he did or said reversed the tide of apostasy that was sweeping the Bride of Christ off her feet. It didn't even help when Paul warned her that the men to whom she was now giving her affections were ministers of Satan, "transforming themselves into apostles of Christ" (2Cor. 11:13–15). And as an aged apostle, sitting in a Roman prison, Paul lamented the apostasy of *all* his converts in Asia (2Tim. 1:15), and that same apostasy was taking place everywhere. By that time, all Gentile believers, with a few exceptions, had rejected Paul's gospel and embraced instead the gospel that promised them supreme earthly wealth and power – as soon as Jesus came back.

Mystery: Babylon the Great

Such was the spiritual condition of believers at the close of the era of the apostles, an era so fraught with heresy that anyone, including the apostle John himself, who believed that Paul's gospel was of God, became *persona non grata* in some, if not most, of the assemblies of believers (cf. 3Jn. 1:9–10). The wrong gospel eventually became orthodoxy for all believers, except for a few dissenting voices, and after almost three centuries of patient suffering with the apostasy of His New Testament saints, God gave them over to the earthly power and wealth they desired, and they blended with Rome, the empire that ruled the world.[83] Believers at last gained the great worldly glory they desired, but at an awful cost. It was, for them, just as the psalmist once said of rebellious Israel: "He gave them what they asked for, but He sent leanness into their souls" (Ps. 106:15).

The doctrine of a Second Advent continued to be taught after believers blended with Rome, but an *imminent* return of Jesus no longer had a great appeal for believers, for they were now enjoying

---

[83] The uniting of believers with Rome fulfilled their dream of earthly glory, and Christians such as Eusebius, Bishop of Caesarea, exulted in it, as is evidenced by Eusebius' sycophantic "Oration and Praise of Constantine".

the privileges and luxuries of the Empire. False teachers drifted away from proclaiming an imminent return of Jesus, for with them, it was just fine if Jesus waited a while to return, for now, they were being honored, envied, and even feared by men. And except for the few believers who dared to condemn the apostasy of the body of Christ,[84] everything seemed under control, and with the Empire's political and military might now at their disposal, the false teachers whom Jesus and Paul saw coming silenced even those few voices.

Unknown to the backslidden body of Christ, what they had embraced was "the abomination of desolation" of which Jesus had warned his disciples on the Mount of Olives (Mt. 24:15). Pursuing worldly gain, the precious virgin of Christ gave herself to men of the world and became the Great Whore of Revelation 17, the religious system known as Christianity, the abomination which made the body of Christ desolate of the grace, power, and knowledge of God that had been purchased for them by the suffering and sacrifice of Jesus.[85]

The Second Advent Will Come

Everything that the prophets said the Messiah would do, Jesus will do, but in God's time, not ours. As John saw in his vision of the end-times, Jesus will return and rescue Israel from all her enemies, and afterward, he will rule over the whole world from Jerusalem. He will bring all the dispersed Jews to their homeland, bless the land of Israel with unheard-of prosperity, and compel the Gentiles to honor the true God with their wealth and abject obedience. Yes, the Son of God is coming again, this time to fulfill the prophecies which he did not fulfill the first time he came. And this time, he will not walk among us as the meek Lamb of God, but will reign over the nations as the fierce Lion of the tribe of Judah.

Now, we will continue our examination of John's revelation.

---

[84] Among these were Montanus and Arius.

[85] For more on this apostasy, see *The Iron Kingdom Series, Vol. 3: The Apostate Fathers*, available for online reading at GoingtoJesus.com.

Chapter 10
The Final Judgment and
the New Heaven and New Earth
Revelation 20:11 – 22:21

New Bodies for Millennial Believers

The Old Testament prophecies concerning the Jews after Jesus returns leads us to conclude that during the Millennial Reign, the Jews, along with the Gentiles who move to Israel, will continue in their natural bodies. They will receive glorified bodies, but apparently, that will not happen until the end of the thousand years when God destroys this entire creation (2Pet. 3:7, 10–13). Isaiah spoke of Jesus giving those new bodies to his Millennial saints when he said that God would do away with "the face of the covering that covers all peoples, and the veil that is spread over all the nations" (Isa. 25:7b). It was only after the Spirit came that it was revealed that the "veil" which "covers all peoples" is flesh (Heb. 10:20). And when God does away with fleshly bodies forever, replacing them with glorious, eternal bodies, it is then that "He will swallow up death forever" and "wipe away tears from all faces" (Isa. 25:8). The new bodies will be given to those believers at Jerusalem (Isa. 25:6–7a), which will be the second time Jesus gives believers new bodies. The first time he grants new bodies to believers was in the first resurrection when he caught up his faithful saints to meet him in the air (1Cor. 15:51–52; Rev. 14:14–16).

¶11. **And I saw a great white throne and Him who sat on it, from whose face earth and heaven fled, and no place was found for them.**

Note 1: Once again, John provides no details of an incredibly important event. However, Peter describes the destruction of this heaven and this earth: "The day of the Lord will come like a thief in the night, in which the heavens, being on fire, will pass away with a roar and be destroyed, and the elements, consumed with burning heat, will be dissolved and destroyed, and the earth and the works that are in it will be burned up" (2Pet. 3:10, 12). Isaiah also saw in a vision that "the heavens will vanish like smoke, and the earth will wax old like a garment" (Isa. 51:6a). On the Mount of Olives, all that Jesus told his disciples of this cataclysmic event is contained in his brief, well-known declaration, "Heaven and earth shall pass away" (Mt. 24:35).

Note 2: If this physical creation is destroyed, then the physical bodies that belong in it will be destroyed along with it. New, spiritual bodies will be given to the saints who are judged worthy to escape the wrath of God, and the sinners who are damned in the Final Judgment and cast into the Lake of Fire will have no body at all.

12. And I saw the dead, the great and the small, standing before the throne. And books were opened, and another book was opened (which is the Book of Life), and the dead were judged by the things written in the books, according to their deeds.

13. And the sea gave up the dead who were in it, and death and hell gave up the dead who were in them, and they were judged, each one, according to their deeds.

Note 1: Death and hell will give up their dead, but the Lake of Fire will never do so. The Lake of Fire is the abode of the damned *after* they have received their eternal judgment. Death and hell are where the damned are held until that day.

Note 2: This is the Day of Judgment to which Paul referred in 2Corinthians 5:10, when he said, "We must all appear before the judgment seat of Christ, that each may receive recompense for the things done in the body, according to what he did, whether good or bad." The result of this eternal judgment is that all creatures will be put where they belong forever, whether it be the Lake of Fire, or the new heaven, or the new earth.

Note 3: The Day of Judgment is when judgment is pronounced, not when it is decided. Our eternal judgment is being determined now, while we live; on the Day of Judgment, however, everyone's judgment will be pronounced.

Note 4: John's warning that our eternal judgment will be determined on the basis of our deeds is consistent with what all the prophets and apostles taught. Every time the basis for eternal judgment is mentioned in Scripture, that basis is said to be our works, not our faith or our gifts. Here are a few examples:

- "You will reward man according to his work" (Ps. 62:12b).
- "God will bring every deed into judgment, with every secret thing, whether it be good or evil" (Eccl. 12:14).
- "The Son of man will come in the glory of his Father, with His angels, and then will he render to each one according to what he has done" (Mt. 16:27).
- "All who are in the tombs will hear [my] voice, and they will come out, those who did good things unto the resurrection of life, but those who did bad things, unto the resurrection of damnation" (Jn. 5:28–29).

14. And Death and Hell were cast into the Lake of Fire. This is the Second Death, the Lake of Fire.

Note 1: The "Death and Hell" of this verse are living beings (hence, the capitalization of their names). Hades was the Greek name for the abode of the dead, as well as for the Greek god who ruled over that abode. John is using the word Hell here (Hades in the Greek text) in the same way. It is the name of a place, but it is also the name of the angel who has authority over that place.

Death and Hell are fallen angels who have been given authority over death and hell (under Christ, of course – Rev. 1:18). That this duo are living beings is seen in the fact that in Revelation 6, John saw Death riding a horse, and Hell was following him. Seeing them as living creatures helps us understand why they will be cast into the Lake of Fire along with all other damned creatures, instead of simply being destroyed, as inanimate objects in this creation will be.

Note 2: Paul said that the last enemy to be destroyed will be death (1Cor. 15:26), and if death itself is destroyed, then no one can die. Those blessed with salvation will live forever in peace and joy, and those who are damned will live forever in torment in the Lake of Fire.

15. And if anyone was not found written in the Book of Life, he was cast into the Lake of Fire.

Note 1: There are two groups who will be cast into the Lake of Fire on the Day of Judgment. The first group is people whose names were never in the Book of Life. The second group is people whose names were once in the Book of Life, but because of disobedience, their names were blotted out (Rev. 3:5). Moses knew of the Book of Life, and when pleading with God to forgive Israel for erecting the golden calf, he said to God, "Yet, now, if you will forgive their sin – but if not, I pray you, blot me out of your Book that you have written" (Ex. 32:32). To which God responded, "Whoever has sinned against me, him will I blot out of my Book." And concerning those in Israel who would reject and abuse him when he came, the Son of God prayed through the Psalmist, "Let them be blotted out of the Book of Life and not be written among the righteous!" (Ps. 69:28).

Note 2: To have one's name in the Lamb's Book of Life is one of the greatest blessings possible. When Jesus sent out his disciples with power to heal the sick and cast out demons, they returned from their mission with amazement and joy at the miracles they found they could do in his name. But Jesus tempered their rejoicing by telling them, "Do not rejoice in this, that spirits are subject to *you*, but rejoice that *your* names are written in heaven" (Lk. 10:20).

Revelation 21

The New Heaven, and New Earth, and New Jerusalem

¶1. And I saw a new heaven and a new earth, for the first heaven and the first earth had passed away, and the sea no longer existed.

2. And I saw the holy city, New Jerusalem, coming down out of heaven from God, prepared like a bride adorned for her husband.

Note 1: New Jerusalem is not the Bride of Christ, as some teach; the faithful saints are his Bride, and he is the Bridegroom. It was not unusual to say that someone or something is prepared as a bride adorns herself with jewels or as a bridegroom decks himself with ornaments (e.g., Isa. 61:10). It was a commonly understood phrase that meant preparations had been made, not that a person or place is an actual bride or bridegroom. With this phrase, John is only telling us that the city has been beautifully prepared for habitation.

Note 2: This New Jerusalem is the city for which Abraham longed, "whose Architect and Builder is God", the city "which has foundations" (Heb. 11:10), and that cannot be shaken because it is not of this creation (Heb. 12:27).

3. And I heard a loud voice from heaven, saying, "Behold! The dwelling-place of God with men! And He will dwell with them, and they will be His people, and God Himself will be with them.

4. And He will wipe away every tear from their eyes, and death will be no more. Neither will there be sorrow, nor crying, nor pain anymore because the former things will have passed away."

Note 1: Isaiah prophesied that God, "will swallow up death forever! And the Lord GOD will wipe away tears from all faces" (Isa. 25:8a), but it is here, not at the first resurrection, that God will do away with all sorrow and pain.

Note 2: This promise of no more sorrow or pain includes an erasing of the memory of lost loved ones (cf. Isa. 26:14). No one could enjoy eternal bliss if he remembered loved ones who refused Christ and were in the Lake of Fire, being tormented day and night forever. God's promise to bless the saved with a loss of memory is a precious one: "The former troubles will be forgotten, and will be hidden from my eyes. For behold, I am creating new heavens and a new earth, and the former things will not be remembered nor come to mind" (Isa. 65:16b–17).

5. And the One sitting on the throne said, "Behold! I am making everything new!" And He said to me, "Write! For these words are true and faithful."

6. And He said to me, "I have become the Alpha and the Omega, the beginning and the end. I, myself, will give freely of the fountain of the water of life to him who is thirsty.

Note 1: As was pointed out in chapter one, throughout John's Revelation, the phrase, "the One sitting on the throne", refers to the Father.

Note 2: The Son will always be our head, our Lord, and our Savior, but on the new earth, the Father Himself will be the Alpha and Omega for His children. Until the end of this age, God has appointed His Son, "the exact representation of His being" (Heb. 1:3), to be the Alpha and Omega for His children. However, in saying, "I have become the Alpha and the Omega," the Father is speaking of the time when the Son will bow at His feet and turn everything back over to Him, so that the Father becomes all things to all His people. Paul prophesied of that day: "Then will come the end, when he [the Son] will hand over the kingdom to God the Father, when he has done away with all government, and all authority, and power. For he [the Son] must reign until He [the Father] puts all his enemies under his [the Son's] feet. And when all things are subdued under him [the Son], then will the Son himself submit to Him who subdued all things under him, that God might be all things to all people" (1Cor. 15:24–25, 28).

7. He who overcomes will inherit these things, and I will be his God, and he will be my son.

8. As for the fearful, and faithless, and sinful, and filthy, and murderers, and the immoral, and sorcerers, and idolaters, and all liars, their portion will be in the lake that burns with fire and sulfur, which is the Second Death."

Details of the New Jerusalem

¶9. And one of the seven angels who had the Seven Vials filled with the Seven Last Plagues came and spoke with me, saying, "Come. I will show you the Bride, the wife of the Lamb."

10. And he carried me away in the Spirit onto a great and high mountain and showed me the great city, the holy Jerusalem, coming down out of heaven from God,

11. having the glory of God. Its brilliance was like a precious stone, as a stone of jasper, clear as crystal,

12. having a great and high wall, with twelve gates, and upon the gates were twelve angels, and names written, which are the names of the twelve tribes of the sons of Israel.

13. On the east were three gates, and on the north, three gates, and on the south, three gates, and on the west, three gates.

14. And the wall of the city had twelve foundations, and upon them were the twelve names of the twelve apostles of the Lamb.

15. And the one speaking with me held a golden measuring rod to measure the city, and its gates, and its wall.

16. The city lay square, its length the same as its breadth. And he measured the city with the measuring rod to be twelve thousand stadia;[86] its length and breadth and height were equal.

---

[86] Twelve-thousand stadia is close to 1,400 miles.

17a. And he measured its wall, one hundred and forty-four cubits,[87]

Note: Having a wall of 210 feet surrounding a city 1,400 miles high may seem senseless, but then, this wall is not for defense but for beauty. One brother also posited that 210 feet might be the wall's width, while its height is unknown.

17b. *according to* **the measure of a man (that is, of an angel).**

Note: Angels and humans have the same general bodily form and measure. This is why people can meet and have dealings with angels without realizing it (Heb. 13:2).

18. And the building material of its wall was jasper, and the city was pure gold, like clear glass.
19. The foundations of the walls of the city were adorned with every precious stone. The first foundation was jasper; the second, sapphire; the third, chalcedony; the fourth, emerald;
20. the fifth, sardonyx; the sixth, sardius; the seventh, chrysolite; the eighth, beryl; the ninth, topaz; the tenth, chrysoprase; the eleventh, jacinth; the twelfth, amethyst.
21. And the twelve gates were twelve pearls; each one of the gates was made of a single pearl, and the street of the city was pure gold, transparent like glass.
22. And I did not see a temple in it, for the LORD God Almighty is its temple, and the Lamb.
23. And the city had no need of the sun or of the moon to shine upon it, for the glory of God illuminated it, and its lamp was the Lamb.

Note 1: The Spirit also spoke through Isaiah about this: "They will neither hunger nor thirst, and heat and sun will not beat upon them. For He who pities them will guide them, and by springs of water will He refresh them" (Isa. 49:10).

---

[87] One hundred and forty-four cubits is about 210 feet.

Note 2: John does not say that there will be no sun or moon; he only says that the city will not need them. Isaiah's description of the new heaven and new earth includes a moon (Isa. 66:23), but the glory and light of God will make the light of the sun and moon of little significance. The sun and moon will not shine in order to give the saints light; they will shine only for beauty. Isaiah spoke of this when he said, "The sun will no longer be for your light by day, nor will the brightness of the moon be for your light, but the LORD your God will be your light and your glory forever. Your sun will never go down, and your moon will not wane, for the LORD will forever be your light, and your days of mourning will be over" (Isa. 60:19–20).

24. And by its light will the nations walk, and the kings of the earth will bring their glory into it.

Note: The kings of the new earth will be men such as Job, Noah, Moses, Samuel, Daniel, Paul, and others whose right-eousness and wisdom will have earned them seats of high honor in the eternal kingdom of Christ on the new earth.

25. And its gates will never be closed by day – and night does not exist there –
26. and they will bring the glory and the honor of the nations into it,
27. and no unclean thing will ever by any means enter into it, nor he who devises an abomination or a lie, but only those who are written in the Lamb's Book of Life.

Note: This wonderful promise of the eternal absence of evil was also foretold by Nahum: "He will make an utter end. Trouble will not rise up a second time" (Nah. 1:9b).

Revelation 22

More about the New Jerusalem

¶1. And he showed me a pure river of living water, sparkling like crystal, coming out of the throne of God and of the Lamb.

2. In the midst of its street and on both sides of the river was a tree of life producing twelve fruit. Every month, each one yielded its fruit, and the leaves of the tree are for the healing of the nations.

Note: There is great similarity between this scene and a vision God gave to Ezekiel: "And on the river, on this bank and that, will grow every tree for food, whose leaf will not wither, and whose fruit will not fail. Month by month, each tree will bear new fruit because of the water which flows out from the sanctuary, and its fruit will be for food, and its leaves, for healing" (Ezek. 47:12).

3. And there will no longer be any curse. And the throne of God and of the Lamb will be in it, and His slaves will minister to Him,

4. and they will see His face, and His name will be on their foreheads.

5. And there will be no more night there, and they will have no need of a lamp or sunlight because the LORD God will shine on them, and they will reign forever and ever.

Final Exhortations

¶6. And he said to me, "These words are faithful and true, and the LORD, the God of the spirits of the prophets, has sent His messenger to show His slaves things that must quickly happen.

7. And behold! I am coming quickly. Blessed is he who keeps the words of the prophecy of this book."

Note: It sounds as if Jesus has begun to speak in this verse, but that is not the case. Angels often speak in the first person when they are delivering a message from God or His Son. It was an angel, you may recall, who spoke to Moses out of the burning bush on Mount Sinai and said, "I am the God of your father, the God of Abraham, the God of Isaac, and the God of Jacob" (Ex. 3:2, 6; Acts 7:30). Angels are merely a conduit for the word of God.

¶8. **And I am John, who heard and saw these things. And when I heard and saw them, I fell down to worship at the feet of the messenger who showed me these things.**
9. **But he said to me, "Do not do that. I am a slave with you and your brothers, the prophets, and with those who obey the words of this book. Worship God!"**

Note: It is interesting that Jesus, still speaking through the angel, considered himself a fellow-slave with John and the prophets and that he would say that he also obeyed the words of this prophecy.

¶10. **And he said to me, "Do not seal the words of the prophecy of this book, for the time is near.**

Note: Unlike Daniel, John is forbidden to seal up his revelation. When Daniel was writing out his prophecy, an angel told him, "Seal the scroll until the time of the end" (Dan. 12:4a). When Daniel pleaded with another angel to help him understand the meaning of the prophecies he had just been given, that angel bluntly responded, "Go, Daniel! The words are shut up and sealed until the time of the end" (Dan. 12:9). John, on the other hand, is commanded *not* to seal his prophecies because the Lamb of God had opened the seals to give us an understanding of the mysteries of the kingdom of God.

11. **He who is unjust, let him be unjust still; and he who is filthy, let him be filthy still; and he who is righteous, let him keep doing righteousness; and he who is holy, let him be holy still.**

Note: These words do not apply to us in our time, for we can still change, for better or for worse. These words apply to the time after the Day of Judgment. From that point on, no one's condition will ever change.

12. **Behold! I am coming quickly. And my reward is with me, to give to each one according to his work.**
13. **I am the Alpha and the Omega, the first and the last, the beginning and the end.**
14. **Blessed are they who keep His commandments so that the right to the tree of life will be theirs, and they may enter through the gates into the city.**
15. **Outside are dogs, and sorcerers, and the immoral, and murderers, and idolaters, and everyone who loves or devises a lie."**

Note 1: Here, "dogs" is most likely a reference to sodomites, as in Deuteronomy 23:18.

Note 2: John says only that these wicked people are "outside" the walls of New Jerusalem (see note 2 under Revelation 14:11), where the Lake of Fire can be seen.

¶16. **"I, Jesus, have sent my messenger to testify of these things to *you who are* over the Assemblies.[88] I am the root and the offspring of David, the bright morning star."**

Note: The "you" in this verse is plural, which means that Jesus sent this Revelation to the seven remaining pastors in Asia, no doubt intending for it to be read by all true pastors everywhere. God will not allow anyone else to understand it and teach it rightly. The understanding of the mysteries of God's kingdom is not given to everyone (cf. Mt. 13:10–17); it is reserved for those whom He has chosen to receive it. When others attempt to explain John's Revelation, or any revelation from the Spirit, the result is a confused mass of contradictory theories.

---

[88] Or, "to *you* for the Assemblies."

¶17. And the Spirit and the Bride say, "Come!" And let him who hears say, "Come!" And let him who is thirsty come. And he who is willing, let him take of the water of life freely.

¶18. I testify to everyone who hears the words of the prophecy of this book: if anyone adds to them, God will add to him the plagues that are written in this book,

19. and if anyone takes away from the words of the book of this prophecy, God will take away his part from the tree of life and from the holy city, the things which are written in this book.

Note: This warning is similar to the one Moses gave Israel: "*You* shall not add to the word that I am commanding *you*, and *you* shall not take away from it, that *you* may keep the commandments of the LORD *your* God which I command *you*" (Dt. 4:2).

¶20. He who testifies these things says, "Yes, I am coming quickly." Amen! Yes! Come, Lord Jesus!

¶21. The grace of the Lord Jesus Christ be with all the saints. Amen.

Appendix

General Order of End-Time Events
Revelation 6–22

1. The Seven Seals.
2. The Seven Trumpets.
3. The Appearing of Jesus (The Resurrection of Life).
4. The Seven Vials (The Seven Last Plagues).
5. The Second Coming of Jesus.
6. The Millennial Reign.
7. The Final Judgment (The Resurrection of Damnation).

Detailed Order of End-Time Events
Revelation 6–22

A. THE SEVEN SEALS.

1. The First Seal is opened.
   a. A White Horse.
   b. A spirit of deception divides the people of God.
2. The Second Seal is opened.
   a. A Fiery Red Horse.
   b. A spirit is sent to take peace from the world.
3. The Third Seal is opened.
   a. A Black Horse.
   b. This has something to do with the economy and food supply of the earth.
   c. Oil and wine unharmed.
4. The Fourth Seal is opened.
   a. A Pale Green Horse.
   b. Through famine, disease, war, and beasts, one fourth of all people die.
5. The Fifth Seal is opened.
   a. A time of great tribulation for the saints.

6. The Sixth Seal is opened.

    a. God plagues men with natural disasters.

7. The Seventh Seal is opened.

    a. Seven angels are given the Seven Trumpets.

    b. More natural disasters; earthquake.

B. THE SEVEN TRUMPETS.

1. The First Trumpet.

    a. Hail and fire, mixed with blood, fall to earth.

    b. One third of all trees and all grass is burned up.

2. The Second Trumpet.

    a. Something like a burning mountain falls into the sea.

    b. One third of the sea becomes blood, and one third of all sea creatures die, and one third of ships are destroyed.

3. The Third Trumpet.

    a. A large, blazing star falls to earth.

    b. One third of all fresh water is ruined, killing many.

4. The Fourth Trumpet.

    a. One third of the sun, moon, and stars are struck.

    b. Days are shortened by one third.

5. The Fifth Trumpet.

    a. Strange, stinging locusts are loosed from the Abyss.

    b. Men are tormented for five months, not allowed to die.

6. The Sixth Trumpet.

    a. An army of at least 100,000,000 slays one third of mankind.

    b. God's Two Witnesses prophesy in Jerusalem for three-and-a-half years.

    c. The Beast arises and kills God's Two Witnesses.

    d. The body of Christ suffers through another time of great tribulation.

7. The Seventh Trumpet.

    a. A voice in heaven declares, "It is done."

    b. A wonder appears in the sky, telling the story of Jesus. It is God's last call to the Gentiles.

C. THE APPEARING OF JESUS (The Resurrection of Life).

1. Jesus appears in the sky on a cloud.
2. Those who are dead in Christ are raised from the dead.
3. Faithful saints still living are also caught up to meet Jesus.
4. Jesus takes the faithful to heaven and presents them to the Father while the Seven Vials of God's wrath are poured out on earth.

D. THE SEVEN VIALS (The Seven Last Plagues).

1. The First Vial is poured out on earth.
   a. A "foul and painful sore" comes upon men.

2. The Second Vial is poured out on the sea.
   a. The entire sea becomes blood.
   b. Every creature in the sea dies.

3. The Third Vial is poured out on sources of fresh water.
   a. All fresh water becomes blood.

4. The Fourth Vial is poured out on the sun.
   a. The sun scorches earth.
   b. In agony, men blaspheme God.

5. The Fifth Vial is poured out on the throne of the Beast.
   a. Darkness fills his kingdom.
   b. Men gnaw their tongues for pain.
   c. Men blaspheme God and do not repent.

6. The Sixth Vial is poured out on the Euphrates River.
   a. The Euphrates is dried up to prepare for the kings of the east.
   b. Three demons like frogs go out to persuade the nations to attack Israel.
   c. The armies of the earth gather at Armageddon.

7. The Seventh Vial is poured out into the air.
   a. An earthquake of unprecedented magnitude strikes.
   b. Every island disappears and every mountain collapses.
   c. The nations attack Israel, killing or enslaving two thirds of the Jews.

E. THE SECOND COMING OF JESUS.

1. Jesus rescues Israel from total annihilation.
2. The Beast's army is butchered by Jesus, and the Beast and the False Prophet are cast into the Lake of Fire.
3. Satan is thrown into the Abyss for a thousand years.
4. The Jews realize who Jesus is, and repent.
5. Jesus washes the Jews from their sins with the holy Spirit.

F. THE MILLENNIAL REIGN.

1. The saints reign for a thousand years with Jesus over the nations that remain on earth.
2. There are occasional rebellions, but Jesus rules "with a rod of iron".
3. At the end of the thousand years, Satan is loosed from the Abyss.
4. Satan deceives the nations, and they attack Jesus and the saints at Jerusalem.
5. The Father rains fire and brimstone out of heaven on the attacking nations.

G. THE FINAL JUDGMENT (The Resurrection of Damnation).

1. Satan is cast in the Lake of Fire where the Beast and the False Prophet are.
2. This earth and this heaven are destroyed.
3. All the remaining dead are raised to face judgment.
   a. Jesus rewards the wicked with eternal torment.
   b. Jesus rewards the righteous with a new heaven and a new earth, and a new Jerusalem.

The Land of Israel as the Wilderness

The following are some of the verses which show that "the wilderness" is sometimes used in prophecy for the land of Israel.

- Of the land of Israel being made a wilderness because of the false prophets and priests who perverted the faith of the nation:

  "Many shepherds have destroyed my vineyard; they have trampled down my heritage; they have turned my precious heritage into a desolate wilderness. They have made it a desolation; it mourns because of me, devastated. The whole land has been made desolate because there is not a man who lays it to heart" (Jer. 12:10–11).

  "I will make her like the wilderness, and lay her waste like a desert, and I will kill her with thirst" (Hos. 2:3b).

  "Your holy cities are a wilderness; Zion is a wilderness; Jerusalem has become a desolate place" (Isa. 64:10).

- Of God turning the Jews over to spirits that made Israel a wilderness because they preferred false teachers to the men whom God sent to them:

  "Thus says the LORD concerning the house of the king of Judah: You are Gilead to me, the height of Lebanon; yet, *I will damn myself* [89] if I do not make you a wilderness of uninhabited cities" (Jer. 22:6).

- Of John the Baptist, who was sent to preach to Israel:

  "A voice crying in the wilderness, 'Prepare the way of the LORD! Make straight in the desert a highway for our God!'" (Isa. 40:3).

---

[89] See footnote 31, page 121.

- Of Jesus rescuing the remnant of Israel who survive the Beast's attack:

  "At that time, says the LORD, I will be God to all the families of Israel, and they will be my people. Thus says the LORD: <u>The people who survived the sword found grace in the wilderness</u>. He will come to give Israel rest" (Jer. 31:1–2).

- Of Jesus giving the spoils of the Beast and his armies to the remnant of the Jews (the "heads of Leviathan" may represent the ten kings who are aligned with the Beast):

  "You crushed the heads of Leviathan. You gave him as food for a <u>people who live in the wilderness</u>" (Ps. 74:14).

- Of God gathering the Jews out of foreign countries to establish their homeland (in 1948), and later, judging them there by using the Beast:

  "I will bring *you* out from the nations and gather *you* out of the countries where *you* have been scattered, with a strong hand and outstretched arm and poured-out wrath! And <u>I will bring *you* to the wilderness of the nations</u>, and there will I enter into judgment with *you*, face to face" (Ezek. 20:34–35).

- Of God returning the Jews to their homeland (the Valley of Achor is within Israel's borders):

  "Therefore, behold, I will entice her, and <u>bring her to the wilderness</u>, and speak to her heart. And I will give to her there her vineyards, and the valley of Achor for a door of hope. And there, she will respond as in the days of her youth, and as in the day when she came up from the land of Egypt" (Hos. 2:14–15).

- Of God blessing the land of Israel after returning the Jews to their homeland:

"[When] the Spirit is poured out on us from on high, then <u>the wilderness will become a fruitful field</u>, and the fruitful field will be deemed a forest, and <u>justice will dwell in the wilderness</u>, and righteousness will dwell in the fruitful field" (Isa. 32:15–16).

"<u>The wilderness and the dry place will rejoice</u>, and the desert will shout for joy and bloom like a rose.... Then shall the lame man leap like a stag, and the tongue of the dumb man will sing, for <u>waters will break forth in the wilderness</u>, and streams in the desert" (Isa. 35:1, 6).

THE "SEVENS" OF REVELATION

The Seven Seals
The Seven Trumpets
The Seven Vials

The Seven Seals
Revelation 6–8:6

The Seven Seals and Jesus' Prophecy on the Mount of Olives

Rev.	End-Time Event	Mt.	Mk.	Lk.
1st Seal 6:2	<u>White Horse</u> A rider with a bow is given a crown and goes out, "conquering and to conquer".	24:4–5	13:5–6	21:8
2nd Seal 6:4	<u>Fiery-Red Horse</u> Wars and unrest are spread.	24:6–7a	13:7–8a	21:9–10
3rd Seal 6:5–6	<u>Black Horse</u> A mystery involving food and money leaves the "oil and wine" unharmed.	—	—	—
4th Seal 6:8	<u>Pale Green Horse</u> 1/4 of earth is given to death.	24:7b	13:8b	21:11a

Only the first four Seven Seals unleash horses. Jesus sets apart the first four end-time events as "the beginning of sorrows".

5th Seal 6:9–11	"Great Tribulation"	24:9–28	13:9–23	21:12–24
6th Seal 6:12– 7:17	<u>Natural Disasters</u> A great earthquake. Sun goes black and moon turns to blood. Stars fall to earth. The sky splits apart. No wind on earth. 144,000 are sealed.	24:29	13:24–25	21:25–26
7th Seal 8:1–6	Silence in heaven for half an hour. Seven Trumpets are given to seven angels standing before God. A golden censor is thrown to earth and a third of the earth is burned up	—	—	—

The Seven Trumpets
Revelation 8:7–14:20

Revelation	End-Time Event
1st Trumpet 8:7	A third of the earth, a third of the trees, and all green grass is burned up by fire and hail mixed with blood that is cast upon the earth from heaven.
2nd Trumpet 8:8–9	A "burning mountain" is cast into the sea, and a third of the sea becomes blood, killing a third of sea creatures and destroying a third of ships.
3rd Trumpet 8:10–11	The star "Wormwood" falls to earth and poisons a third of the earth's supply of fresh water, killing many people.
4th Trumpet 8:12	A third of the sun, moon, and stars is stricken, and they do not shine for a third of every day and night.

**Woe! Woe! Woe to those who live on the earth
because of the remaining sounds of the trumpet
of the three angels who are about to sound!**

Revelation	End-Time Event
5th Trumpet 9:1–12	The key to the Shaft of the Abyss is given to an angel from heaven. Smoke from the Abyss darkens the sun, and men without the seal of God are tormented by creatures from the Abyss for five months.
6th Trumpet 9:13–11:14	Chapter 9: Four angels are loosed from the River. A 100,000,000-man army kills a third of all mankind. Chapter 10: The 7th Trumpet events are mentioned. Chapter 11: God's Two Witnesses are slain by the Beast, who ascends out of the Abyss.
7th Trumpet 11:15–14:16	Chapter 12: The Son of Man's sign appears in the sky. Chapter 13: Details of the reign of the Beast are given. Chapter 14: The Rapture of faithful saints takes place.

The Seven Vials
Containing the Seven Last Plagues
Revelation 16:1–21

Revelation	Where the Vials are Poured Out	End-Time Event
1st Vial 16:2	The Earth	Horrible sores erupt on humans who took the mark of the Beast.
2nd Vial 16:3	The Sea	The sea becomes like blood. Everything in the sea dies.
3rd Vial 16:4–7	Rivers and Fountains of Water	Rivers and fountains become like blood. The angel over the waters rejoices.
4th Vial 16:8–9	The Sun	The sun's heat is greatly multiplied.
5th Vial 16:10–11	The Throne of the Beast	The kingdom of the Beast is darkened, and men gnaw their tongues for pain and blaspheme God.
6th Vial 16:12–16	The Euphrates	The Euphrates River is dried up for "the kings from the East". Unclean spirits go out to gather the nations to Armageddon.
7th Vial 16:17–21	The Air	An earthquake leaves no islands or mountains. Large hail comes down out of heaven.

THE "BEAST"
IN DANIEL AND REVELATION

Introduction

After some end-time events were revealed to Daniel, he asked an angel about the timeline of those events, but the angel was blunt: "Go, Daniel! The words are shut up and sealed until the time of the end" (Dan. 12:8–9). This disappointing command to Daniel stands in stark contrast to the commandment given to John near the end of Revelation: "Do not seal the words of the prophecy of this book, for the time is near" (Rev. 22:10). The prophecies of the end-time were "shut up and sealed" for the prophets and wise men who came before Christ. Now, however, the Lamb of God has prevailed to open the seals, and we are invited to understand the end-time events that John saw.

In John's Revelation, the Beast appears during the time of the 6th Trumpet, just before the Lord Jesus appears in the clouds to catch away his faithful saints. In Daniel, chapters 2 and 7, the Beast is also spoken of and is again described as the last kingdom of man before the Second Coming of Jesus.

In Daniel 2, God gave King Nebuchadnezzar a dream in answer to the king's desire to know what would happen on earth after he died. Nebuchadnezzar saw in his dream a giant image of a man, with its body parts made of various materials. The head was made of gold, the chest and arms were of silver, the thighs were of brass, the legs were of iron, and the toes were a mixture of iron and clay. Then Nebuchadnezzar saw a Stone smash down upon the image and crush it to such fine powder that it was carried away by the wind. The Stone then became a fifth kingdom, one that would last forever. Elements of the dream, along with Daniel's interpretation of them, are shown in Table 1.

Table 1
The Beast in Daniel 2

Daniel 2	The Image	Daniel's Interpretation	Daniel 2
2:32a	Head of gold	1st Kingdom: Babylonian Empire	2:37–38
2:32b	Chest and arms of silver	2nd Kingdom: "inferior" to the 1st Kingdom [Medo-Persian Empire]	2:39a
2:32c	Belly and thighs of bronze	3rd Kingdom: [Greek Empire]	2:39b
2:33a	Legs of iron	4th Kingdom: "strong like iron" [Roman Empire]	2:40
2:33b	Feet and toes: a mixture of iron and clay	Ten kings, some strong and some weak, will reign as part of the 4th Kingdom in its latter days.	2:41–43
2:34–35	A stone cut out without hands smashed the image into powder and became a great mountain that filled the earth.	5th Kingdom: "In the days of those kings, the God of heaven will set up a kingdom that will never be destroyed . . . It will break in pieces and put an end to all these kingdoms, and it will stand forever."	2:44

Facts about Table 1:

1) The dream concerns the future, from Daniel's perspective.
2) The 4th Kingdom will subdue every other kingdom.
3) Near the end of the 4th Kingdom, ten kings will be part of it.
4) Note that the 4th Kingdom will be in power when Jesus returns.

The following Table will show that the 4th Kingdom of Daniel 2 is the 4th Beast of Daniel 7:

Table 2
The Beast in Daniel 7

Daniel 2	4th Kingdom	4th Beast	Daniel 7
2:28	"God is making known **what shall be** in the latter days."	"The 4th Beast **shall be** the 4th Kingdom which will be on earth."	7:23
2:40a	**"The 4th Kingdom will be strong like iron"**	"The 4th Beast **had great iron teeth**."	7:7a
		"The 4th Beast **whose teeth were of iron**."	7:19a
2:40b	"As iron breaks to pieces and shatters everything, **it will break to pieces and bring ruin**."	"It devoured, and **broke in pieces**, and trampled the rest with its feet."	7:7b
		"It devoured, **broke in pieces**, and trampled the rest with its feet."	7:19b
2:41	"The feet and the [ten] **toes** will be partly of potter's clay and partly of iron."	The 4th Beast had **ten (pairs of) horns**.	7:7c
2:44a	"in the days of those kings"	The ten (pairs of) horns of this kingdom are "ten kings who shall arise."	7:24
2:34, 2:44–45	God gives **an eternal kingdom** to the "stone".	God gives **an eternal kingdom** to "one like a son of man".	7:13–14

The facts from Table 1 which match Table 2:

1

From Table 1: The dream from Daniel 2 concerns the future, from his perspective.

From Table 2: The vision from Daniel 7 concerns the future, from his perspective.

2

From Table 1: The 4th Kingdom will subdue every other kingdom.

From Table 2: The 4th Beast will subdue every other kingdom.

3

From Table 1: Ten kings will be part of the 4th Kingdom at the end of its time.

From Table 2: Ten kings will be part of the 4th Beast's reign.

4

From Table 1: The 4th Kingdom will be in power when Jesus returns. Jesus is the "stone cut out without hands" which filled the earth.

From Table 2: The 4th Beast will be in power when Jesus returns. Jesus is the "son of man" who receives an eternal kingdom from God.

Conclusion: Since there cannot be two kingdoms dominating the world at the same time, the 4th Kingdom in Daniel 2 must be the 4th Beast in Daniel 7.

The following Table will show that the Beast in Revelation 11 and 13 is the Beast in Revelation 17:

Table 3
The Beast in Revelation 11, 13, and 17

	Revelation 11, 13	**Revelation 17**	
11:7	The Beast came **from the Abyss**.	The Beast came **from the Abyss**.	17:8
13:1	The Beast had **ten horns**.	The Beast had **ten horns**.	17:12
13:1	The Beast had **seven heads**.	The Beast had **seven heads**.	17:3
13:1	On the heads of the Beast were **names of blasphemy**.	The Beast was full of **names of blasphemy**.	17:3

- Table 1 and 2 showed that the 4th Kingdom in Daniel 2 and 7 are the same.

- Table 3 showed that the Beast in Revelation 11 and 13 is the Beast of Revelation 17.

The following Table will show that the Beast in Revelation 11, 13, and 17 is the same as the 4th Kingdom/Beast in Daniel 2 and 7:

Table 4
The Beast in Daniel and Revelation

	Daniel	**Revelation**	
7:3	The 4th beast came **from the sea**.	The Beast came **from the sea**.	13:1
7:1–7, 17	The 4 Beastly King-doms 1 - **a lion** with eagle's wings. 2 - **a bear** with 3 ribs in its mouth. 3 - **a leopard** with 4 wings and 4 heads.	The Beast 1 - like **a leopard**. 2 - had feet like **a bear**. 3 - **a lion's** mouth.	13:2
7:7d; 7:24b	The 4th beast was "**different from all the beasts before it**."	"And they worshipped the Dragon, saying, '**Who is like the Beast**?'"	13:4
7:23	"And it shall devour **the whole earth**, and it will tread it down and break it to pieces."	"Authority was given to him **over every tribe and people and language and nation**."	13:7b
7:7c	The 4th beast had **ten horns**.	The Beast had **ten horns**.	13:1; 17:3
7:24a	"**The ten horns are ten kings**."	"**The ten horns are ten kings**."	17:12a
7:24b	"**who shall arise**"	"**who have not yet received a kingdom**"	17:12b
The End of the Beast's Reign			
7:25b	"They shall be given into his hand until **a time, and times, and half a time**." (Three and a half years)	"Authority was given to him to wage war **forty-two months**." (Three and a half years)	13:5b

7:22a	"until the Ancient of Days came"	"The Lamb will conquer them because he is Lord of lords and King of kings."	17:14
7:11	"The beast was slain and its body destroyed when it was given to the burning fire."	He loses the war against Jesus, and is "thrown alive into the Lake of Fire."	19:19 –20; 20:10
7:22b	"Judgment was given to the saints of the Most High."	"Judgment was given to them."	20:4a
7:18	"The saints of the Most High will receive the kingdom, and they will take possession of the kingdom forever, even forever and ever."	"And they will reign forever and ever."	22:5c

Mystery: Different from All Kingdoms

Twice, Daniel said that the 4th Kingdom was different from the kingdoms that went before it (Dan. 7:7, 19). Daniel was able to compare the first three to certain animals, but in the case of the 4th Beast, he could only relate to a few body parts, namely, its teeth, its feet, and its ten horns. Other than that, Daniel apparently had nothing on earth to which to compare it.

All kingdoms have laws, and customs, and military might by which they attain to power and by which they maintain and/or expand their dominion. They all tax, build, educate, have an economy, and secure their territory. So, how did this kingdom differ from the others? Daniel did not say. Nor does Revelation tell us. But both Daniel and John were utterly astonished at what they saw.

Mystery: Both a King and a Kingdom

Tables 3 and 4 showed that the Beast of Revelation is the same as the 4th Kingdom/4th Beast of Daniel 2 and 7 (the Roman Empire). The following Table will show that the Beast is also the "little horn" of Daniel 7:

Table 5
The "Little Horn" in Daniel and
the Beast of Revelation

	Daniel	**Revelation**	
7:8a	A little horn uproots three of the ten horns (ten kings) and becomes **the eighth horn**.	The Beast is **the eighth horn**, but he is one of the seven.	17:10–11
7:8b 7:11a	The little horn has eyes like a man and "**a mouth speaking great thing**s."	"There was given to him **a mouth speaking great things**."	13:5a
7:25a	"And he will speak words **against the Most High**."	"And he opened his mouth **in blasphemy against God**."	13:6a
7:21 7:25b	The little horn "**waged war against the saints and prevailed against them**."	The Beast will "**make war against the saints and to overcome them**."	13:7a

Table 5 shows that the "little horn", the Beast, is actually one of the seven kings who preceded him, that is, he reigned on earth at some unknown point in the past, was taken from earth, and will return. An angel explained to John, "The Beast that you saw was, and is not, and will ascend out of the Abyss, and he is headed for damnation. And the inhabitants of the earth will marvel, whose names are not written in the Book of Life from the foundation of the world, when they see the Beast that was, and is not, and yet, will be" (Rev. 17:8).

The Beast's seven heads, according to the angel, represent "seven kings; five have fallen, one is, and another has not yet come, and when he comes, he must continue a little while. And the Beast who was, and is not, even he himself is the eighth, but he is one of the seven" (Rev. 17:7, 9–11a). So, the Beast is a man who has reigned on earth, then was taken from the earth for a time, and will return to reign on earth again shortly before Jesus returns.

The 2000-Year Gap

Not a single prophecy exists which plainly foretold of a two-thousand-year period of spiritual blindness for the Jews after the First Advent of the Messiah. Joel (2:23), Zechariah (10:1), and the apostle James (Jas. 5:7) spoke of two outpourings of the Spirit on Israel, and James and the other apostles clearly expected the time between those outpourings to be short. An early and latter rain fell in Israel every year, and it is likely that believing Jews saw that as a sign that Jesus would return within a year's time. Were they wrong to expect that, or did God change what should have happened because of the Jews' unbelief? Is this large gap between the two Advents the way it was meant to be, or is it only the way God made it in response to Israel's unbelief? Either way, the Jewish nation, in the main, proved itself unworthy of the promises the first time the Son of God came to them.

God foresaw this two-thousand-year gap between the two Advents of His Son. But was that gap His original plan for Israel, or was it the result of unbelief on the part of the Jews? In spite of the thousands in Israel who believed in Jesus (Acts 21:20), the number of Jews who rejected him far exceeded them, and that may have been the determining factor in Jesus not returning quickly. It can be argued that God always planned for the Gentiles to have the same amount of time (two thousand years) that Israel had with Him (from Abraham to Jesus) and that the glorious prophecies for Israel were never meant to be fulfilled in the apostles' time. Then again, it may be that the prophecies of glory for Israel would have been fulfilled quickly if Israel had recognized their Messiah and believed in him.

The author of Hebrews referred to his time as "these last days" (Heb. 1:1), and he said that Christ had made his sacrifice at "the close of the ages" (Heb. 9:26). That may very well have been true. However, God "works all things according to the counsel of His own will" (Eph. 1:11), and the scriptures bear witness to the fact that God's will can change – and His people's conduct is the reason He changes it. Both Paul and Peter taught that the fulfillment of prophecy can be delayed or hastened by the conduct of God's people (2Cor. 10:6; 2Pet. 3:12). In truth, all of world history has been determined, for better or for worse, based on God's relationship with His people, and it will continue to be determined by that relationship until the end.

What Is Slander and How Does It Work?

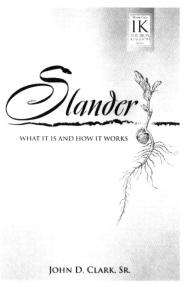

"He who hides hatred with lying lips, and he who utters slander, is a fool."

The writers of the Bible understood slander in ways that modern dictionaries do not capture. A dictionary will tell you that to slander means "to make a false spoken statement that damages a person's reputation."

Biblical stories of slander reveal that slander can be verbal or non-verbal and that slander often uses truth to accomplish its purpose. Slander, as found in Scripture, is a most effective tool of unclean spirits; it has a very high success rate both in the world and in the body of Christ.

Slander, book one in The Iron Kingdom series, lays the foundation needed to understand slander in its most perfect form: the religious system called Christianity.

Jesus Alone Can Save.

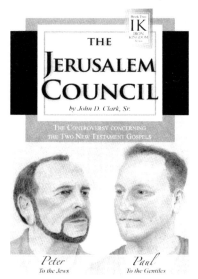

Peter
To the Jews

Paul
To the Gentiles

The aged apostle Paul wrote to Timothy, "All they in Asia have forsaken me." And such was the case in the Assemblies of God everywhere, for before the apostles died, the body of Christ fell into apostasy. Today, the body of Christ remains confused and divided, and the confusion and division can be traced back to the issues debated in the Jerusalem Council in Acts 15. Few perceive what was at stake when the leaders of the Assembly in Jerusalem convened this special Council.

This book takes the reader through the likely arguments that were made at the Council and explains why both sides were desperate to win the day. It also reveals that while Paul's argument was accepted by the leaders of the Council, the body of Christ as a whole eventually rejected Paul and his gospel.

God Is, First of All, a God of Relationships.

What love the Father had for us, to transform us desperately sinful creatures into saints and to re-create us as His children, worthy to live forever! God sent His Son to give us life so that we might know Him, and by revealing Himself through His Son, God accomplished the impossible in us.

The revelation that from the beginning there existed a beloved Son lets us know that above all else, God desires loving relationships. That desire lies at the heart of everything God has ever done, and nothing in Creation contradicts that truth.

God Had a Son before Mary Did examines the significance and glory of the "mystery of God", the mystery of the Son, which God kept secret from the foundation of the world until He revealed it in the person of Jesus Christ.

When Were the Disciples Born Again?

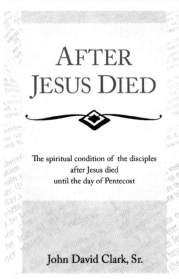

If anyone on earth was born again after Jesus died, and before Pentecost, surely his disciples were - but they were not. If anyone on earth understood his purpose and doctrine after Jesus died, and before Pentecost, surely his disciples did - but they did not. *After Jesus Died* shows that the Bible leaves no reasonable alternative to those two conclusions.

When we carefully study the disciples' actions and words in the time between Jesus' death and the day of Pentecost, we are forced to conclude that they were not born again until they were baptized with the Spirit on Pentecost morning. May God give us the same grace that He gave to his disciples to escape spiritual blindness and to walk with Jesus in his light. "The God who commanded light to shine out of darkness has shone in our hearts to give us the light of the knowledge of the glory of God in the face of Jesus Christ."

Who Is in Charge of Our Suffering?

Let those who suffer according to the will of God commit their souls to Him in well doing, as unto a faithful Creator.
1Peter 4:19

John David Clark, Sr.

"And we know that all things work together for good to them that love God, to them who are the called according to His purpose."

Are you hurting? Have you suffered a crushing loss? We all suffer from disappointment, misunderstanding, and betrayal. What are we to think? How do we respond?

In *Suffering and the Saints,* we will read the Biblical stories of men and women whose faith survived desperate situations. But this is more than a collection of stories. We will pay close attention to what they thought about their suffering and how they perceived God's part in it. Only by understanding what they knew and patterning our faith after theirs can we respond as they did, finding the strength to overcome evil with good, as they did, proving again that all things work together for good for those who are the called according to God's purpose.

The Relationship Must Come First.

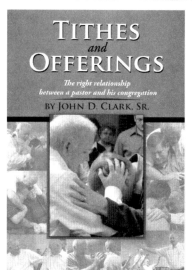

The right relationship between a pastor and his congregation

This is not a book about money. Understanding tithes and offerings is necessary, but the more important issue is the proper relationship of a pastor and his flock, both his responsibility toward them and theirs toward him.

Upon reading this manuscript, one lady commented, "Every sentence will be a new thought to God's people." That may not altogether be the case, but this book certainly will bring new thoughts to those who read it. The lack of understanding about how to deal with God's money has caused much confusion, but be warned; the truth of the matter will challenge your heart. Although the issue of tithes and offerings is a minor matter, as Jesus himself said (Mt. 23:23), if that part of our spiritual life is not in order, every other part of our spiritual life is adversely affected.